ISBN 978-1-330-23219-4
PIBN 10059046

1 MONTH OF
FREE
READING

at
www.ForgottenBooks.com

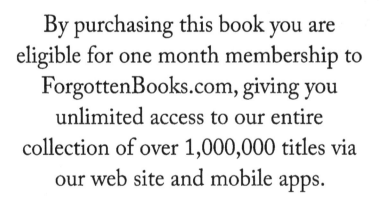

By purchasing this book you are eligible for one month membership to ForgottenBooks.com, giving you unlimited access to our entire collection of over 1,000,000 titles via our web site and mobile apps.

To claim your free month visit:

www.forgottenbooks.com/free59046

THE
STUDY OF SHAKESPEARE

BY

HENRY THEW STEPHENSON

AUTHOR OF "SHAKESPEARE'S LONDON" AND "THE
ELIZABETHAN PEOPLE"

NEW YORK
HENRY HOLT AND COMPANY
1915

THE QUINN & BODEN CO. PRESS
RAHWAY, N. J.

TO
MARGARET LOUISE STEPHENSON

PREFACE

For some fifteen years I have conducted classes in the study of Shakespeare at the University of Indiana. I early found that great advantage was derived from an intimate knowledge of the social conditions that obtained at the time the plays were written. My attempt to furnish some assistance in this direction by the publication of an account of Shakespeare's London and of the people of Elizabeth's generation has given me confidence in the preparation of a handbook designed differently from many now in use.

Though criticism of the plays forms the larger part of the following pages, I have had no intention of writing a volume of criticism. The book is not intended to be read on its independent merits, but in conjunction with a study of the texts. Though I hope it will be of interest to those already familiar with the plays of Shakespeare, it is primarily addressed to students.

Inasmuch as it is intended to be an assistance, I have not felt it necessary to discuss the obvious. Oftentimes a mere suggestion is sufficient to start the reader aright so that he will discover all that is necessary without further assistance. For instance, I have frequently observed a class which read *The Taming of the Shrew* without the least comprehension of its meaning. To the members of the class

CONTENTS

THE STUDY OF SHAKESPEARE

CHAPTER I

SHAKESPEARE'S BIOGRAPHY

THE poet's father was John Shakespeare of Snitterfield, who married in 1557 Mary Arden of Wilmcote, near Stratford. Some five or six years before his marriage John Shakespeare moved from Snitterfield to Stratford, where he was living at the time of the poet's birth. Stratford was then a small but flourishing country town on one of the main thoroughfares to London; and John Shakespeare soon became one of its prominent citizens.

In 1552 he was living in a house in Henley Street, either the house now known as the poet's birthplace, or the one adjoining. He set himself up in business as a trader with a miscellaneous assortment of wares, a fact which doubtless accounts for his designation among older historians as a glover by one, a butcher by another. During the next few years he was prosperons in a worldly way, occupying successively several important offices in the gift of the municipality.

The poet was the third child and first son of John Shakespeare. He was baptized in the parish church, April 26, 1564. It was then customary for this ceremony to take place as soon after birth as possible.

There is, however, no authority for the usually accepted date of his birth, April 22 or April 23.

Stratford possessed a good free grammar school, which Shakespeare probably entered about 1571. Instruction was principally carried on in Latin, a language the rudiments of which were known to the poet, though he seems never to have become a proficient scholar. There is no reason to believe that he ever studied Greek. A reading knowledge of Italian was probably picked up after leaving Stratford. The acquirement of his knowledge of French may have begun at Stratford and have been continued by himself in later years. He possessed no claim to be called " one skilled in the tongues "; on the other hand, he certainly possessed a good foundation in Latin, French, and, perhaps, Italian. Doubtless he read little. The Bible was probably to him the most accessible book in English. Though his plays contain many biblical allusions, they suggest, as Mr. Lee puts it, " youthful reminiscence and the assimilative tendency of the mind in a stage of early development rather than close and continuous study of the Bible in adult life." * It should be remembered in this connection that the service of the Church of England provides for the continuous reading of both the Old and the New Testament.

Shakespeare was still a schoolboy in 1575 when Queen Elizabeth visited Robert Dudley at Kenilworth. He was, however, probably withdrawn from school in 1577, when but thirteen years of age, to be apprenticed to his father. This move was proba-

* Sidney Lee: *A Life of William Shakespeare.* Revised edition. Page 17.

bly due to the declining family fortunes. For some years John Shakespeare's fortunes and his prominence in civic affairs had been on the wane. Records of his borrowings and of the sale of some of his property show that in a worldly way he was in distress. Never again did he regain his former position of importance.

Shakespeare's marriage in 1582 has given rise to endless speculation. The whole subject has been treated in detail by Mr. Lee. The facts, stripped of all inference, are as follows: Anne Hathaway was the poet's senior by eight years; the marriage was arranged and solemnized in a hasty and irregular manner, mainly at the instigation of the friends of the bride; within six months a daughter was born to the poet. In after life Shakespeare did not scruple to live away from his wife and family for the better part of twenty years, though he visited Stratford occasionally, and at last returned to his home and family to spend the years that followed his retirement from the London stage.

While still a resident of Stratford, Shakespeare acquired a familiar knowledge of outdoor life. In his plays the art and practice of falconry is at his tongue's end. He knew about horses and dogs. Flowers were his familiar friends. He knew every superstition and all the folklore of the countryside. Above all, he knew the country characters and their pranks.

In fact, association with a group of these country characters in one of their ribald escapades was, according to persistent tradition, the cause of his leaving Stratford. The hall and park of Charlecote was the most pretentious estate in the immediate neigh-

borhood of his home town. Shakespeare, in company
with other idle fellows, raided the deer park at
Charlecote. For this they were severely prosecuted by
the owner of the park, Sir Thomas Lucy. In retalia-
tion Shakespeare is said to have written a ballad which
so incensed Sir Thomas that he redoubled his perse-
cutions. In order to escape, Shakespeare fled from
Stratford. In later years he vented his spleen by
caricaturing Sir Thomas Lucy in the person of Justice Shallow of *The Merry Wives of Windsor.*

Traditions that attempt to fill up the gap of the
next few years in the poet's life are wholly without
a proved foundation. It is idle to guess where he
went; and what he did is not known. He probably
left Stratford in 1585. We next hear of him in
London about 1590, under circumstances that imply
that he had been there for some time and was already
firmly footed in the theatrical world.

During Shakespeare's career there were many companies of actors; not nearly so many, however, as the
numerous names applied to them would suggest.
There were two companies of men actors of far
greater prominence than any others. One was under
the associate management of the money lender, Philip
Henslowe, and his son-in-law, the great actor, Edward
Alleyn. From their patron, the Lord High Admiral,
they were known as the Admiral's Men.

The other and more notable company was the one
to which Shakespeare belonged. It is known by
many names. Leicester's early company, under the
patronage of Robert Dudley, Earl of Leicester, became at his death in 1588 Lord Strange's Men. They
became known later, in all probability, by the name

of his subsequent title, Lord Derby. Under successive patrons this company was known as Lord Hunsden's Men, and as the Chamberlain's Men. After the accession of James in 1603 they were known as the King's Men. Shakespeare is known to have been a member of the company as early as 1594; and there is no reason to doubt the probability that he was connected with it from the beginning of his theatrical career.

What Shakespeare's first duties about the playhouse were we do not know. When he appears again in history after his flight from Stratford he is an actor of minor rôles, and a maker-over of old plays, with, perhaps, a play or two of his own to his credit. For many years he continued to act, taking subordinate parts in some of his own plays. For the next twenty years, however, his biography, as known to us, is mainly the record of the succession of his dramas.

It is easy to piece out in broad lines the history of his life during this period of twenty years. He never became a great actor. He soon, however, passed beyond the apprentice stage of play writing. From a maker-over of old plays he soon became a writer of original plays, for some years mainly in imitation of the established writers of the day. Then he broke loose from the trammels of imitation to write the long list of dramas on which his fame rests to-day. A study of his plays shows him a constant student. Books he read, to be sure, and many of them; but it is as a student of the life about him that he stands pre-eminent. A consideration of plays following the Essex Rebellion discloses a temporary morbidness that to many implies some unfortunate connection with that ill-starred attempt to supplant Elizabeth. Another dark page in his history is disclosed vaguely to some by the description of an intrigue set forth in the sonnets. But this is a shadowy inference at the best.

Meantime he was growing rich. He derived a revenue, not only as play writer and play actor, but also as sharer in the company's profits. The latter was probably his chief source of income. About 1610 or 1611 he retired from the theatrical world. He had from time to time purchased properties in Stratford, among them the most prominent private house in town. To New Place he returned to live the remaining years of his life.

Shakespeare died at Stratford, April 23, 1616. On April 25 he was buried in the parish church. His wife and his two daughters, Judith [Quiney] and Susanna [Hall] survived him. By 1623, the year the Folio Edition of his plays was published, a bust of the poet was placed in Stratford church. This is one of the two likenesses that are known to have been in existence at such an early date. The other is the portrait engraved on the title page of the First Folio.

Besides his worldly goods Shakespeare left a book of sonnets, a few minor poems that are doubtfully attributed to him, two long narrative poems, and the plays. The list of plays shows Shakespeare's versatility. Nine of them are history plays, among which are the very best of their type; there are a couple of farces, one of which is, perhaps, the best produced during the generation. There are numerous comedies and tragi-comedies. But upon the great series of tragedies which began with *Julius Cæsar* and ended with *Coriolanus* Shakespeare's position rests supreme.

CHAPTER II

A GENERAL VIEW OF LONDON

ROUGHLY speaking, mediæval London began with the building of the White Tower by William the Conqueror, and ended with the great fire of 1666. Throughout this long period changes were made from year to year; but, after the great religious establishments were once built, the face of London changed so slowly that the picture of one generation is the picture of the next. The most sudden sweeping change was made at the Dissolution of the Monasteries, and the period of most rapid expansion was the reign of Elizabeth. It is the London of the latter half of the sixteenth century and the beginning of the seventeenth, the most brilliant period in its history between Hastings and the Fire, that the following pages essay to present.

Three hundred years ago the relative importance of London to the rest of England was even greater than it is to-day. All the theaters and all the publishers of note were in London or in the immediate vicinity. The court was held for most of the time at Westminster. There was but one Royal Exchange in the kingdom. All persons of any pretense to wealth or influence possessed their town house or inn. The city set the manners and furnished the news for the whole island; it was, indeed, the heart of the kingdom.

In order to draw a fancy picture of the Elizabethan city as Shakespeare knew it, one who is familiar with the modern metropolis must blot from his mind all present associations—not only in regard to size, but also in regard to outward aspect, and in the manners and customs of the people; for in these respects the city of that day was wholly different from the city of this.   It should be remembered that the fire of 1666 practically swept away all but the suburbs of Elizabethan London.   Hardly a town in the world of ancient origin preserves so few of its original structures as does the capital of England.   One can go about the city to-day and encounter practically nothing besides the street names that reminds him of times before the Fire.   Roughly speaking, a line connecting the Tower, Crosby Hall, Christ Church, Ludgate Circus, and the approach to Blackfriar's Bridge includes the part of the city destroyed by the great conflagration.   And this area, though it is but a small part of the city we know, constituted the major part of the city in 1600.*

In the latter part of the sixteenth century a Dutch traveler by the name of Hentzner visited England, and afterward wrote a very interesting account of his foreign travels.   He visited London, and his quaint account of the sights is full of the local color of which we are so desirous.   Let us for a moment station ourselves where he must have been when he first caught a glimpse of what was then, as it is to-day, one of the chief cities of the world.

We are on the Surrey side, approaching London

* The part of the modern metropolis known as The City approximates in area the Elizabethan city.

along the old Roman road which lèads to the bridge. Perhaps before Hentzner crossed the river he visited St. Mary Overies. If he had ascended the Tower he would have seen a splendid sight. Across a river that was as unlike the modern Thames as imagination can picture lay the bustling city. The river was clear and shining, sparkling with swans that swam gracefully in miniature fleets of snowy whiteness. Behind, on either side, and beyond the busy capital were green fields spotted with flowers or covered with golden grain and emerald turf. The city itself was nestled upon three hills. On an eminence to the right rose the many-towered walls of the citadel surrounding the lofty White Tower of William the Norman. Two small valleys rendered visible by the dip in the red-tiled roof line separate it from the great cathedral pile of St. Paul's. This church was the glory of all England. No other cathedral in the kingdom was so beautiful, the source of so much pride; and one who looks at the modern structure that occupies its site sighs with deep-felt regret over the ignominious contrast.

What perhaps impressed the Dutch traveler most was the innumerable collection of spires that rose from the densely populated city. The Dissolution of the Monasteries had not fallen lightly upon London; in fact, it had left it, as Mr. Besant says, a city of ruins. For all that, the parish churches had been spared. Hardly one had fallen in the national game of snatch-grab that followed the Dissolution. Stow tells us that there were no less than a hundred and twenty, and all of these were provided with towers or steeples. Yet, high above the clustered mass of slender spires rose the great bulk of the cathedral. Its lofty, graceful spire, however, had been burned some years before, and only a mutilated stump replaced it.

If we pause for a moment to listen we can hear the mingled peals of bells and the roar of the city, for it was even more noisy then than now. People lived in the streets and used them constantly as a daily convenience that is suggested to one by modern Paris, not by London.

Immediately beneath us lies the only bridge across the Thames. London Bridge of those days was a little east of the present structure; in fact, it crossed the river just where St. Magnus' Church now stands. It was an arched bridge of nearly a score of arches, no two of them exactly the same in width. About the piers were timber frameworks of wood that so encroached upon the waterway that the flow while the tide was rising and falling was greatly impeded. Such obstacles were thes- lozenge-shaped "starlings," that the backing up of the water at mid-tide produced a fall beneath the bridge of several feet. Pennant alludes to the sound of the falling waters in the following words: "Nothing but use could preserve the rest of the inmates who soon grew deaf to the sound of falling water, the clamors of watermen, or the frequent shrieks of drowning wretches." The old plays sometimes refer to the sound of the bridge being heard over the whole city. This natural waterfall was pressed into use to operate a set of force pumps that supplied water to a large part of the city. Much of the local travel that is now carried on in cabs was then performed upon the river in small boats. The cry with which one hailed a waterman was Westward ho! or Eastward ho! according to the direction. If, in the journey, it was necessary to cross the bridge at mid-tide the passenger had to land and wait. Sometimes they " shot " the bridge, that is, took their chances of mishap and went over the fall. The danger that attended this kind of rapid transit gave rise to the proverb: London Bridge was made for wise men to walk over and fools to go under. When the Princess Elizabeth, afterwards the Queen, was conveyed a prisoner to the Tower, it was necessary for the boatman to row about in the neighborhood of the bridge for an hour before it was deemed safe to " shoot."

What to us appears the most peculiar feature of this old bridge was not the starlings or the noisy river, but the covered way or arcade that capped the arches throughout the entire length. From end to end, with the exception of two small openings, London Bridge was covered with houses that inclosed and roofed a narrow street: dwellings above and shops below. There were many kinds of shops, but in the time of Elizabeth the bridge was especially noted for the manufacture of pins, and the fair dames of London often bargained among the narrow stalls above the water for this indispensable article of dress.

At the southern end of the bridge was a huge towered gate-house whose principal use in the days of Queen Bess was to afford a resting place for traitors' heads. Imagine the trait of character that prompted the people to flock to an execution by the hundred, in holiday attire, and afterward gaze unshocked upon a score of bloody heads on pikes, grinning ghastly from the battlemented tower. About midway on the bridge was a handsome chapel. Beneath the last three arches of the northern end were the pumps for forcing water to which allusion has already been made. At the London approach was another tower, almost in ruins by the third quarter of the century, and taken down by the end.

Unless Hentzner hailed a boat at the stairs of the Bear tavern by the bridge foot with the cry of Northward ho! he must have entered the city along the gloomy bridge. The roadway through this structure was scarcely wider than a single cart, and in the press one had to exercise considerable ingenuity to escape collision, the bridge being always a busy thoroughfare. At two places only were open spaces where people could stand for safety.

Instead of following the Dutch traveler to his tavern, let us take a general view of the outward appearance of the city in methodical order. The city, as has been said, was then comparatively small; it was also comparatively open in the manner of building. For, though the streets presented solid and continuous lines of house fronts, there were gardens behind most of them. In fact, many of the city blocks resembled open courtyards occupied on the four sides with buildings. There were numerous churches, and about most of them burying grounds of considerable size. Furthermore, it was but a short walk to the country in any direction. Ten minutes was sufficient for a person to reach the open fields from any part of London afoot. Hunting and hawking were still common sports of the neighborhood and were carried on as near the center of the city as the British Museum or the Liverpool Street Station.

Elizabethan London, which in area corresponded closely with the modern City, was surrounded by a wall that remained almost intact on three sides till a time long subsequent to that under description. Even so early as the days of Fitzstephen the river side of the wall had disappeared, leaving no trace of its existence except in such names as Dowgate and Billingsgate. The course of the Elizabethan wall was from the north side of the Tower ditch, along the Minories in a northwesterly direction to Aldgate; then, curving west and north, followed Camomile and Wormwood Streets and London Wall. The angle of the wall at the northwest corner is still marked by the existing base of the tower which stands in the church-yard of St. Giles, Cripplegate. From this point the wall turned directly south along the present Noble Street, west, crossing Aldersgate Street, and south-west between St. Bartholomew's the Great and Christ's Hospital to a point west of Newgate prison. Thence it ran south to Ludgate Hall, west to Ludgate Circus, and south again to the river.

The wall was built, except for a small portion, upon the foundation of an earlier Roman wall. The more recent structure was partly of rough stone and partly of tile, and was capped by a battlemented wall of brick and stone. At short and irregular intervals were small towers in addition to the fortified gate-house. None of these smaller towers has survived, nor is there any accurate description of them. The base of one in St. Giles churchyard has been mentioned and another was discovered after a fire about a century ago. It was two and twenty feet in height, but not complete.

There were several gates: the Tower postern, Aldgate, Bishopsgate, Moorgate postern, Aldersgate, Greyfriar's postern, Newgate, and Ludgate. These, with the exceptions of the posterns, were huge towered structures, with, usually, a triple passage: one for vehicles, the others for pedestrians. The latter were closed at night by heavy doors, the former by ponderous portcullises. Newgate and Ludgate were used as prisons, the others often as private dwellings for those who guarded the gates.

The wall on the outer side was bordered by a ditch two hundred feet across; on the west side, however, the place of the ditch was taken by the Fleet River. Of old time the ditch not only was a defense, but also supplied most of the water and much of the fish used in the city. In Elizabethan times, however, it had become too filthy for such purposes, and was, moreover, encroached upon in many places, filled up with débris, turned into garden plots, and otherwise marred and displaced, much to the chagrin of the old historian Stow.

This relic of mediæval life had been of real service to the city in the time of Queen Mary, and actually formed an obstacle that turned to naught the ill-starred rebellion of Essex; yet, in spite of these facts, the wall was an obsolete and useless feature of London life. It was no longer necessary as a protection, and, in consequence, the city began to spread beyond the limits of its confines at the beginning of the reign of Elizabeth. By the end, the jurisdiction of the Lord Mayor extended over the adjacent ground north of the river in every direction for a distance varying from one to three-fourths of a mile. All this area, however, was not wholly occupied by buildings. On the east, running northwest from the Tower, was a single row of houses along the Minories. The same was true of much of the north side of the city; but in the immediate vicinity of the gates the populated portion extended along the high road for some little distance. There was, Stow tells us, a continuous line of houses along the river east of the Tower for half a mile or more; and the road from Bishopsgate was well occupied all the way to Shoreditch Church, which was well outside the city limits. Northwest of the city in the vicinity of Smithfield, and the church and hospital of St. Bartholomew's, a considerable hamlet had sprung into existence. The Strand was lined upon the south side with palatial residences all the way to Westminster, though the mayor's jurisdiction stopped then, as it does now, at Temple Bar. The north side of the Strand was built upon for the first time during the reign of Elizabeth.

The population of the city of that day cannot be accurately given; but a fairly trustworthy estimate can be obtained. The city contained in all likelihood not far from one hundred thousand people, with as many more in Westminster, Southwark, and the neighboring suburbs to the north and west. It is interesting to note the foreign population at this time. In 1567 there were 40 Scots, 428 French, 45 Spaniards and Portuguese, 140 Italians, 2,030 Dutch, 44 Burgundians, 2 Danes, and 1 Liegois. In 1580 there were 2,302 Dutch, 1,838 French, 116 Italians, 1,542 English born of foreign parents, and 664 not specified.

The increase of native population kept pace with the foreign increase, a tendency the government tried hard to interrupt. A proclamation of Elizabeth forbade the erection of any new buildings upon hitherto unoccupied sites within three miles of any of the city gates. The same proclamation forbade more than one family to live together in the same house. The noble persons were fast removing their mansions to new locations without the walls, and the last-mentioned provision of the above proclamation was directed against the popular custom of turning the abandoned mansions into tenement houses, crowded and filthy fosterers of the plague. The reason given for this proclamation and some others of a similar nature, which, however, were frequently violated, was to prevent the danger arising from disease and disorder, both important factors in the Elizabethan life; but there can be but little doubt that under the surface of these building regulations lay a substantial jealousy, if not an actual fear, of the rapidly growing wealth and power of the city corporation.

Within the area bounded by the old wall the city was divided by a few grand thoroughfares, but, for the most part, by narrow and filthy streets. They were dark and dingy from the projecting upper stories of the gabled houses that shut out most of the light, and dirty under foot, while one in passing was not infrequently deluged with the house-maid's slops from an upper window. Most of the streets were poorly paved, or not at all, with a kennel half full of stagnant water in the center. Sometimes there was no specially prepared footway; often such a convenience was little more than indicated by a low line of posts. The public streets were made the dumping grounds for all sorts of rubbish. Scalding Alley owed its name to the habit of scalding chickens there for sale in the neighboring market of the Poultry. So little was the value of correct sanitation known that as late as 1647 the following permission is recorded in the official reports of the Royal Hospital: "No man shall cast urine or ordure in the streets afore the hour of nine in the night. Also he shall not cast it out but bring it down and lay it in the channel." It is not to be wondered at that the people often encountered the blue cross on a doorpost, the sign of plague, or that statutes required every householder to build a fire opposite his house three times a week in order to purge the atmosphere.

The houses that lined these streets were of various kinds. There were still standing many of the fine old mansions of the nobility that retained the appearance, though no longer the reality, of stone fortifications. One of the finest of these remained almost until yesterday—Crosby Hall. The houses of contemporary build were usually of brick and timber, eked out with lath and plaster, and constructed on a less pretentious scale. The woodwork of the fronts was often grotesquely carved and painted, and the roof usually gabled towards the street, as is still to be seen in the Staple Inn.

The windows were generally composed of small panes of glass imbedded in lead, and opening casement-wise; while each story of the house projected several feet beyond the line of the story below. Often a street of fair width on the ground showed but a narrow sky line above, the house fronts being so close together that people could shake hands across the space. In addition, shop-keepers often built pent-houses against their lower walls for the display of goods, thus encroaching still further upon the narrow passage.

One is particularly struck by three details in connection with the houses of old London: (1) The number of churches, to which allusion has already been made. (2) The frequency of taverns. It would be useless to attempt to catalogue the city taverns. Besides the scores that are famous, there were other scores and scores. Often and often Stow finishes the description of an unimportant street with the words, "containing many fair houses and divers taverns." (3) The proximity of shops of the same nature. Until quite recently Holywell Street, Strand, presented an aspect typical of Elizabethan London. Both sides of the street were lined with the shops of petty dealers in second-hand books, one adjoining the other throughout the whole length of the street. In Elizabethan times this custom was carried out over the whole city. Thus the pin makers were upon London Bridge, the apothecaries in Bucklesbury, the goldsmiths in Cheapside, etc. Only the ubiquitous tavern possessed no local habitation.

Then as now the smaller streets were named in connection with their proximity to larger streets. As there were no numbers in use, each house was indicated by a sign, and much ingenuity was required to diversify them. These signs were occasionally painted upon the house fronts, or carved in the stone-work; but more commonly they hung out over the street, suspended from elaborate wrought-iron brackets.   Originally a sign had indicated an individual shop-keeper's trade, but, just as the number of a house remains to-day unchanged with change of ocenpant, so the Elizabethan sign was generally permanent.   Thus came about the state of affairs that Addison ridicules in *The Spectator*.

"I would enjoin every shop-keeper to make use of a sign that bears some affinity to the wares in which he deals.   A cook should not live at the 'Boot,' nor a shoemaker at 'The Roasted Pig,' and yet for want of this regulation I have seen a goat set up before the door of a perfumer and the French King's head before a sword cutter's."

The streets of London were poorly lighted at night, or not at all.   Various acts provided that householders should at regular intervals hang out lanterns; but these lanterns did little or no good, for they were only horn boxes containing a dim candle.   Even so, the acts were seldom obeyed, and one of the common street cries was that of the watchman reminding a delinquent householder that his lantern was not in place.

The watchman, who was, too often, not at all unlike Dogberry and his companions, went his rounds armed with a huge halberd, and was about as useless for the preservation of order as the numerous "Statutes for Streets," which among other things forbade persons to cry out at night, to blow a horn after nine o'clock, to whistle, to cause a disturbance, or to do a thousand and one other necessary acts.   From time to time special attempts were made to improve the efficiency of the police, especially in regard to the arrest of "sturdy beggars," the pest of Elizabethan London.

But, do what they could, the fact remained that one always wore his side arms for protection, and took his life in his hands, when he stirred abroad after nightfall.

In connection with the streets of London one might mention the water supply of the city, since so great a part of it was drawn from the public conduits in the streets. Till the thirteenth century London depended for its water supply wholly upon the neighboring brooks and springs and upon the Thames. With the growth of the city, however, the smaller streams became polluted and, in 1236, the citizens were given permission to convey water in pipes from Tyburn to Cheapside. In 1285 was commenced the great lead-lined cistern with a castellated structure over it that was known as the Great Conduit in Cheap, to which the water was conveyed a distance of three and a half miles.

There were in and about London many springs and wells that were turned to account in serving other conduits; and there was also a system of pipes supplied by a pump under London Bridge. Besides the conduits in Cheapside, the principal conduits throughout the city were as follows: the Tun upon Cornhill, the conduit in Aldermanbury, the Standard in Fleet Street, the Standard without Cripplegate, the conduit in Gracechurch Street, the conduit at Holborn Cross, the Little Conduit at the Stocks Market, the conduit at Bishopsgate, the conduit in London Wall opposite Coleman Street, the conduit without Aldgate, the conduit in Lothbury, and the conduit in Dowgate.

An annual custom in connection with the conduits

is thus described by Stow: "And particularly on the 18th of September, 1562, the Lord Mayor and others . . . rid to the conduit heads for to see them after the old custom (of annual inspection), and after dinner they hunted the hare and killed her, and thence to dinner at the head of the conduit . . . and after dinner they went hunting the fox."

The vehicles encountered in the streets were mostly the carts of costermongers, still more clumsy wagons, men on horseback, chairs, and coaches. The latter, however, were of infrequent use, having been but recently introduced. It was considered so effeminate as to be almost a disgrace for a man to be seen riding in a coach, unless it were the occasion of some civic or royal ceremony.

Stow in many places expresses his heartfelt enthusiasm for the city, such enthusiasm as a native Londoner born within sound of Bow Bells would feel. Elsewhere, however, the same Stow bewails the following state of affairs in the streets of his native city:

"But now in our time, instead of these enormities, others are come in place no less meet to be reformed, namely purprestures, or encroachments on the highways, lanes, and common grounds, in and about this city; whereof a learned gentleman and grave citizen hath not many years since written and exhibited a book to the mayor and commonalty; which book whether the same have been read by them and diligently considered upon, I know not, but sure I am nothing is reformed since concerning this matter.

"Then the number of cars, drays, carts, and

coaches, more than hath been accustomed, the streets
and lanes being straightened, must needs be dan-
gerons, as daily experience proveth.

"The coachman rides behind the horse tails, lash-
eth them, and looketh not behind him; the drayman
sitteth and sleepeth on his dray, and letteth his horse
lead him home. I know that, by the good laws and
customs of this city, shodded carts are forbidden to
enter the same, except upon reasonable cause, as
service of the prince, or such like, they be tolerated.
Also that the fore horse of every carriage should be
led by hand; but these good orders are not observed.
Of old time coaches were not known in this island,
but chariots or whirlicotes, then so called, and they
only used of princes or great estates, such as had
their footmen about them; . . . but now of late years
the use of coaches, brought out of Germany, is taken
up, and made so common, as there is neither distinc-
tion of time nor difference of persons observed; for
the world runs on wheels with many whose parents
were glad to go on foot."

The close crowding of the city and the timber
framework of the buildings gave rise to the two great
dangers of the Elizabethan city: fire and plague.
People are prone to think of the great plague which
Defoe described as the only plague to which the
metropolis has been subjected; but, as a matter of
fact, this dread disease visited the city about once
in thirty years. It was not an uncommon happening
to have the court moved inland because of the danger
of infection, and it furnished the cause of many of
the brief closures of the theaters long before the
Puritans carried their way on moral grounds. Cam-

den asserts that in 1563 there were 21,530 deaths from plague in London alone.

The streets of Elizabethan London were proverbially noisy, not only from the busy, jostling traffic, but also from the innumerable street cries heard upon every hand. It was the custom for an apprentice to stand in the door of his master's shop and to solicit trade of the passers-by with the cry of "What do you lack?" A foreigner, who was likely to be ridiculed by the common people wherever he was met in those days, or any other person who examined articles without making a purchase, was liable to the sarcastic chaff of the disappointed 'prentice; and if the customer answered impudently he was likely to have the whole brotherhood down upon him with their clubs in a trice. Sir Walter Scott in *The Fortunes of Nigel* has given an excellent picture of the Elizabethan shop, the rude behavior of the apprentices, and a subsequent riot.

In the days of Elizabeth they declare by act of common council that in ancient times the lanes of the open city have been used and of right ought to be used as the common highway only, and not for bucksters, pedlars, and hagglers to stand or to sell their wares in, and to pass from street to street, hawking and offering their wares. The preventive acts of Elizabeth, however, chiefly illustrate the abuses in full operation notwithstanding the violation of the law; hence we are not surprised to find a number of forbidden street cries alluded to in the old plays, among which are the following: "Old clothes, any old clothes "—" Buy, sell, or exchange, hats, caps, etc."—" Any kitchen stuffs, have ye, maids "—(the latter was the cry of those who collected refuse for the manufacture of soap and candles). " Ballads, Almanacks," was the frequent cry of the itinerant book-seller. Heywood, in *The Rape of Lucrece,* under the head of cries of Rome, gives a series of amusing illustrations of the London cries of his own day. Many others are to be found in the second act of *Bartholomew Fair.* Suffice it to say here that they were of innumerable variety, representing nearly every trade imaginable, and were heard like a constant chorus in the streets.

The principal thoroughfares of London were as follows: (1) From Newgate, across the city by Cheapside to Aldgate. (2) From Bishopsgate, south by London Bridge to the Surrey Side. These were the only thoroughfares that crossed the city completely. (3) From Ludgate to the Tower by way of Candlewick Street, interrupted, however, by the necessity of going through or around the churchyard of St. Paul's. (4) Thames Street, that ran parallel to the river from Blackfriars to the Tower.

CHAPTER III

THE PLAYHOUSES

As early as the time of Henry the Seventh companies of players constituted a part of the households of the great noblemen of England. The players were attached to the musical part of the establishment; and presented the morality plays and the interludes, the forerunners of the Elizabethan drama. When the services of the players were not needed by the master the actors were allowed to wander about the country at will. The most adaptable place to be found in the rural districts for dramatic purposes was the interior of the village tavern. During the years just previous to 1576 a small group of London taverns had become in reality the theaters of the day.

The English tavern of those days contained a central quadrangular courtyard entered through a large doorway at one end. About this court were galleries, one above the other, at the level of each story. When a play was to be performed, the actors would erect a temporary platform upon trestles at the end of the court, and extending back beneath the first gallery. From this gallery they would hang draperies so as to convert the back part of the platform and the court into a sort of dressing room. The spectators of the play stood about in the open court, or sat upon stools placed in the galleries. As we shall see in a few moments, this impromptu arrangement contains all the essential features of the earliest Elizabethan theaters.

The principal London taverns thus used were the Bull and the Cross Keys, both in Gracechurch Street, and the Bel Savage on Ludgate Hill. The Blackfriar's tavern should not be confused with later theaters of the same name. There was another Bull in Bishopsgate Street, and one " Nigh Paul's " about which nothing else is known. So, too, was used the Boar's Head in Eastcheap, the gathering place of Falstaff and his merry companions.

By the end of the third quarter of the century Puritanism had taken a fair hold on the people of London. This is no place to describe in detail the long factional quarrel which resulted in the expulsion of the players from the city. Suffice it to say that the long dispute culminated in an order from the town council prohibiting the performance of plays within the jurisdiction of the Lord Mayor. So the actors set to work at once to build theaters. The first two to be built were north of the city wall. Soon, however, the Bankside, on the opposite shore of the river, became more popular. It is now alone associated with the original performance of most of the greatest Elizabethan plays.

The first playhouse to be built was The Theater, erected in 1576 by James Burbage, once a carpenter, later a play-actor. Of the construction of The Theater practically nothing is known. No picture or detailed description of it is extant. It must, however, have been a ramshackle affair, for, in regard to it, one of the Lord Mayor's proclamations refers to " the perils from ruins of such weak buildings." And it was subsequently demolished quickly and with ease. In December, 1598, or January, 1599, The Theater was taken down and the material, so far as possible, used in the construction of Shakespeare's new playhouse on the Bankside, the Globe.

The other theater north of the city was probably built the same year—1576. It was near at hand, and from what scanty information we have of it, one fancies it much like The Theater. Its name, the Curtain, does not imply the use of a curtain therein. The name was derived from a military fortification, a curtain, on whose site it was built.

The Rose, the earliest of the Bankside theaters, was built by Henslowe, probably before 1592. It was circular, whereas most of the other Bankside theaters were hexagonal or octagonal. It was also a very low building in comparison with the others. The flagstaff rises from the interior, and the usual hut is lacking. This flag and hut, as we shall see, are very important details in the construction of the early theaters.

When The Theater north of the city was demolished the materials were carried across London Bridge to Southwark, where they were incorporated in the new Globe. This was in 1599, in all likelihood. The theater became the home of Shakespeare's company. Here he acted minor parts in his own plays, and here appeared for the first time the great series of his tragedies from *Julius Cæsar* to *Coriolanus*. It served as the model of the Fortune to be referred to later, so little need be said of its construction here. It **is** sufficient to say that it was a relatively tall building, open to the sky, and that it possessed a double-gabled hut from which projected the flagstaff. These huts will be spoken of later. They constitute one of the Elizabethan theatrical enigmas.

This theater was burned to the ground in 1613 during a performance of *Henry the Eighth*. It was, however, immediately rebuilt and remained in existence till 1644, when it was taken down to make room for a pile of tenements.

The original site of the Bear Garden contained a circular inclosure for the baiting of bulls and bears —hence its name. The first bear ring, we know not when, was rebuilt rectangular in form. In 1606 it was again rebuilt by Peter Street, who had already built the Globe. And in 1613 it was again rebuilt in its final form. For a short time the new theater was known as the Hope, but it soon returned to the use of its more venerable name.

Farther west was the Swan. Though one of the largest theaters, it was not long, and never exclusively used for plays. Like the Lear Garden, it possessed a movable stage which could be taken down when the interior was to be used for bear-baiting. Though one of the minor theaters, it is of great historical importance. This is due to the fact that a view of the interior which has come down to us is the only contemporary picture of the interior of an Elizabethan playhouse extant.

In 1599 the Rose theater was falling into decay. Again Peter Street was called upon to build a theater, this time the Fortune, this on the city side of the river, not on the Bankside. The contract for

INTERIOR OF THE SWAN THEATER

building the structure has been preserved and forms the basis of the graphic reconstructed drawing given opposite page 32. This square theater was burned in 1621, and rebuilt as a round brick building.

The other of the two theaters belonging to Shakespeare's company was called the Blackfriars.* It was on the city side of the river, and was known as a private theater, that is, it was smaller, higher-priced, more select, and roofed over. This latter detail necessitated some kind of artificial lighting during the performance, notwithstanding the fact that the plays were given in the daytime.

It was common practice in those days for the players to parade the streets of London with music on the day of performance. As there was then but one bridge across the river and Bankside on the opposite side from the city, persons on their way to the theaters often made use of the numberless small ferry-boats that plied upon the river. As the playhouses were open to the sky bad weather often prevented a performance—hence the value of the flag appearing in all the early representations. This flag could be seen across the river from the city side. If, for any reason, an advertised performance was abandoned at the last moment, the flag was lowered. Thus the would-be theater-goer would be saved the trouble of crossing the river to a disappointment.

General admission was collected at the outer door. The increased price of the best seats was collected

* Recent discoveries have revealed the existence of an earlier theater by this name. A convenient account of the matter is to be found in *The Elizabethan Playhouse and Other Studies*, by W. J. Lawrence; Lippincott, 1912.

inside. Prices, of course, varied with the occasion,
and with the theater. Admission was sometimes as
low as a penny (about twenty cents, for money was
then worth about ten times its present value). A
good seat, however, frequently cost a shilling, that
is, about two dollars in our money. Prices for a first
performance were usually double. The plays were
performed by daylight in the afternoon.

Once within the doorway of the theater the spectator found himself within a large, circular inclosure
into which projected the stage. The floor of the
central area, called the " yard " was the bare clay or
turf, and was not furnished with seats. About the
yard were three galleries, one above another, divided
into sections called " rooms." The lower rooms could
be reached by steps from the yard as well as from
a door in the rear of each room. The music room,
so often referred to in the old plays, was probably
one of these rooms nearest the stage. Later, however, as structural improvements were introduced,
the portion thus called and reserved for the use of
the musicians was in all likelihood a continuation on
either side of the upper stage, which will be described
later. The people who occupied the yard were called
" groundlings," because they stood on the ground.
They were the commoner sort of tradesmen, apprentices, and petty venders, loose women, pickpockets,
and the like. The better sort of quietly disposed
people sat in the rooms. Respectable women sometimes accompanied their husbands to the rooms, but
on such occasions they always went masked. Not
to do so was a sign of loose morals.

The stage projected into the yard, was rectangular,

and occupied about one-fourth of the area. In the earlier theaters the stage was an open platform upon trestles, later it was boxed in, and in one or two of the theaters it may have been provided with a railing. At any rate, from its projecting position it was open to the view of the audience from three sides. This necessitated all entrances and exits being made from the back or very near it. The stage, however, was not wholly given up to the actors. It was upon either side of the stage that the gallants placed their stools, often arriving late for the mere fun of making a disturbance. These were the most expensive seats in the house, corresponding in a way to the box seats of to-day.

The space directly behind the stage was occupied by a three-story structure. The stage doors opened into the dressing rooms on the first floor. The second story was like a room with the front wall removed, so that its interior was visible to the audience. It was called the upper stage, or the upper gallery. In it were originally represented those parts of the play that were supposed to be separated from what was being acted on the lower or main stage. Before the added improvement of a rear or inner stage on the ground floor, we should imagine the Juliet in the famous balcony scene as appearing on the upper stage, while Romeo stood on the stage proper. The play before the king and the court in *Hamlet* was acted on the upper stage. In the history plays the defenders of the city walls and ramparts would appear on the upper stage, and the besiegers on the stage proper below.

The third story of this rear structure was the hut

that was visible from the outside of the building, and whose use can only be guessed at. It seems almost too elaborate to have been built merely to shelter the bugler before he came out to announce the beginning of the play. Nor is its erection justified on the score that it was a mere support for the flagstaff. This point, however, will be returned to later.

From a point above the upper stage a canopy projected forward sufficiently to cover one-third or one-half of the lower stage. It was called the " heaven," or the " shadow," and served partly as a shelter for the actors in inclement weather.

All of these chief structural points are illustrated in the interior of the Swan, the only contemporary picture of the interior of an Elizabethan theater that has come down to us.

What is certainly a more trustworthy guide to the interior construction of these theaters in the zenith of their fame is the drawing of the interior of the Fortune opposite this page. It is constructed by a modern draughtsman from all the data obtainable, including the builder's contract for the Fortune. Note that the space between the stage and the ground is concealed from the sight of the audience. Such a scene as that of Hamlet at the grave of Ophelia could be adequately represented on this stage, but not on the stage of the Swan, where the spectators could see beneath the floor. Note the two doors, one at either side towards the rear of the middle stage.*

* The portion of the stage proper from the columns that support the shadow forward towards the audience is referred to as the front or the outer stage. From this point

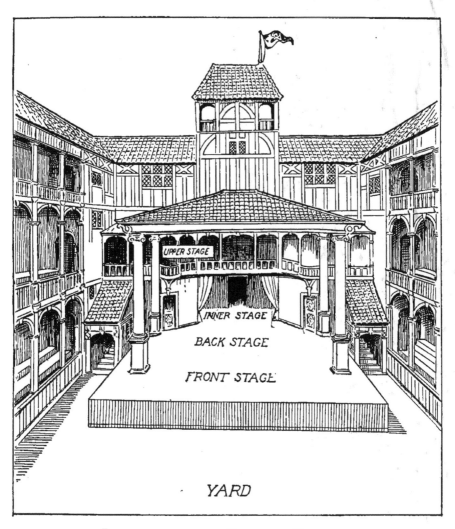

UPPER STAGE

INNER STAGE

BACK STAGE

FRONT STAGE

YARD

INTERIOR OF THE FORTUNE THEATER

In a moment reference will be made to the traverse curtain. This curtain was drawn across so as to cut off the rear stage from the middle stage. Probably there was another traverse drawn between the columns supporting the shadow which could be used to cut off the middle stage from the outer stage.

From the same data has been constructed the plan shown opposite page 34. Notice that when either of the traverses is drawn there is nothing to indicate any division of one stage from another. It is all one space, with a slightly irregular shape.

The cross-section of an Elizabethan theater shown facing page 38 is the result of one of those attempts to incorporate what is known as generally applicable into a typical drawing rather than to make a representation of any particular theater. Note the provision made for sub-stage effects. Also notice that scenes upon painted cloths could be let down from rollers contained in the triangular spaces above the middle stage. And there is fairly presumptive evidence that something of the sort was actually done.

Now let me describe the usual form of stage presentation in Shakespeare's time. After a bugler had announced from the hut by three calls of the bugle at intervals of a minute that the play was about to begin, the prologue entered. He was dressed in a black cloak and crowned with bay leaves. When the prologue had finished his speech, which usually contained an apology for the stage effects, or an

in the opposite direction to the wall of the tiring house is referred to as the back or the middle stage. In the center, and beyond this towards the rear, was a space yet to be described which is referred to as the rear or the inner stage.

explanation of what was to follow, or some other matter in connection with the play, he withdrew, leaving the stage to the possession of the actors. The place of the scene was in some cases indicated by a placard or " title."

It is known that a title was often hung out to indicate the name of the play. It was the custom then to decide, oftentimes, at the last moment, what play was performed. Sometimes the bill was quickly changed at the will of the audience. More difference of opinion exists among critics as to the use of the title to represent the scene. In earlier times the staging was much cruder than in later years. There was what was known as multiple staging, where one part of the stage represented one location, another another, and so on. In such cases titles were probably hung up. If the actor made his exit through one door labeled Rome, or entered through that door, the audience understood the scene as at Rome. But as improvements in the theaters were introduced and the staging became more realistic, this practice became less and less used. It is probable that the title was used very little in the height of the Elizabethan age to represent the location of the scene.

As the play progressed the end of the scene was usually marked by the clearing of the stage for a moment, or the drawing of one of the traverse curtains. The end of the act was frequently marked by dancing or by music. In some plays specific directions are given in this regard. In others there is no indication of the fact. The time of duration of a play in those days precludes the possibility of many or long intermissions. Some places show that the inter-

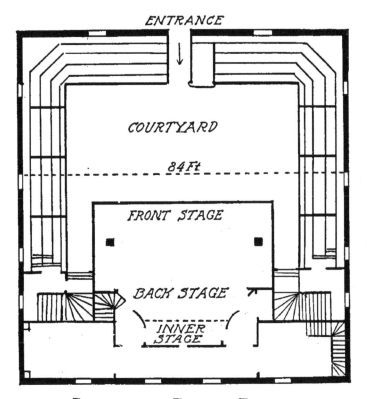

PLAN OF THE FORTUNE THEATER

act music began before the act was quite finished, and continued till after the next act was begun, thus minimizing the actual time of intermission. It is probable that the Elizabethans did not consider the division into acts as a structural necessity, and that intermissions were introduced sparingly for the purpose of relief to the audience, or changing of setting.

At the end of the play was music and a sort of comic aftermath known as the jig. The verses at the end of *Twelfth Night* constitute such a jig. Elsewhere in the present volume the last act of the *Merchant of Venice* is explained as an expansion of the customary jig. This diversion, we suppose, followed even a serious tragedy.

The Elizabethan writers constantly refer to the poverty of their stage effects. Doubtless they spoke in comparison with the costly machinery of the court masks. At all events, these statements seem to have been sometimes taken a trifle too seriously by critics. The Elizabethans were certainly rich in properties. The following are taken from the numerous lists quoted by Fleay and others.

The castle for Lady Peace or Lady Plenty, and the prison in which Discord is watched by Argus; frozen heads; Turk's heads; a monster in which Benbow played; women's masker's hats; fisher's masker's nets; spears for play of Cariclia; holly for Dutton's play; holly for forest; fishermen's trays; palmer's staff; vizard for ape's face; key and hailstones for Janus; altar for Theogines; Andromeda's picture; black physician's beard; palmer's hair; two squirts for Paul's children; the monarch's gown; a basket to hang Diligence in in the play of Probia, etc.

In February, 1577, a play was prepared for court
presentation in which a " counterfeit well " was carried from the Bell in Gracious Street. Artificial
horses often figure in the old plays; a box-tree is
used in *Twelfth Night;* Slitgut climbs into a tree in
Eastward Hoe; Isabella cuts down the arbor in *The
Spanish Tragedy;* ordnance was constantly shot off
in the history plays; in *Locrine* there is a crocodile
stung by a snake and both of them fall into the water;
tents are pitched in many of the history plays;
tables, chairs, beds, boxes, chests, piles of rock, etc.,
etc., are frequently mentioned.

The greatest money outlay referred to in the expense accounts of Henslowe is for costumes. The
clothes worn by the actors were often magnificent.
They were, however, Elizabethan garments. Costuming in the modern sense of the word was then
unknown. Julius Cæsar wore an Elizabethan doublet,
and alludes to it in the lines of the play. Richard
the Third wore Elizabethan armor. One of the earliest notices of the actual use of garments in accordance with correct historical setting relates to that ill-
starred performance of *Henry the Eighth* in which
the Globe Theater was burned to the ground.

Wright, in *The Second Generation of Actors,* says
that there were no scenes in Elizabethan times, and
it is impossible to disprove his assertion absolutely.
There is reason to believe, however, that there was
some scenery in the modern sense of the word. There
are numerous passages in the old plays where people
point to and discuss certain things in a way that
would seem far more unreal if the actor were pointing to nothing in particular than if the descriptive

passage were altogether left out. The burlesque in *A Midsummer Night's Dream,* performed by Bottom and his companions, loses its point if we imagine that there was no scenery on the Elizabethan stage to become the subject of a burlesque.*

The Elizabethans were not shocked by certain situations that would seem impossibly incongruous to us; but this fact is hardly warrant for supposing that they altogether lacked the sense of congruity. While searching about for a cheap substitute for the elaborate scenery of the court masks that was so familiar to the Elizabethans, one is struck by the mention of painted cloths among their expense accounts. These were the popular substitutes for tapestry and interior hangings of all kinds, decorated with pictures, often narrating whole stories by a series. Such properties the players had, for we find them mentioned in their lists. Why should they possess them if they did not use them? Why should not many of the passages that so readily apply to a visible scene have been uttered with the scene described actually present in the form of a painted cloth covering the back of the stage? The hut above the upper stage, or stage gallery, seems to have been too pretentious a structure to have served no other purpose than that of a flagstaff support, or a standing ground for the bugler. It may have contained rollers by which the painted cloths were let down. The idea of elaborate stage scenery was not unknown to the Elizabethans, though barred from the public stage by expense. Nor is it possible to un-

---

* The full significance of this fact in relation to *A Midsummer Night's Dream* was first pointed out to me by one of my students, Mr. Russell Sharp.

derstand the rapid development in construction and staging after the Restoration unless we imagine a beginning in earlier times. Such facts, at least, lend probability to the surmise that the Elizabethans had crude representations of scenes other than what were merely suggested by suitable properties.

There was, we know, a fair-sized space closed off at times by a curtain which could be drawn open at will. This space seems to have been about ten by twenty-five feet and was located at the rear of the stage. There was also a middle space with two doors opening to it in such a position that exits and entrances could be managed independently of the inner stage. This is what we call the middle stage. There must have been secondary curtains. One was the traverse used to shut off the inner stage. The others were probably merely draperies temporarily placed for the occasion of need. Possibly there were side curtains used, to be referred to elsewhere.

The entrances to the inner stage were from the side. It is possible, however, that this convenience existed only in the more up-to-date theaters. The gallery was certainly in existence from an early time, and was usually called the upper stage. This also could be cut off from the view of the audience by a curtain. I am not so sure that the upper stage was directly over the inner stage. Possibly it projected over it slightly, but this is a detail of minor importance. A window in the back part of the inner stage enabled one to look out into space and to suggest by his words a prospect that the audience could not see.

There is fair presumption that windows existed above the doors that opened upon the lower stage.

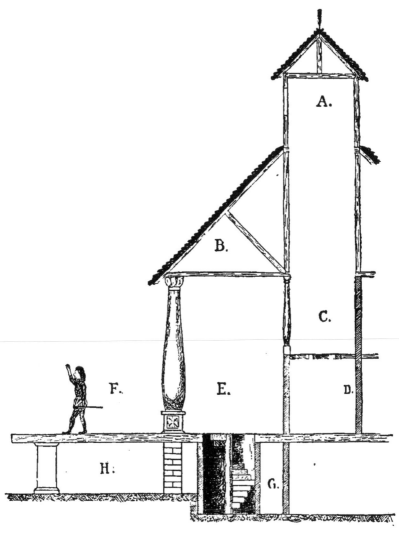

CROSS-SECTION OF THE ELIZABETHAN STAGE
(Adapted from a print by Brodmeier)

A. Loft, possibly used for painted cloths.
B. Loft for properties and machinery.
C Balcony Stage.
D. Rear Stage.

E. Inner Stage.
F. Outer Stage.
G. Steps for Trap, etc.
H. Space under Front Stage.

From *The Development of Shakespeare as a Dramatist* by George P. Baker
(The Macmillan Company)

This is an important detail in staging such scenes as the balcony scene in *Romeo and Juliet,* as this arrangement would allow both actors to stand sideways to the audience, a much more effective position than that in which one faced and the other stood with his back to the audience.

Scenes in Elizabethan plays are of two kinds. There are those having an indefinite location, or, at least, a location which enables them to be easily staged without accessory properties; and also those scenes that do require the setting up of various properties and paraphernalia. The former are called outer scenes because they were acted on the outer stage with no scenic accompaniment; and the latter inner scenes because they made use of the middle and inner stages where the properties had been set in preparation.

And this is the point. While an outer scene was being acted with the traverse curtain hiding the inner stage the setting of the inner scene to follow was being put into place. At the proper time the traverse was drawn and the scene acted on the inner and outer stage combined. At the end the curtains were again drawn shut. While scene three was being acted on the outer stage the setting of scene two was being taken away and that of scene four put in place. And so on alternately. It must not be assumed that this principle was followed with such monotonous regularity as is suggested by the above. See the discussion of *The Merchant of Venice,* where it is shown that the same inner scene is returned to again and again throughout the first three acts of the play.

This conception of the method of staging Elizabethan plays removes two stumbling-blocks that have hitherto been in the way. First, the rapidity with which an Elizabethan play was performed, for we know that the duration of a performance was scarcely longer than it takes to pronounce the lines, is accounted for. Second, the old idea that everything in the way of change upon the stage was performed in plain sight of the audience not only contradicts and renders unintelligible many of the contemporary stage directions but also suggests intrusions and distractions necessary to the changing of properties which would have entirely upset the unity if not the gravity of the piece.

If I were constructing a new picture of an Elizabethan stage I should attempt to include one detail which, though of great importance, has been thus far altogether ignored. I refer to the fact that part of the audience sat upon the stage itself. And this detail is of twofold importance. Elizabethan men wore clothes that for variety of form and brilliancy of color exceeded the fashion even of party dress among women of to-day. What hostess to-day could give a ball and decorate her drawing-room in advance so that the colors would harmonize with the colors of the gowns worn by her expected guests? Yet those who have had anything to do with theatrical affairs know how necessary it is to plan harmoniously every detail of the stage picture from costume to drapery, and paper on the wall. Now this possibility was denied the Elizabethan stage manager, who could never estimate in advance the unknown quantity of many gaily-dressed young men on the stage itself in close proximity to the actors.

On the other hand, this very fact gave him one splendid opportunity denied the modern playwright. I once saw *The Merchant of Venice* played in a small country town by a troupe of barnstormers. In the great trial scene, impressive as it was even under such circumstances, the ticket seller, two ushers, and a village lad were pressed into service to make up the unruly rabble of spectators in the court-room. At another time I saw the same play put on the stage by Sir Henry Irving. In his production a score of trained persons, carefully costumed and drilled in their parts, appeared in this scene with never a line to speak. I was impressed at the time with the relative expense of this detail. This, however, is what the Elizabethan stage manager found ready to hand. Actors and people wore the same kind of clothes, though they might differ in cut and color. Nothing was seen in the audience that might not have appeared on the stage. In *The Knight of the Burning Pestle* a member of the audience climbs upon the stage, and it is some time before it becomes apparent that he is in reality one of the actors. If an actor stepped suddenly among the spectators seated along the sides of the stage he could not be distinguished by general appearance from one who had just risen to his feet from among the stage portion of the audience. Thus the stage manager could always count upon merging his small handful of actors on the stage into the larger group of spectators, also on the stage, without the least hint of discord, just as the real scenery of a modern stage merges into the painted perspective at the back.

And now let us look for a moment at the character

of the audience in an Elizabethan playhouse. For, perhaps, it was largely due to this unruly audience that Ben Jonson was put upon the shelf and his rival Shakespeare kept alive for us to to-day.

That was a cruel, boisterous, half-savage age. The people were superstitious; they believed ardently in witchcraft, ghosts, and fairies; many of the sports both of boys and of men were cruel to a degree with which we now have no sympathy. Branding in the face, slitting the nose, clipping the ears, even hanging, were penalties inflicted for petty crimes. Men wore swords as a habit and were accustomed to taking the law into their own hands. From such a people we must expect noisy behavior in the playhouse, though they were, in many respects, much more appreciative of the drama than the modern audience.

The people who sat in the rooms were, as a rule, well enough inclined. The characteristic scenes happened in the yard and on the margins of the stage. The former, having no seats, tempted people to move about during the performance. Doubtless a person bent on crossing the yard used his arms and elbows freely, and trod on people's toes. If the audience was in a good humor this sort of behavior would provoke a general laugh; but, likely as not, there would be angry blows, sometimes a general row.

During the play venders of apples, cakes, ale, tobacco, etc., hawked their goods about the yard and in the galleries. Sometimes a deeply tragic part would be interrupted by a cry of "Pickpocket! Caught!" The play would be stopped while the luckless cutpurse was hustled out of the theater.

The gentlemen on the stage were little better. It

was thought a clever trick to come in late enough to interrupt the prologue with a lot of noise in placing one's stool. Once in their seats the gallants did not scruple to bandy words with people in the yard, flirt with women in the rooms, or interrupt the players during a speech. We are told that sometimes these gallants crowded so close upon the stage that the players came forward and appealed to the audience to know whether more room was not needed in which to act. If the play for the day was not liked, the actors were pelted and hooted off the stage.

Among the numerous pamphlets of Elizabethan times, none is so racy, so amusing, or so useful as a bit of social history as *The Gull's Hornbook.* The following is taken from the direction of a young gallant about to go to the theater.

"Whether therefore the gatherers of the Publique or Private Play-house stand to receive the afternoones rent, let our Gallant (having paid it) presently advance himself up to the Throne of the Stage . . . on the very Rushes where the Commedy is to daunce, yea, and under the state of *Cambises* himself must our feathered *Estridge* like a piece of Ordnance, be planted, valiantly (because impudently) beating down the mewes and hisses of the opposed rascality.

"By sitting on the stage, you may (with small cost), purchase the deere acquaintance of the boyes; have a good stoole for sixpence; at any time know what particular part any of the infants present; get your match lighted, examine the play suits, lace, and perhaps win wagers upon laying it is copper, etc.

"And to conclude, whether you be a fool or a Justice of the peace, a Cuckold or a Capten, a Lord-Maiors sonne, or a dawcock, a knave or an under-Sheriff; of what stamp soever you be, current or counterfeit, the stage, like time, will bring you to most perfect light and lay you open:

neither are you to be hunted from thence, though the Scarecrows in the yard hoot at you, hiss at you, spit at you, yea, throw dirt even in your teeth; 'tis most gentleman like patience to endure all this, and to laugh at the silly Animals: but if the *Rabble,* with a full throat cry away with the foole, you were worse than a madman to tarry by it; for the gentleman and the foole should never sit on the stage together. . . .

"Present yourself not on the Stage (especially at a new play) untill the quaking prologue hath (by rubbing) got color into his cheeks, and is ready to give the trumpets their Cue, that hees upon point to enter; for then it is time, as though you were one of the *properties,* or that you dropt out of ye *Hangings* to creep from behind the Arras, with your *Tripos* or three footed stoole in one hand, and a teston mounted between a fore-finger and a thumb in the other; for if you should bestow your person upon the vulgar when the belly of the house is but half full, your apparell is quite eaten up, the fashion lost, and the proportion of your body in more danger to be devoured than if you were served up in the Counter amongst the Powltry; avoid that as you would the Bastome. It shall crown you with rich commendation to laugh aloud in the middest of the most serious and saddest scene of the terriblest Tragedy; and let that clapper (your tongue) be tost so high, that all the house may ring of it. . . . As first, all the eyes in the gallery will leave walking after the Players, and onely follow you; the simplest dolt in the house snatches up your name, and when he meets you in the streets, or that you fall into his hands in the middle of a Watch, his word shall be taken for you; heele cry *Hees such a gallant,* and you passe . . .

"Before the play begins, fall to cards; you may win or loose (as fencers do in a prize) and beat one-another by confederacie, yet share the money when you meet at supper; notwithstanding, to gul the *Raggamuffins* that stand aloofe gaping at you, throw the cards (having first torn four or five of them) round the Stage, just upon the third sound, as though you had lost; it skills not if the four knaves ly on their backs, and outface the Audience; theres none such fools as dare take exception at them, because, ere the play go off, better knaves than they will fall into the company.

" Now, sir, if the writer be a fellow that hath both either epigrammd you, or hath had a flirt at your mistress, or hath brought either your feather, or your red beard, or your little legs, &c. on the stage, you shall disgrace him worse than by tossing him in a blanket, or giving him a bastinado in a Tavern, if, in the middle of his play, you rise with a screwd and discontented face from your stoole and be gone; no matter whether the scenes be good or no; the better they are the worse do you distaste them; and, being on your feet, sneak not away like a coward, but salute all your gentle acquaintance, that are spread either on the rushes, or on stooles about you, and draw what troup you can after you; the *Mimicks* are beholden to you, for allowing them elbow roome; their poet cries, perhaps, a pox go with you, but care not for that, theres no music without frets.

" Marry, if either the company, or the indisposition of the weather bind you to sit it out, my counsel is then that you turn plain Ape, take up a rush, and tickle the earnest eares of your fellow gallants, to make other fooles fall a laughing; mew at passionate speeches, blare at merrie, find fault with the musicke, whew at the childrens Action, whistle at the songs, and above all, curse the sharers. . . ."

Though *The Gull's Hornbook* is a comical satire, Dekker truly represents the time. Yet the Elizabethan audience was not all bad. Their rudeness was, in the main, good-natured, not a rudeness due to malice. Furthermore, the Elizabethans knew a good play when they saw it. Many a poor comedy that satisfies the popular taste to-day would never have got safely through the first night three hundred years ago. This fact has much to do with the general excellence of the Elizabethan drama. After all, there was manifested in the audience of that day the gen-nine spirit of true sport, of every fellow for himself, and give the Devil his due, that has always character-ized the English, whether of the time of the Armada or of Waterloo.

So far I have attempted to give the generally ac-cepted picture of the Elizabethan stage. Let me end the chapter by reference to one of the mooted points about which there are two opinions.

In the study of Shakespeare's plays the present writer lays great stress upon two points as con-tributive above all others to thorough appreciation: 1. A knowledge of the social life and conditions of the people at the time the plays were written. 2. An understanding of Elizabethan staging. It is true that the effect of modern stagecraft is often ruinous to Shakespeare's plays. They were written for other conditions. The modern dress is an awkward misfit. Wherever possible or necessary, I have attempted in the following pages to suggest the Elizabethan setting.

This chapter has shown from what scanty material much of the story of Elizabethan staging has been constructed. The question may be put as to some of the suggestions contained in the following pages as to how I know it was done that way. To be truthful, I do not know. But I bear the following constantly in mind. We know enough of the Elizabethan court masks to know that stage scenery as elaborate as any used to-day was then in use. We know that this was debarred by expense from the public stage. We also know that the Elizabethans were extremely imitative, imaginative, and ingenious. We know in general the construction of their playhouses. We have many lists of their properties. Oftentimes we can read almost to a certainty between the lines that certain things were done upon the stage, though we do not know just how they were done.

To my mind the situation suggested by these facts reduces itself almost to a mathematical problem. If one of us can easily invent such a staging for an Elizabethan scene as any ingenious person could construct out of what we know they had in those days, is it unfair to assume that the ingenious Elizabethans did as well, if not better? More likely better. They were more used than we are to making a little go a great way.

One point in particular needs a note in this connection. Not only do many of the Shakespeare scenes imply a considerable setting, but some of them also imply a darkened stage. Consider the last act of *The Merchant of Venice*. Innumerable allusions cry out for a darkened stage. It may be urged that the stage was not darkened and that these references are put in for the sole purpose of suggesting night. In many cases this situation is doubtless true. But is it true here? My own feeling is that the number of references is so large that all value as suggestion on a light stage would be lost through overdoing. Furthermore, some of the points, such as the failure of one person to see or recognize another when he first comes upon the stage, could be easily managed more effectively in other ways if the stage were light. Does not the fact that it was not done otherwise imply that the stage was not light?

There appeared in the *Century Magazine* for December, 1911, an article by Mr. Corbin. In this he calls attention to the canopy over the stage, frequently

referred to as the Shadow, or the Heavens. He con-
jectures that some canvas arrangement could be
spread from the shadow which would effectually close
the open top of the theater, thus producing a considerable gloom upon the stage. I might further cite a
phrase from *Henry the Sixth,* " Hung be the heavens
with black," to show that arrangements were actually
in use for dropping hangings from the stage canopy.
It would be easy, by means of a few wires stretched
across the top of the playhouse, a roll of canvas, and
a bundle of rings, to sufficiently darken the space
below as it is to-day to control by the same means
the light in a photographic studio. It is no com-
pliment to the Elizabethans to assume that they lacked
the ingenuity to do so. (See the discussion of *The
Merchant of Venice* for a further treatment of this
subject.)

CHAPTER IV

QUARTOS AND FOLIOS

PLAYHOUSE owners in Shakespeare's day considered it unwise to publish plays. Plays, however, got into print in spite of opposition. Oftentimes a play was so popular that its publication would be a profitable venture to any printer who could get hold of a copy of the play. Laws were so loose and public opinion so lax that there was little likelihood of punishment as the result of publishing a play without permission. On such occasions, actors and managers guarded their written copies of the plays zealously. If neither love nor bribery could procure a copy for the piratical publisher, he resorted to actual theft in the open playhouse. That is, he would send a man to take down the play while it was being acted. As shorthand writing was not then developed to the extent it is to-day this process usually resulted in very imperfect copies.

On the other hand, as plays were usually short-lived upon the stage, managers willingly resorted to publication when the play was no longer popular on the stage. In such cases, however, the publication followed the original production of the play by several years.

There is, however, an interesting and unique exception. Two quartos of *Hamlet* appeared very

promptly after the appearance of the play on the
stage, and both before it had in any way lost its
popularity. Various theories have been advanced to
account for this fact. I incline to believe that the first
quarto, which seems to be a very imperfect copy of
the play as we know it, is the result of a piratical
publisher's theft in the playhouse, as described above.
And that the second quarto, an excellent copy, was
published with the authority of Shakespeare's company in order to protect itself against the spurious
first quarto.

However, the plays that in one way or another
got into print during Shakespeare's lifetime were published in quarto form. They were thin pamphlets, so
called because the sheet after printing was folded
into four. The average size of the page was about
six by nine inches. During Shakespeare's life and
the intervening years before the publication of the
Folio sixteen plays were published in quarto form.
Some of them appeared successively in several editions. These plays were:

1594 Titus Andronicus.
1597 Richard II.
1597 Richard III.
1597 Romeo and Juliet.
1598 1 Henry IV.
1598 Love's Labour's Lost.
1600 Merchant of Venice.
1600 Henry V.
1600 2 Henry IV.
1600 Midsummer Night's Dream.
1602 Merry Wives of Windsor.
1603 Hamlet. (Mutilated copy.)
1604 Hamlet. (True copy.)
1608 King Lear.

1608 Pericles.
1609 Troilus and Cressida.
1622 Othello.

Before 1557 there was very little supervision over publication. A guild of publishers, called the Stationers' Company, exercised practically no authority over its members. Later a law was passed making it illegal for any one not a member of the Stationers' Company to operate a printing press. During the greater part of Elizabeth's reign no book could be printed till it was licensed by the Stationers' Company. When permission was granted the fact was entered upon the company's register. Thus the Stationers' Register * affords many interesting details regarding the early publication of Shakespeare's plays. Gradually the company acquired the power and developed the will to protect the printers to whom it licensed books. It paid, however, little or no attention to the author or his rights. Though he had some recourse in the courts, the process was so cumbersome and expensive that it was seldom resorted to. Thus, even under the protection of the Stationers' Company the publication of a book fit for publication at all was merely a question of the possession of the manuscript, with or without the author's permission.

Shakespeare retired from London to Stratford several years before his death in 1616. After his death, seven years elapsed before any one thought of publishing a complete edition of his plays. The work was done, however, in 1623. The volume which then appeared is known as the First Folio, or, merely, the Folio.

* Abbreviated S.R.

The following account of the Folio is abridged from Mr. Sidney Lee's life of the poet. In 1623 the first attempt was made to give to the world a complete edition of Shakespeare's plays. Two fellow-actors and intimate friends, John Heming and Henry Condell, were nominally responsible for the venture, but a small syndicate of printers and publishers undertook all pecuniary responsibility. The First Folio was printed at the press in the Barbican, which Jaggard * had acquired of Roberts. Upon Blount * probably fell the chief labor of seeing the book through the press. It was in press throughout 1623, and had so far advanced by November 8 that on that day Edward Blount and Isaac Jaggard obtained formal license from the Stationers' Company to publish sixteen of the hitherto unprinted plays it was intended to include. Four other hitherto unprinted dramas for which no license was sought figured in the volume, namely, 1 and 2 *Henry VI, King John,* and *The Taming of the Shrew;* but each of these plays was based by Shakespeare on a play of like title which had been published at an earlier date, and the absence of a license was probably due to an ignorant misconception on the part either of the Stationers' officers or of the editors of the volume as to the true relations subsisting between the old pieces and the new. The only play by Shakespeare that had been previously published and was not included in the First Folio was *Pericles.*

The volume consisted of nearly one thousand double-column pages, and was sold at a pound a copy. From the number of copies that survive it may be

* Members of the syndicate referred to.

estimated that the edition numbered five hundred. On the title page was engraved the Droeshout portrait. Commendatory verses were supplied by Ben Jonson and others. The dedication was addressed to the brothers William Herbert, Earl of Pembroke, the Lord Chamberlain, and Philip Herbert, Earl of Montgomery, and was signed by Shakespeare's friends and fellow-actors, Heming and Condell.

There is no doubt that the whole volume was printed from the acting versions in the possession of the manager of the company with which Shakespeare had been associated. But it is doubtful if any play was printed exactly as it came from his pen. The text of the First Folio is often inferior to that of the pre-existent quartos.

The plays are arranged under three heads, comedies, histories, and tragedies, and each division is separately paged. As a specimen of typography the First Folio is not to be commended. The misprints are numerous and are especially conspicuous in the pagination. The sheets seem to have been worked off very slowly, and corrections were made while the press was working, so that copies struck off later differ from the earlier copies. One mark of carelessness on the part of the compositor or of the corrector for the press, which is common to all copies, is that *Troilus and Cressida,* though in the body of the book it opens the section of the tragedies, is not mentioned at all in the table of contents, and the play is unpaged, except on its second and third pages, which bear the numbers 79 and 80.

The number of surviving copies exceeds one hundred and eighty, of which one-third are now in America. Only fourteen are in a perfect state, that is, with the portrait printed (not inlaid) on the title page, and the fly-leaf facing it, with all the pages succeeding it intact and uninjured. (The fly-leaf contains Ben Jonson's verses attesting the truthfulness of the portrait.) Of these, the finest and cleanest is the "Daniel" copy which belonged to the late Baroness Burdett-Coutts. It measures thirteen inches by eight and a fourth. On March 23, 1907, the copy of the First Folio formerly in the library of the late Frederick Locker-Lampson fetched at Sotheby's £3,600 (about $18,000). This is the largest sum yet realized at public auction.

The second, third, and fourth folios, usually referred to by the abbreviations, F_2, F_3, F_4, appeared in 1632, 1663, 1685. To all intents and purposes each of these folios is a reprint of the preceding.

An accurate reprint, though not a facsimile, of the First Folio has recently been issued by Crowell and Co.

CHAPTER V ·

SHAKESPEARE'S VERSE

MR. DOWDEN says that the highest passion of all finds its expression in prose. This assertion seems at first sight to be in accordance with our ideas. Prose seems to be more the language of nature than verse. Mr. Dowden cites some of the speeches of King Lear as illustrative. ` Is the illustration, however, quite apt? If tested by Shakespeare's other plays the situation does not seem to fit. Some of the most intense moments of passion are phrased in verse. Note the words of Hamlet, " Absent thee from felicity awhile," etc. This fact is true even in *King Lear*. Prose is used in parts of *King Lear* because the king is going mad. His thoughts are incoherent. The very essence of verse is coherence, therefore it is out of harmony with such a situation. Shakespeare, almost of necessity, depended sometimes upon prose, and not always prose of the most orderly sort.

Some characters in the plays are essentially unpoetic and are made to speak prose; yet Enobarbus, the blunt-spoken common soldier in *Antony and Cleopatra*, recites that most wonderful description of Cleopatra in her barge.

Frequently Shakespeare desired to imitate the language of ordinary conversation, and made use of prose. On the other hand, there are passages in which he accomplishes the same task in verse with no diminution in the naturalness of effect.

Sometimes the poet seems to make use of prose for no other purpose than to emphasize the contrast with other passages spoken in verse: as where Hamlet describes the make-up of the human frame.

The fact of the matter seems to be that no rule is discoverable which uniformly applies to when Shakespeare did or did not use prose or verse. My belief is that he used one form or the other as the spirit moved him, that is, intuitively, in whichever form his thoughts naturally expressed themselves, and that no rule or method of procedure occurred to him in advance. He was inspired by momentary preference and intuition.

Much has been written concerning the form and quality of Shakespeare's verse. Blank verse was then in its infancy, not yet having been fully reduced to rule. To the student of metrics the whole subject presents a wealth of exceptions that may well occupy such an one's attention to the exclusion of more important matters. To the student who is interested in the actual plays, rather than in the study of meter for its own sake, the subject is not so intricate. In fact, for our present purpose, it may be reduced to a few simple statements.

Shakespeare wrote at a time when blank verse was comparatively new in English poetry. It had not been practised and pruned to the extent we find it in Tennyson. Then, too, Shakespeare wrote blank verse for people to speak, for actors who took all sorts of liberties with pronunciation, and who were able and often found the opportunity to fill up a gap with a significant gesture. Hence we may expect to find it composed very loosely.

The normal line of Shakespeare's blank verse consists of five iambic feet. The lines are unrhymed. The end of a line corresponds with a pause in the sense. Lines differing from this normal type are, however, almost as frequent as lines composed strictly in accordance with it.

The principal variations are as follows: In early plays many lines are rhymed. We find that the comparative number of rhymed lines steadily decreases as we follow the list of plays in chronological order. In the early plays we find much doggerel and many stanzas. This practice also decreased as Shakespeare grew older, though songs are introduced into the plays till the very end. Lines shorter and longer than five feet often occur, the latter more frequently when a line is divided between two speakers. Lines in which there is no sense pause at the end frequently occur. They are called " run-on " lines to distinguish them from " end-stopped " lines. Run-on lines occur more frequently in the later plays.

There are still other frequent variations. The iambic foot consists of two syllables, the first unaccented, the second accented. The order of accent may be reversed in any foot, sometimes in two or more feet of the same line. An unaccented syllable may be added to any foot, more frequently at the end of the line. Such extra syllables are much slighted in pronunciation. After a pause an unaccented syllable is often dropped. One should frequently imagine such a gap accompanied on the stage by a pause just long enough to enable the actor to continue the original rhythm when he resumes his speech. Occasionally the purpose of such a break is to produce an intentional jar. Sometimes lines of an altogether different form are introduced for the sake of variety.

Scansion of Shakespeare's verse is often facilitated by a knowledge of Elizabethan pronunciation. Space can be afforded here for only a few references to the more important details of this subject.

Contractions, such as th' for the, and expansions, such as i-on for ion, are not necessarily indicated in the text. Where they are not indicated they must be supplied by the reader's sense of rhythm. The more important rules of pronunciation are:

The loss of an unaccented syllable before a consonant is common.

'gainst = against.
'venge = avenge.

Sometimes a prefix beginning with a consonant is thus lost.

'fore = before.

An initial vowel is often dropped and the consonant combined with the preceding word.

what 's = what is.
they 're = they are.

Such combinations as the following are common:

I've = I have.
he 'th = he hath.
let 's = let us.
before 's = before us.
defy 's = defy us.
'tis = it is.
is 't = is it.

Most of the above contractions are still in frequent use; but in Shakespeare's plays we must often introduce them even when not indicated in the printed text.

The final letter is often omitted.

i' the = in the.
th' lad = the lad.
o' me = oh, me.

Many words of several syllables are contracted by elision.

prison = prisn.
perilous = perlous.
heartily = heartly.
opening = opning.
prisoner = prisner.
reckoning = reckning.
Antony = Antny.
ordinance = ordnance.
desperate = desprate.
temporal = tempral.
general = genral.

Words containing v and th are often slighted in pronunciation, thus:

devil = del or de'il.
evil = eil.
ever = ere.
even = ene.
whether = where.
whither = whire.
hither = here.
thither = thire.

On the other hand, words were often expanded in pronunciation.

marriage = marri-age.
celestial = celesti-al.
Christian = Christi-an.
valiant = vali-ant.
familiar = famil-i-ar.
conscience = consci-ence.
suspicion = suspici-on.
chariot = chari-ot.
gracious = graci-ous.
determined = determin-ed.

The word spirit when pronounced sprite retained all the dignity of the former word, and was synonymous with it. Hamlet speaks of his father's ghost as a sprite. The rhythm will guide the reader to a one- or two-syllable pronunciation, whether the word be spelled in the text spirit, sprite, or spright.

This is is frequently contracted into *this*. And there are many other similar words and phrases. But enough are cited for the purpose of illustration.

Many words are accented differently: access', auth'orized, aspect', com'plete, cano'nized, envy', pio'neer, portents', perse'vere, perse'verence, rheu'-matic. Most of these words are also found with their present pronunciation.

Words like fire, dear, hour, were frequently dwelled upon sufficiently to make them count for two syllables. The rolling of the r was a characteristic detail of Elizabethan speech.

In closing this brief note on the subject of meter I should call attention to the fact that not every line of verse in Shakespeare can be satisfactorily scanned with any degree of regularity. In many cases this fact is probably due to the corrupt state of the text.

The whole subject is well summarized thus by Mr. Manly:

"In reading Shakespeare, slurs, elisions, resolutions, and contractions occur and must be reckoned with. But they are always found to be such as harmonize with the proper recitation of the lines and not mere artificial products of forcing the rhythm into a system." (Intro. *Macbeth,* xxxiv.)

CHAPTER VI

CHRONOLOGICAL LIST OF PLAYS

I⊤ has not been easy to determine the dates of Shakespeare's plays. In fact, there is general agreement as to the dates of each play within a limit of one or two years in most cases. Different critics, however, disagree oftentimes as to the exact date to which this or that play is to be assigned.

The date of a play is an inference based upon many facts. The evidence of early or late style is taken into consideration. The dates contained in the Stationers' Register are often important. So are the dates of the quartos. Sometimes a play refers to known historical facts, to other books whose dates of publication are known, or quotes from another play whose date of composition is established. This kind of *internal* evidence implies a date after which the play cannot have been written. Some other piece of writing may refer to the play itself. If the date of this piece of writing is known it sets a date before which the play must have been written. This is known as *external* evidence. The sifting of all such evidence has led to the present chronology.

The introductions to the Tudor Edition of the plays recite the evidence of the dates there assigned, which have been quoted in the following list:

1590-91   1 Henry VI.
1591-92   2 Henry VI.

1592	3 Henry VI.
1592-96	Richard III.
1594-95	King John.
1595-96	Richard II.
1597	1 Henry IV.
1597-98	2 Henry IV.
1599	Henry V.
1613	Henry VIII.
1591	Love's Labour's Lost.
1591	The Comedy of Errors.
1592	Two Gentlemen of Verona.
1594-95	Midsummer Night's Dream.
1594-97	The Taming of the Shrew.
1596-97	The Merchant of Venice.
1598-1601	All's Well That Ends Well.
1599-1600	As You Like It.
1599	Much Ado About Nothing.
1599-1600	The Merry Wives of Windsor.
1601	Twelfth Night.
1601-02	Troilus and Cressida.
1603-04	Measure for Measure.
1607-08	Pericles.
1609-10	Cymbeline.
1610-11	The Winter's Tale.
1610-11	The Tempest.
1594	Titus Andronicus.
1594-95	Romeo and Juliet.
1599	Julius Cæsar.
1602-04	Hamlet.
1604	Othello.
1606	King Lear.
1606	Macbeth.
1606-08	Timon of Athens.
1607-08	Antony and Cleopatra.
1608-10	Coriolanus.

CHAPTER VII

DRAMATIC STRUCTURE

EVERY one who reads a play realizes that much of the effect produced depends upon the local color, the words and phrases used, scenery and properties, suggestions, bits of foreshadowing, cross-references, etc. All such details, however, are manufactured by the playwright late in the process of constructing a play. They are, figuratively speaking, scattered over or hung upon the skeleton of the play. A description of what is meant by this skeleton involves the subject of dramatic structure. In other words, the structure of a drama may be compared to the framework of a building on which are engrafted the decorations.

There are differences in this framework according as the play is of one type or another. Let us postpone the consideration of such differences for the present and consider as the type a play which is to be taken seriously. Such a play need not necessarily be a tragedy, though hardly an out-and-out farce.

It is necessary, however, first to consider a few general details.

What is meant by dramatic? A drama is a story. The essence of the drama is action—but all action is not dramatic. Action is dramatic only when it leads to more action. Yet this action need not be physical action. It may be mental. Thus an argu-

64

ment which leads to physical action is dramatic, as Antony's oration over Cæsar's body. Or, a discussion that changes the ideas of persons in the play and thus leads them to action is essentially dramatic, as the soliloquy of Lady Macbeth after reading her husband's letter. Pure passion, even inaction, may be dramatic if it is made the means of leading to more action.

A drama should contain a dominant idea. Because one cannot lay aside a drama as one can a novel, but must listen to the end at one sitting, the play must be a unit. That is, there must be some one thing that is begun, carried on, and brought to a conclusion during the performance. This is usually called the *idea*.

Think of the novels you have read. Can you sum up each one in a single sentence? *The Prisoner of Zenda*—yes; *Vanity Fair*—no. A good drama can be thus summed up. It has a well-defined theme, a topic sentence, so to speak. Thus in *Macbeth:* the conflict between Macbeth and fate in the person of Macduff in which the character of the former is gradually depraved till it leads to his downfall. In *Richard the Second:* the overthrow of a weak, wicked monarch by one whose opposite characteristics better fit him to rule as king.

It is also well to remember that many rules of dramatic technique depend upon the mechanical and physical conditions under which the play is produced. Many structural differences between the Elizabethan plays and the plays of to-day are due to architectural differences between the old and the new theaters. The rapidity of performance allows the audience no time to stop and think, hence omissions, contradictions, etc., may be tolerated in a play that would be altogether out of place in a novel. This rapidity of performance prevents one from weighing details too critically; it enables the dramatist to juggle with the feelings of his audience in a way utterly impossible under other conditions. The tiring of the audience physically, mentally, and emotionally accounts for the requirement of greater brevity and more rapid action as the end of the play approaches. And as the audience wishes to leave the playhouse fully satisfied, every question raised by the play must be disposed of before the curtain falls.

We have suggested what sort of material is essentially dramatic. A mere mass of dramatic material, however, does not constitute a dramatic story. The story of a drama differs in one important detail from what may be a good story for a novel. A dramatic story must have a beginning and an end.

As these words are used with a technical significance, it is necessary to explain them. Recall for a moment the story of *Vanity Fair*. Is there any particular reason for beginning the story at the point where Thackeray takes it up? There is none. The story could just as well have been begun later; or, had Thackeray so wished, he could have begun a volume earlier. So, too, the story could have been ended sooner, might possibly have been thereby improved. Also, as affairs are at the end of the volume, it would be possible to go right on with many more events. In other words, as we look back over the history of Becky Sharp we find no part of it cut out as a single piece, standing alone, for treatment here.

This story is without beginning or end in the dramatic sense.

Consider, by way of contrast, the story of Hamlet's life, both as we have it in the play and as we have it pieced out by our fancy. As our imagination roams over his whole life we suddenly pause at one significant event, the supernatural revelation of a crime. This event begins a new era in Hamlet's life. The results of it bring new forces into play. Then they play themselves out. When this is done there is nothing left to write about. The early history of Hamlet could not be incorporated into the play without becoming an unnecessary drag. Nor can one conceive a sequel to Hamlet. It is this sharply defined initial occurrence, and the equally sharp finality of the conclusion that constitute in the dramatic sense the beginning and the end. Thus, every good dramatic story is capable of being isolated from its chronological surroundings as a whole—that is, it has a beginning and an end. And both, so to speak, are final.

Furthermore, every dramatic story involves a struggle. Sometimes it is a struggle between ideas; but more frequently between two people or between two groups of people. At any rate, the idea of a struggle is always present. And the presentation of this struggle on the stage follows a regular course. The reader must be sufficiently informed in regard to preliminary events to understand what follows (the introduction). Then comes the initial event, the beginning, out of which the story grows (the exciting force). One element of the struggle involved gradually rises into prominent significance (the rising action) till it reaches (the turning-point), the place where it begins to find the other element of the struggle too strong to be withstood. While the balance of power swings the other way (the falling action) we approach the end of the play, the technical end referred to above (the catastrophe).

Before calling attention to some of the minor details concerning the presentation of this arrangement, it is necessary to dwell for a moment longer on the technical terms contained above in parentheses.

The peculiar nature of dramatic production entails a certain way of opening the narrative. It should be remembered that the audience has no control over the speed of production. If, in reading a novel, one becomes confused, one can pause, re-read, turn back, or ponder as deliberately as one wishes. This opportunity, however, is denied the playgoer. The presentation of the play goes right on without interruption. If the audience is confused, there is no time to stop and straighten matters out. Hence, one of the absolute requirements of dramatic story-telling is perfect clearness from start to finish.

This requirement implies an *introduction*. The dramatist cannot plunge into the middle of his story. He must begin at the beginning, in fact, a little before the beginning. No matter how sharply defined the technical beginning of the play, its full comprehension presupposes something. Some details must be known which lead up to and account for it. Furthermore, the audience must become acquainted with the principal characters, and know something of their personalities as well as of their relations to each other. And the story will be much more effectively received if the audience is put in the proper mood, acquainted from the start with the keynote of what is to follow.

It is the purpose of the *introduction* to furnish all this material in the briefest possible space consistent with clearness and completeness.

Then comes the *exciting force*. This is the technical beginning spoken of above, the initial event that sets things going. It must stand out prominently, be of sufficient importance of itself, and the following events should grow out of it in accordance with the law of cause and effect. Every plot detail that follows should be traceable more or less directly back to this event. The *exciting force* excites the quiescent conditions of the introduction into action.

The *rising action* can be disposed of in a few words. It is merely the logical development of the story from the appearance of the exciting force to the climax of interest known as the turning-point. This scanty definition will seem more sufficient after reading what follows descriptive of the turning-point.

As the phrase *turning-point* suggests, something in the drama turns at this point. Let us see what it is. As has been said, every dramatic story involves a struggle between two forces. And this struggle is so presented that at first one of the forces is dominant and, throughout the rising action, seems mounting to success. At the turning-point, however, we begin to see that the present success is temporary and that ultimately the other force will prevail. The turning-point, then, is the place where the success of one element of the struggle begins to find itself powerless before the ultimate success of the other element of the struggle.

In *Hamlet,* for instance, the struggle is between Hamlet and Claudius. Late in the first act, after the introduction, the exciting force appears in the form of the ghost's revelation to Hamlet. As a result, Hamlet is bent on just revenge. During the rising action the story develops. Hamlet formulates and puts into action "The Mouse-Trap." Hamlet, however, so mismanages this little device that Claudius reaps an advantage. He is immediately roused into action. Henceforth, throughout the falling action Claudius is the aggressor, directing his heretofore quiescent energy against Hamlet. The "Mouse-Trap" scene where Hamlet's aggressive behavior reaches the maximum and immediately sinks before the energy of Claudius, may be called the turning-point of the play.

The *falling action* of the second half of the play corresponds to the rising action of the first half. It is the logical working out of the new turn of affairs that has been ushered into existence by the turning-point.

The *catastrophe* is the end. It should correspond with the end of the play, all minor details having been disposed of previously; and it should also come as a climax of interest.

Oftentimes the climax of an Elizabethan play is followed by a brief passage that is usually omitted to-day. The entrance of Fortinbras and his soldiers at the end of *Hamlet* is such a passage. It was inserted by Shakespeare not for dramatic purposes, but for mechanical. The absence of a drop curtain in the theaters of that day made some such device necessary in order to rid the stage easily of the dead bodies.

The familiar diagram representing the structure of a drama is given below. *AB* represents the introduction. The exciting force appears towards the end of this part or soon afterward. *BC* is the rising action. *C* is the turning-point. *CD* is the falling action. *D* is the catastrophe. The introduction and the exciting force usually appear in the first act of an Elizabethan play; and sometimes the rising action is started. The turning-point is usually in the third act. In *Othello,* however, it is delayed to the fourth,

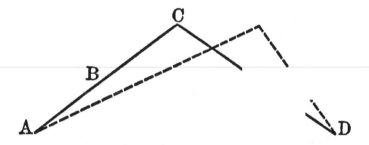

a condition more nearly represented by the dotted lines in the diagram. The catastrophe, as has been said, occurs at the end of act V. Thus, acts II. and IV. are more or less transitional. Here, if anywhere, a slight lull in the interest becames tolerable. The action, however, must proceed more rapidly towards the end.

Many of the Elizabethan plays were first printed without any indication of division into acts—a fact which implies that no very great significance was attached to the act-division. In fact, the division of a play into acts was a mere imitation of the outward form of Seneca's plays which furnished the earliest Elizabethan models. By the time of Shakespeare the five-fold division was followed almost as a habit, hardly at all for its structural significance. In Shakespeare an act is seldom more than a mere fifth of the play. Beyond what is said above relative to the function of each of the five acts it is impossible to go. Rarely does an act of Shakespeare correspond to an integral unit of structure. And when it does it seems to do so by accident.

The scene, however, is more likely to be a structural unit. Yet even in this case less significance seems to attach to such divisions than in a modern play. Many of the early play texts omit the division into scenes as well as the division into acts. For all that, the scene is in the majority of cases an integral unit.

In dramatic parlance the word scene is used with varying significance. 1. It represents what may be seen, and is akin to scenery. 2. A new scene, as in French plays of to-day, is marked every time the number of persons on the stage is increased or diminished. 3. According to Elizabethan practice a new scene is indicated whenever the stage is completely cleared. 4. The word is often used to denote any portion of a play that is a unit in itself—that represents fully one brief step or portion in the development of the story. This may include a dozen scenes if the text is printed according to the French custom alluded to above.

In Elizabethan times the scene very nearly corresponded to what is mentioned last above. Yet we sometimes find a text scene that includes more than one such scene.

Yet, in the majority of cases, an Elizabethan scene is a distinct unit, with a structure somewhat similar to the play as a whole—that is, it begins quietly with an introduction, rises to a climax, and falls away to a quiescent close.

There is one kind of scene that requires especial mention. Often there is a scene that implies a continuation in another place or after a lapse of time. If one scene followed the other immediately the effect would be unsatisfactory. The audience would not appreciate the gap. The insertion, however, of a short, irrelevant scene diverts the attention for a moment, and thus emphasizes the lapsing interval, or the change of place. Such *division scenes* are of frequent occurrence in the Elizabethan drama.

Just as the above device seems to emphasize interruptions, so many other devices serve to preserve the continuity of the parts. Thus, hints, or bits of foreshadowing of what is to come, are freely used. Often the close of one scene outlines plainly what is to follow in another; and the opening of one frequently recapitulates what has happened earlier.

The student may encounter difficulties in applying the structure outlined above to many of the plays of Shakespeare. It might as well be acknowledged at once that the structure of certain plays is faulty. This is especially true of the history plays. In the first part of the chapter on *Richard the Third* it is pointed out that these plays belong in a class by themselves. In them another interest was paramount to the dramatic interest. The loose structure of *Henry the Sixth* is more characteristic of the series than the accidentally symmetrical structure of *Richard the Second*. And again, the earlier plays of Shakespeare display less structural skill than the plays of his maturer years.

The analysis of plays composed of several distinct threads often presents difficulties. In *King Lear,* not an easily analyzed play at the best, we should expect to find the structural points referred to above appearing both in the Lear and in the Gloucester stories. In *The Merchant of Venice,* on the other hand, the different stories are so closely interwoven as to make their structural separation impossible. (It is pointed out in Chapter XV. that act V. of this play is structurally unusual.)

And then again, these rules are not applied so rigorously in comedy as in tragedy writing. The mood in which we listen to a comedy is naturally less serious, the mind is less critical, and the dramatist not under so great a responsibility in regard to logical sequence.

(It is a good example for the student to work out the structure of each play studied. In the following chapters hints as to the structure are given from time to time.)

CHAPTER VIII

HOW TO READ A PLAY

I HAVE frequently encountered students who are discouraged over the fact that a certain period of time spent upon a play is not so productive of results as the same amount of time spent upon the study of any other form of literature. That is, a student will read thirty or forty pages of a novel in an hour and be able to give a pretty good account of himself in the class-room. If, however, he reads a play at the same rate his knowledge of it is inconsiderable. This is as it should be, but few students, and too few teachers, realize the situation. I would impress upon the student at the outset that play reading is slow in comparison with any other kind of reading.

Let us look for a moment into the actual conditions. No one would deny that three men can do more work in a given time than one man. If one man would do the work of three he must take more time to it. In the playhouse, three senses are at work all the time:—eye, ear, and mind. With the eye one sees the persons, their motions, their positions, their dress, and the stage setting. By means of the ear one is alert to tones of voice, inflections that often give the meaning rather than the actual word, etc. Mentally the audience is constantly interpreting the word symbol into what it conventionally stands for.

When, on the other hand, one reads a play in the study, all impressions are received primarily through the eye and the printed word. The sense of sight is doing the work that in the playhouse engaged the eye, the ear, and the mind. Is it to be wondered at that the process takes more time?

When one reads a play one must be alert at all times to supply the missing points. How easy it is when reading to lose track of a character upon the stage who for the time being has nothing to say. This would be impossible on the stage. How easy it is to recognize a character whose former entrance had been announced in the text merely by a printed stage direction! In the playhouse we have actually seen him, we remember his dress, his features, the tones of his voice. If we forget his name, that is a mere bagatelle. It is unnecessary to say more in order to make plain the fact that when we read a play we are acquiring only a part of the dramatic presentation. It is the purpose of this chapter to suggest a few practical hints which will sharpen the average reader's attention, thus helping him to supply those parts that are inevitably present in a stage production.

In the first place, I should say, read, read, and reread. A thorough familiarity with the text is absolutely essential. In every case the play should be read through at a comfortable rate of speed before one begins the actual study of details.

Make first a careful study of the dramatis personæ. Do not merely glance over the list. Read it carefully again and again. Read it aloud so that the abbreviations of the speakers' names used in the text will be at once familiar. Note whether the list is comparatively long or short. What is the proportion of men to women? Are the characters of high or low rank? Ask the dramatis personæ every imaginable question and try for an answer.

It is a good plan, before beginning the study of the text proper, to turn over the pages of the play, reading the captions of the scenes, the people present at the beginning of each scene, the entrances and exits, and other stage directions. One can often in this way surmise the general setting of the play, which are the important characters, what are inner and outer scenes, etc.

Next, read the first act through, on the way performing conscientiously several tasks. 1. Make a brief written synopsis of the story part of each act. 2. Note what characters enter; and how soon the entire dramatis personæ have appeared. 3. Does one character, or do several, stand out above others more prominently? 4. What details are introduced which are manifestly to inform the reader concerning the part of the story which has gone before, but which does not form a part of the story as actually dramatized? 5. What is the setting? 6. By what means is it presented to the reader? 7. What are the characters who are not speakers doing with themselves? 8. Make out frequent plans to show where the characters should stand to the best advantage. 9. Above all, try to imagine the gestures, the manner, and tone of voice in which each remark is spoken. Reading aloud is good practice. 10. To whom is a remark addressed and how is it received? 11. Is it an inner or an outer scene? 12. If the latter, try to imagine the actual Elizabethan setting. To ask and answer these and similar questions is time well spent, although it may prevent the reading of more than a few pages in a given time.

Having thus acquired a fair familiarity with the first act it would be well to read it over again, just as carefully but with a new object in mind. Persons take part in every dramatic story. It is the supreme gift of the dramatist to delineate character. In reading a play we have in the actual words but a small portion of what the dramatist depends upon for the delineation of his characters. In other words, we lack, when reading the text, all that the art of acting adds to the mere words. We should do our best to supply the omission.

In this second reading of the first act one should note every detail which serves to indicate the personality of the characters in the play. What they say may be an indication. So may what they fail to say. The way in which their remarks are received by others, as well as others' opinions of them will help us to formulate our knowledge. As early in the reading of the play as possible attempt to formulate the personality of each character. In most Elizabethan plays, and in nearly all of Shakespeare's, the chief characters are pretty well drawn by the end of the second act. The remainder is reiteration and amplification, merely a filling out, with the plot becoming more and more prominent towards the end. Occasionally, however, as in *Macbeth,* a character is continually changing throughout the play. In such a play there should be no relaxation of the continual scrutiny of the character's acts and words.

As it is advisable to make a written synopsis of

the story, scene by scene, so it is equally advisable to make frequent brief written statements of the personality of each character. Such written notes have no permanent value, hardly even the value of a class exercise. Their purpose is to order one's thoughts, or, oftentimes, merely to reveal the hazy condition of them, thus spurring one to the effort to clear the matter up.

When one has read each of the five acts slowly and carefully as indicated above, one is fairly on the road to a comprehension of the play. For all that, one is yet far from the end of the journey.

In reading the play again one should give general consideration to several matters that have been heretofore examined in fragments. Note how much space is given to the introduction relative to the rest of the play. Does the story run smoothly throughout? How many crises are there in the narrative interest? Is the story completely finished at the end? Which thread is left to the last? How and where have the minor threads been disposed of?

Note the relative number of important characters. One is often surprised to find how few characters in one of Shakespeare's plays are of prime importance. How are the characters grouped? Is there one of great importance in each group? Is one character set over against another so as to contrast with it? Or is one made almost similar to another? If so, do they appear together or separately?

It is not to be understood that these identical questions should be asked and answered in regard to every play; but rather that they are illustrative of what the alert student will be asking continually. The actual phrasing of an answer, either orally or on paper, is so conducive to clear thinking that I consider it imperative.

By this time the reader, in the case of some plays, will be so familiar with the characters that further study is unnecessary. In such a play as *Twelfth Night,* the characters are so clearly and so simply portrayed that one thoroughly familiar with the lines of the play can hardly escape their true significance.

Other plays, however, contain characters so complex and so enigmatical that special study from this point of view is necessary. I know of no practice so valuable as re-reading in succession only those scenes in which the characters appear. Ponder each speech carefully. At any place where the significance is not fully grasped try to imagine the situation. Fancy who is present, what the person would be thinking about, what has recently happened to him, what is he planning for the future. Under such circumstances, what would he do? This will frequently suggest the true meaning of what he actually does do and say.

It would be well to analyze the plot of each play and try to imagine the Elizabeth staging, as set forth in chapters devoted to these subjects.

In the following pages an effort is made not to repeat more than is necessary. Thus, the Elizabethan staging is discussed in detail in regard to only a few plays, or parts of plays. Yet it is assumed that the student will think over such matters in regard to all the plays. Oftentimes the critical part of a character is discussed in some part of the notes on the text. Though nothing further may be said, it is supposed that the student will order his thoughts relative to the presentation of the character as a whole. Above all, it is well to make comparisons. If a question is asked in regard to one play, try to fit it to another, recall similar passages elsewhere, etc., etc.

There is a point in the study of every art where mechanical application seems to reach its limit, and taste and intuition begin to play their part. Just here is where the rules set by an instructor fail to be of use. Careful drill will sharpen one's wits, but one must exercise them for one's self. Repeated exercise will develop one's taste, gradually creating the knowledge of good and evil. A knowledge of dramatic good and evil is the only road to a sane appreciation of Shakespeare's plays. But for guidance in the last steps of the process the student must depend upon himself.

CHAPTER IX

A BRIEF WORKING BIBLIOGRAPHY

THE following is not a bibliography for the study of Shakespeare; rather a very condensed list of books of use to the average school-teacher, or to the reader who desires to carry his study of Shakespeare beyond the limits suggested in this volume.

EDITIONS

There are numerous school editions of individual plays on the market. In this day and generation there is no excuse for a poorly edited edition of one of Shakespeare's plays. So far as the present writer is concerned, who has examined most of these editions, he is inclined to say that the imprint of a well-known publisher is synonymous with accurate, scholarly editorial work. This edition may involve special features more attractive to the individual instructor than that one. Among them, however, I find it impossible to discriminate.

The Cambridge Edition, edited by Professor Nielson, and published by The Houghton Mifflin Co., is from the standpoint of editorial work and typographical make-up the best one-volume edition on the market.

The Eversley Edition, published by the Macmillan Co., in ten volumes, has but few notes (on the page, however, with the text).   The introductions to the plays are excellent.   On the whole, it is the best reading edition of the plays for general use that has come to my notice.

The references in the present volume are to the Tudor Edition, published by The Macmillan Co., one play to the volume.   The edition seems to strike the happy medium between under and over editing. Typographical details are of the highest quality. A style of binding cheaper than the standard recommends it to those who would economize carefully in the choice of a class text.   Take it all in all, it is the present writer's favorite edition for all such purposes as are implied by a use of the present volume.

The Dowden Edition, published by The Bobbs-Merrill Co. of Indianapolis, is very fully edited.   It is certainly the best edition for the advanced student who is interested in the textual interpretation of the plays.

Though as yet far from completion, the Variorum Edition, published by Lippincott and Co., is the final word in regard to the plays that have appeared. They are treated both textually and critically.   Its expense, however, in many cases implies its use as a library reference book.

Miscellaneous

Bartlett's *Concordance,* published by The Macmillan Co., is the standard concordance.   Its references are to the Globe Edition of the plays, also published by The Macmillan Co.   The text, however, of this one-volume edition limits it to occasional use.

Luce's *Handbook to Shakespeare's Works* (The Macmillan Co.) contains in briefest space the largest amount of information regarding the plays. Though each play receives a brief critical treatment, the volume is mainly a storehouse of valuable facts.

Shakespeare's London and *The Elizabethan People* (Henry Holt and Co.), both by the present author, are an attempt to portray the social manners and customs of the metropolis at the time of Shakespeare.

The standard biography is *A Life of William Shakespeare,* by Sidney Lee, The Macmillan Co.

CHAPTER X

RICHARD THE THIRD

I. THE HISTORY PLAY AS A TYPE

DURING the decade from 1575 to 1585 England as a great national power was slowly coming to its own. Even before the victory of 1588 Englishmen had begun to realize their strength and to feel proud of their birthright. Along with this new feeling of manhood grew up an intense national desire on the part of Englishmen to know themselves and their past. This desire was catered to by prose writers, as in Holinshed's *Chronicle,* by the poets who produced histories of England in verse, and by the playwrights. From their hands came a long series of dramatic productions whose first and foremost purpose was to popularize history for the sake of instruction. These history plays, then, were akin to the purpose novel of to-day. At any rate, the information concerning history came first in importance, dramatic quality second. While criticising them from the dramatic standpoint, this fact should never be lost sight of.

Shakespeare's task in producing a history play (except in those cases where he revised an earlier play) was little more than translating the narrative of Holinshed into dramatic dialogue. In some cases the original formless story, as in *Henry the Sixth,* re-

85

sulted in an equally formless play. In others, however, notably in *Richard the Second,* the original material, almost by accident, shaped itself into a symmetrical dramatic composition.

Different writers of history plays varied greatly in their methods of procedure. In Greene's *James the Fourth* the historical element is so secondary as almost to exclude this play from the class. Other writers were manifestly politicians who seemed to garble facts intentionally in order to effectively present their own particular views. Shakespeare among them all seems to be the fairest in his dealing with history. He displays no particular bias; he presents his source accurately in the main, only departing from fact in trivial details that do not alter the tenor of general truths.

It is a fact that he gives in *Richard the Third* a picture of the king which is believed by modern historians to be false. But it should be remembered that Shakespeare gives the picture held by his own generation of the last of the Plantagenets. We cannot accuse the dramatist of wilfully distorting the picture.

On the other hand, we can find no evidence that Shakespeare was an historical student in the modern sense of the word. His later history plays show him to be not only a clear but also a deep thinker on historical subjects. But the plays nowhere afford the least indication of the modern spirit of investigation. Research was unknown to him. He did not go to original sources, he did not try to discover both sides, he did not try to weigh all the evidence and judge impartially. He merely took what was the currently accepted historical account for granted. This he transformed into the best dramatic terms possible.

What the history play really was is best illustrated by a comparison of three plays on the same subject— namely, the reign of King John. The first of the three is not really a history play at all. The second is a true history play, written, however, before the type had passed beyond its crudest stage. The third, Shakespeare's *King John,* is a play written but a few years before the type reached its highest development.

1. John Bale's *King Johan,* though not a true history play as we are now using the term, is the earliest Elizabethan play whose subject-matter is drawn from English history. It was probably written about 1550.

"The play opens with a speech by the king in which he declares his determination to do justice. England, as a widow, implores his help against the clergy, but this confidence is interrupted by Sedition, who is strongly clerical in his sympathies. Nobility, Clergy, and Civil Order come in and discuss the state of the kingdom, and Clergy makes a hypocritical submission. Dissimulation and Sedition take counsel and bring in Private Wealth and Usurped Power to their aid. They procure the election of Stephen Langton as archbishop (here we touch history) and soon after we have the Pope cursing King John for his attacks on the church. This closes act 1. In the second act we find the clergy preparing to resist the king. . . . In a subsequent scene we are shown John's submission to Pandulph, and the hard terms exacted of him, but Sedition is not satisfied and procures a fanatic monk to murder the king. . . . But now come on Verity and Imperial Majesty. The memory of the king is vindicated, and the play ends with compliments to Queen Elizabeth." *

* Pollard: *English Morality Plays.*

The play reminds us of the Elizabethan drama in only two points.

First: The author loses no opportunity to abuse the Roman Catholic clergy. In fact, the play is a religious tract. Bale, the author, though educated in a monastery and in holy orders, had married and had preached against the celibacy of the clergy. For this he was obliged to leave the country. He returned, however, and found protection, only to be driven out again at the accession of Queen Mary, but to return to his native country a second time at the accession of Elizabeth. His hatred of the Roman church, which was due to the harsh treatment he had received at its hands, is everywhere evident throughout the play. In this expression of the personal feeling of the author regarding current events the play reminds us of the Elizabethan drama.

It also reminds us of the Elizabethan drama in another though unimportant way: namely, it closes with a flattering tribute to the queen. This custom, which was frequently practised in Shakespeare's day, has in this play already found its birth.

In general, however, the play of *King Johan* is altogether unlike the Elizabethan drama. In the first place, it is written in a rough, halting meter which is hard to read and harder to listen to. The lines are arranged in long, jingling couplets that for the most part rhyme two and two. It differs from the Elizabethan plays in another vital characteristic. It contains little or no action worthy of dramatic presentation. It is full of long, tedious dialogues which are either epic in their character, or are mere arguments and debates concerning the present condition of England.

In other ways the play is unlike the more finished drama of Shakespeare's day. It possesses no unity whatever, let alone a unity of action, which implies an orderly arrangement of incidents based upon the law of cause and effect. There is no attempt to bind the parts together by means of the ordinary dramatic conventions, such as foreshadowing, cross-linking, etc. It almost entirely lacks human interest, and fails utterly to appeal to the passions of the audience, which appeal is the main asset of Shakespeare and his contemporaries. But slight knowledge of history is made use of; and there is displayed practically no individuality of character.

A mere glance at the dramatis personæ reveals its greatest departure from Elizabethan traditions. Of the nineteen characters, only five or six represent persons; and of them, only the king has a personality of his own, and that none too well defined. All the others who take part are the personified abstractions of the Morality plays: Clergy, Nobility, Private Wealth, Treason, etc. It is this that links the play hard and fast to the preceding era, notwithstanding the fact that it deals with material that is distinctly within the province of the history play.

This brief review of a play that is not one of those we have under consideration is necessary to a clear conception of the birth of the history play itself.

2. The second play of the three here considered was published in 1591, though written, doubtless, much earlier. In the period that elapsed between Bale's *King Johan* and *The Troublesome Reign of*

King John the great religious struggle had come to a head. Though the play may have appeared before the great emancipation of England in 1588, the country already knew its power, and the patriotic wave was on the rise. People had become interested in the history of their ancestors. For all that, none of the great Elizabethan plays had appeared. The drama was still crude, the rules of structure not yet formulated.

By this time the drama had begun to fill in part the place of the modern periodical and popular textbook. It was akin, as has been said, to the novel of purpose. And its purpose was well defined: namely to instruct the people in the history of England.

The Troublesome Reign of *King John,* which is written for the most part in blank verse, shows a great advance over *King Johan.* It opens with a scene that presents a definite point of beginning for the plot. Chatillon, the French ambassador, enters to King John and his court to claim the crown of England for John's nephew Arthur, who is with the king of France. John, of course, refuses the justice of the claim. Chatillon departs, vowing war and vengeance.

There follows a very clumsy scene. Robert and Philip enter, each claiming to be the heir of Sir Robert Falconbridge. The debate hangs on the parentage of Philip. Robert asserts that Philip is the son of Richard Cœur-de-Lion. His only proof is the resemblance of Philip to the former king of England. King John resolves to solve the difficulty by applying to Philip and to his mother. Both vehemently deny his bastardy. Then, for mere form's sake, the question is put again. This time Philip assents just as positively that he is the son of the king. King John is satisfied. He recognizes Philip Plantagenet, and confirms Robert as heir to Falconbridge. The only hearing that this incident has on the play is that later Philip becomes one of John's staunch henchmen.

Here we see plainly illustrated the lack of care in planning one scene to prepare for the next. The law of cause and effect is not followed. There is no reason for Philip's denial changing into an affirmation. No pressure is brought to bear to make him change his attitude. Likewise, there is no attempt to justify the king for believing Philip, who has just proved himself a liar. The author must have felt the crudeness, for he makes the widow of Falconbridge acknowledge later that Philip is not her husband's child.

Crude as this presentation is, it is far ahead of *King Johan*. There are no personified abstractions. The author starts at a definite point in the plot, and realizes the necessity of introducing all the principal characters early in the play. There is shown a considerable knowledge of the then-accepted history of the time; and the desire to present it for its own sake is evident from first to last.

For instance: when the two kings meet in France before Angiers much space is occupied by explaining in detail the political situation, and the claim of Arthur. Lest the audience should not take it all in at once, the matter is re-explained when the king summons Angiers to surrender.

The town, however, refuses to surrender. There is a good deal of fighting. At last it is proposed that the Dauphin marry John's niece. This is agreed upon. The two kings are reconciled. Arthur's claim is merely ignored. To all intents and purposes the play seems to be at an end.

For all that, the play is by no means finished. It begins all over again. Just as Chatillon appeared at the beginning to make trouble between John and France, so Cardinal Pandulph now enters to make trouble between John and Rome. He upbraids the king for opposing the election of Stephen Langthon to the See of Canterbury—a thread of interest for which the audience is in no way prepared. John continues his refusal. He is excommunicated. The rest of the play is occupied with his struggle against the Pope.

So far as the facts of history were then known, this play popularizes with sufficient accuracy the principal events of the reign of King John, but with one important exception. There is no reference to the signing of the Great Charter. Yet it is a true history play in purpose and in subject. Its defects of form are the defects of the drama of the day, then in its crude infancy.

Let us now see how the master hand of Shakespeare, yet in its immaturity, however, has treated the same theme.

3. *King John,* by far the most important and dramatically the most perfect of the three plays, may be discussed in relatively fewer words because it is so familiar. It shows a great advance in plot construction and continuity of action. It begins and ends sharply. Though there is no marked balance and symmetry of structure, it possesses a connected and

continuous action. One scene leads up to the next. Most of the significant situations grow out of the preceding. No better illustration can be cited of increased skill in this respect than the scene where Falconbridge establishes his identity. In *The Troublesome Reign* the whole matter is accomplished at the expense of inconsistent character portrayal. In *King John* the situation is developed naturally and convincingly. Everything happens in accordance with realistic character. One feels no dismay due to plot-ridden personalities. Throughout the play historical situations are sufficiently but not over-explained. As a last improvement we note that the abrupt end and new start in the midst of the former play has been done away with.

Improvement in plot, however, does not mark the main advance of this play. The difference in character drawing is almost immeasurable. The people are realistic. Every member of the dramatis personæ is an individual. So valuable is this quality that the fact of Shakespeare's having found the plot almost completely worked out for him in advance becomes negligible. The play is his own creation.

To recapitulate: Shakespeare shows great advance in the art of character drawing, telling a story, and dramatic technique. He adds, however, no detail characteristic of the type which is not to be found in *The Troublesome Reign*. One play is as characteristic of the type as the other. Shakespeare has merely improved the type.

II. Shakespeare's History Plays

A consideration of all of Shakespeare's plays shows him to be the man of the hour. He did not originate. He took what he found and bettered it. This assertion is equally true of the history plays. What is set forth above relative to *King John* is true of all of them. The type was the vogue. Shakespeare took it up. And he has given us the best of it.

Shakespeare wrote or participated in ten history plays. Two are excluded from the following discussion: *King John* because enough has been said of it above; *Henry the Eighth* because it was written in collaboration after a lapse of many years, and does not properly belong to the present consideration.

As a matter of convenience for discussion the remaining eight plays are divided into two groups which possess decidedly different characteristics. I call the three parts of *Henry the Sixth* and *Richard the Third* the York plays; *Richard the Second,* the two parts of *Henry the Fourth,* and *Henry the Fifth* the Lancaster plays. The first group was written before the second and possesses marked differences.*

In the York plays we find that narrative is of the first interest. It is as if Shakespeare set to work on that most objective of all histories, Holinshed's *Chronicle,* with but one task before him: namely, to dramatize the story, to present the simple narrative. We find little or no attention given to questioned motives beyond the desire to make the dramatic char-

* There is a difference of opinion as to whether or not *Richard the Third* preceded *Richard the Second.* I am of the opinion that it did, but the question is of minor importance in the following discussion.

acter plausible on the stage. We find little moralizing, little reflection on the great issues at stake, no appreciation of the inner political significance of the material dealt with. In other words, Shakespeare is concerned with the outward, pictorial, and spectacular aspect of the facts of history, not with their inner significance.

The York plays deal with a threefold theme: 1. The fall of the House of Lancaster. 2. The rise of the House of York. 3. The fall of the House of York. Thus, in the four plays devoted to Henry the Sixth and Richard the Third we find the old story of the Wars of the Roses dramatized for popular instruction.

The Lancaster plays, though written later, deal with an earlier period. They are *Richard the Second*, two parts of *Henry the Fourth*, and *Henry the Fifth*. In them we find that the interest in mere narrative is no longer supreme. The dramatist has developed a real interest in the meaning of historical events. And he has infused these plays with this new spirit. He reads Holinshed more critically, he is constantly reading between the lines. He is fully aware of the fact that the objective narrative is superficial. History is a matter of deeper moment than a series of pictures to be enjoyed as a spectacle. There has been born in his mind the attitude that gives rise to modern constitutional histories rather than to picture books.

The theme of this set of plays is also threefold: 1. Who is responsible for civil war? 2. The influence of personal character in determining history. 3. A king's responsibility to his people and to his God.

Though three of the history plays are considered in detail later, it is not possible here to work out all of the above propositions. I hope later to supplement the present volume with chapters dealing with the remaining plays of Shakespeare. For the present, however, a few suggestions must suffice for the omitted plays.

In the York plays we note improvement in technique. The four plays, to be sure, are not distinct dramas, each with a symmetrical structure of its own. They form, on the other hand, an almost continuous story. There is little skill shown in binding the parts together, or in linking various threads. The character drawing is at times the crudest, in others, as in *Richard the Third,* more finished. The stage handling of battle scenes improves steadily. The law of nemesis is observed throughout. On the other hand, there seems to be little recognition of graded punishment. Death is the constant penalty. There is no account taken of the inalienable rights of the commonalty. The plays deal with kings and princes, peers and potentates. Common people are usually introduced merely for comic effect.

The Lancaster plays, on the other hand, are altogether different. There is plenty of action. The narrative is not stinted, but it is not supreme. There is a steady improvement in the minor details of dramatic technique. The rights of the common people are here taken into consideration, the final conclusion, voiced in *Henry the Fifth,* being that they are supreme. The king is as worthy of punishment as the commonest person in the kingdom. Thus *Richard the Second* is not so much concerned with telling the story of Richard's deposition as in showing that he lost his crown because he disregarded the rights of his people. Again, Bolingbroke rebels against his sovereign. Was that right? The ultimate success of the House of Lancaster answers yes. The trials and remorse of King Henry himself answer no. In other words, Henry succeeded because he did what was best for England; he was punished because he used questionable means.

These and other questions of principle are what are worked out in the Lancaster plays, culminating in *Henry the Fifth,* Shakespeare's picture of The Happy Warrior.

III. SHAKESPEARE'S RELATION TO MARLOWE

When Shakespeare began his stage career in London as a reviser of old plays, Christopher Marlowe was not only at the zenith of his career but also universally recognized as the foremost dramatist of the day. He had already inspired a set of imitators, among whom we find Shakespeare. The latter had imitated Lyly, or was soon to do so, in comedy. So he took Marlowe as his model in history and tragedy. So close is this imitation in *Richard the Third* that occasional critics have advanced the idea that in reality it is a play by Marlowe.

Though in one way Shakespeare is the most original of poets, it cannot be denied that he was a crafty imitator. It is, however, impossible ever to follow his imitation far. Thus we soon find him outgrowing his model. The Marlowesque character of Richard the Third was followed (I think) by the character of

Richard the Second, conceived and portrayed from a different point of view and in a different way. In fact, the often referred to resemblance between Marlowe's *Edward the Second* and Shakespeare's *Richard the Second* has never appeared to me. And in a later chapter I have tried to show that *Richard the Second* really indicates Shakespeare's emancipation from the Marlowe tradition.

IV. Notes on the Text

Act I., Scene i., line 1, etc. The opening soliloquy. Soliloquys in Elizabethan plays were used for two purposes. In the first place, the soliloquy was the conventional way of expressing one's unspoken thoughts. In such a case, though the audience hears the words, it fancies them unspoken. The actor is really supposed for the time being to be lost in silent meditation. The spoken words merely constitute the dramatist's `device for getting the silent thoughts before the audience. We are not to look upon the person who soliloquizes as one who is in the habit of talking to himself aloud. Hence, such a soliloquy represents the inmost personality of the speaker.

The soliloquy, however, is frequently used for another purpose. All that the dramatist has to say to the audience must proceed through the lips of the various characters. So long as they speak for themselves there is no difficulty. On occasion, however, the dramatist longs for the novelist's privilege of speaking to the audience in his own person. Though seldom so used to-day, the Elizabethan playwright often used the soliloquy for this purpose. There are times when the soliloquy is not really indicative of the speaker's thoughts at all, but in reality represents some thought in the mind of Shakespeare which he desires to convey to the audience.

The soliloquy of Lady Macbeth uttered after reading her husband's letter is truly characteristic. On the other hand, the soliloquy in which Prince Hal informs the audience that he will eventually throw off his trivial personality and become the great king is not consistent with the character at all. It is Shakespeare's hint to the audience, forestalling possible criticism of an adverse kind for making light of the character of Henry the Fifth.

It is always necessary to bear this double use in mind; and it is not always easy to determine which application to make.

In the present soliloquy we have a very accurate description of the character of King Richard. However, the sentiments expressed are hardly indicative of the thoughts that would be passing in his mind. Many men are given to accurate self-analysis; but the character of Richard as set forth in *Henry the Sixth* and in this play is hardly one that would prompt such a self-judgment. We are compelled to think of the soliloquy as proceeding from Shakespeare rather than from Richard himself.

Note also the unusual condition of a play opening with a speech by the main character.

I. i. 145, etc. Does Richard's gleeful talk of his own wickedness sound natural? or does it seem to be a mere pose? Watch the character of Richard carefully throughout the play. Does he take himself more seriously towards the end?

I. i. 161, 162. Note the rhymed couplet at the end. In the chapter on verse it is pointed out that Shakespeare used rhyme less and less as time went on. This rhyme, however, is of a peculiar nature. It is introduced for the purpose of giving the actor a sort of vocal flourish at the last moment to assist his exit. Such *rhyme-tags* were used by Shakespeare even after he had practically discarded the ordinary use of rhyme.

I. ii. In this scene Richard meets the body of Henry the Sixth mourned by his daughter, the Lady Anne. She knows that both her husband and her father have been murdered by Richard. She hates him viciously. Richard meets her. In the course of a short conversation she turns the body of the king over to him willingly, and practically acknowledges favorable progress in Richard's suit for her hand.

Briefly stated in this way the situation seems impossible. Even the daring Richard would hardly have attempted it under ordinary circumstances. No woman for whom we entertain the sympathy that we have at times for Anne could have capitulated so ignominiously. As the scene reads it is thoroughly unconvincing.

Before a modern audience, the scene on the stage is no more effective. To portray Anne as an unfeeling doll who could do such an act naturally is to sacrifice other vital moments in the presentation of her character. Nor, were she such, would Richard have felt the necessity of marrying her as a detail in the safety of his plans. No matter how well the part of Richard is acted, this scene is one to be overlooked when we are searching for plausibility.

I think, however, that to the Elizabethans the
scene was very different in its effect. The above
objections did not appear to Shakespeare's audience.
In other words, the situation seen through Elizabethan eyes was thoroughly plausible.

The Elizabethans believed implicitly in a personal
devil. They believed that he manifested himself in
all sorts of ways in the ordinary daily life of the
people. Horatio's first impulsive thought was that
the apparition which beckoned Hamlet was not his
father's ghost but the devil in disguise. So here,
I think, the Elizabethans understood the victory of
Richard as due to the devil, not merely to his own
wicked personality.

In I. iii. 228 Queen Margaret calls him elfish
marked, and says (line 229), " Thou that wast sealed
in thy nativity . . . the son of hell." In the present
scene (ii. 45) Lady Anne remarks, " And mortal eyes
cannot endure the devil "; a statement the truth of
which she is soon going to exemplify in her own behavior. She continues (line 46), " Avaunt, thou
dreadful minister of hell." And in line 67 she speaks
of Richard's hell-governed arm.

Later, when Richard offers Anne his sword she
still hates him, offers at him, but her arm is powerless. In the moments that follow, her behavior is
exactly that of one who is bewitched. Richard himself (line 237) attributes his power, the result of
which is a surprise even to him, to the devil. And
in IV. i. 66, etc., Anne in looking back finds her own
behavior to be incomprehensible from any rational
point of view.

I think the Elizabethans considered Richard to have

exercised the perfectly natural power of magic over Anne.

I. iii. What is the situation of the queen's kinsfolk? and how will their situation be altered by the death of Edward?

I. iv. None of the plays written in the maturer period of Shakespeare's workmanship is so devoid as *Richard the Third* of characters with whom we fully sympathize. In this respect Clarence of this play stands almost alone. This pathetic scene belongs to him. Note how it is supplemented by the words of Edward in II. i.

The death of Clarence is a mere detail in Richard's plan to sweep away all impediments to the throne. Being a mere detail, the space given to it in this scene and in the next is out of all proportion to its importance in the full development of the story. Nevertheless, this scene and the next are among the best scenes of the play. We could hardly spare them even if their condensation improved the compactness of the play as a whole.

II. i. 79. Stage direction, "they all start." Note the intense dramatic effect of Richard's sudden announcement of the death of Clarence. Try to picture the group on the stage and how each one takes the news. In the first place, Richard is the guilty party. He is thoroughly in command of himself. Yet, according to the letter, the king, though now repentant, is actually responsible. (How much good is there in Edward's character?)

What of Buckingham at this point? In line 83 he asks Dorset, "Look I so pale as the rest?" What does this line mean? It has been suggested that he is one of the guilty parties and fears that he shows it in his face. If so, would he have referred to the fact? "Rest" refers to the queen's kindred. Their guilty looks are referred to in line 135. But they are really not guilty. Is it possible that Buckingham is as yet so little in with Richard's plans as not to know that he lies in line 135? If so, Buckingham may fear that he will be the next victim of the queen's kindred, and therefore asks whether he shows his fear by the paleness of his face.

Again, the passage may have no character significance at all, being merely a dramatic device to call attention to the others and to suggest their looks. It should be remembered that a miscellaneous group of actors cannot turn suddenly pale at will. There are traditions that some of the great actors have been able to control the color of their features, but it is a rare accomplishment, not to be depended upon under ordinary circumstances. Without this line, the audience would not notice the pale group upon the stage, but with it, it is easy to imagine their appearance.

II. i. 100. Derby's request for his servants in regard to a trivial matter serves to emphasize Edward's following speech concerning the similar but momentous situation involving Clarence. Here is where Edward appears to the best advantage in the play; and his speech beginning with line 102 is one of the finest passages.

II. ii. 70, etc. There is a symmetrical artificiality about this passage that we miss in Shakespeare's later plays. In the early years of the generation blank verse was more bombastic and acting probably more stilted than in later years. Lyly, too, had done more than any other dramatist to popularize word-play and artificial balance both in sentence structure and in the larger details of dramatic structure. (See the double speeches of the ghost to Richmond and to Richard later in the play, and the two orations before the armies.) The artificial character of this passage is probably due more to the example of Lyly than to that of Marlowe, whose manner in general is so closely followed in this play.

II. iii. " 2 Cit.," etc. Speeches attributed to a vague, indefinite person, as Second Citizen, usually indicate rumor and hearsay. That is, the ideas expressed are not held by these particular citizens but by any and all citizens in general.

II. iv. The lines spoken by children in Shakespeare's plays should not be scrutinized too carefully from the standpoint of naturalness. It was a dramatic convention of the day to represent children on the stage as more precocious than we generally find them in real life. Just as to-day the bright sayings of youthful prodigies often suggest an adult origin.

III. ii. 22. Note that Catesby is playing a double part. Though really Richard's man, he is pretending to be Hastings'. The latter shows his confidence by the free expression of his intentions, lines 43-45.

III. iii. This is a division scene. (See chapter on Dramatic Structure.) At the end of scene ii. the group of speakers is proceeding to the Tower. After a short lapse of time they appear at their journey's end in scene iv. If the two scenes followed each other immediately the effect would be unnatural. This would be less unnatural on the modern stage, for there would probably be a darkening of the theater for a moment, a change of scene, etc., before the resumption. The place of this mechanical interruption is taken by the conventional Elizabethan division scene.

III. iv. 60. We already know that Richard will play false with Hastings if Hastings does not agree to his plans. Richard already knows the position of Hastings when the former leaves the stage with Buckingham. (Line 43.) Now they are returning. What did they do while absent in conference?

The scene that follows was stupidly conceived and is clumsily carried out. Were the details due to the suggestion of Buckingham or is Richard wholly responsible for the plot? Richard has already expressed the opinion that Buckingham is a gull. Would the former have followed the latter's suggestion as to such a clumsy device? If it is due to Richard himself, consider whether it is natural for him to plan so poorly, or whether the whole thing merely represents Shakespeare's inability to design a better form to the matter. Again, is it possible that this clumsy, ill-timed act is what first suggests to Buckingham his future desertion from the standard of Richard? He may here begin to think that such a man is not a safe one to follow further. Yet Buckingham goes still further in co-operation with Richard. Or did Shakespeare intentionally plan the detail thus to emphasize the sweeping power of Richard's personality over every one—it is not necessary for him to be careful.

The above contradictory and inharmonious list of suggestions is introduced partly for the purpose of illustrating how necessary it is to consider all possible sides of a situation before deciding just what is the real effect of the passage.

III. v. 5, etc. Note how suggestive this passage is of the Elizabethan manner of tragic acting.

III. v. 47. Here and elsewhere in the play the Lord Mayor is a gull, a mere tool, without a mind of his own, blown willingly by the wind here and there. Yet there is no reason to believe that Shakespeare intended any reflection on the office of the city magistrate. The Lord Mayor is merely one of those minor characters necessary to the development of the plot. His character is not worked out with any degree of care.

III. vii. 240. Richard becomes king. This is the height of his desire. Almost immediately his fortunes begin to decline. This may be looked upon as the turning-point of the play.

The student should observe the character of Richard carefully throughout the remainder of the play. There is no apparent difference in his personality; but Shakespeare himself seems to have undergone a change. He seems to be taking the task of character presentation more seriously. In the first part of the play Richard seems to be playing at being wicked. His jocose remarks imply a mere game. From here on he is seriously wicked, in desperate straits, and thinking carefully. Note also how similar many points in his subsequent career are to those of Macbeth. For instance, Richard is no sooner king than he begins to fear lest he shall be unable to maintain his own. (See IV. ii.)

IV. ii. 5. So far Richard has waded through crime in order to reach the throne. He has been wholly intent upon the needs of the present hour. He seems to have taken no thought for the morrow. But now he sees that he has only just begun. The most desperate chances are really yet before him.

IV. ii. 24. In reading below relative to the character of Buckingham the student should weigh this passage carefully. Richard's surprise at Buckingham's coldness is shared by the audience. So far he has been such a patient tool in the king's hands that his present opposition is altogether unexpected. And there is no sufficient reason for it. One possible explanation is suggested in connection with III. iv. 60. Or is Buckingham shrewd enough to foresee the drift of events, and is preparing to desert? Or is Buckingham, bad as he is, unwilling to go quite so far?

IV. ii. 34. It hardly seems natural for the king to consult a lad relative to the choice of a murderer, or that the lad would have one ready at hand.

IV. iv. 425. Note the similarity of the preceding passage to I. ii. There is, however, a great difference. Instead of with Anne, Richard is here dealing with the queen, a woman of the world who is not to be easily taken in by him. She has already made her plans for the future. Her seeming agreement with Richard is but a ruse to gain time. Line 431, however, shows that the king is thoroughly deceived. Is the audience aware of the true situation?

V. iii. The history play was popular as early as 1585; and it reaches the crest of its vogue by 1600. During this period we find a steady advance in the staging of battle scenes from the mere crude suggestion of the earlier plays to the elaborate setting of *Henry the Fifth*. This play is midway in the prog-

ress.   The present scene may have been staged as
follows:

The middle stage is bare, with possibly the stock
drop let down at the back representing the open
country.   Soldiers come in and pitch Richard's tent,
say on the right side of the stage.   This must be a
real tent, perhaps only half a tent.   At any rate,
Richard must enter it and be seen therein.   Later
Richmond's tent is pitched on the opposite side of
the stage.   These tents represent the opposing camps.
The distance between them must be fancied great
enough to embrace the intervening territory.

The ghosts subsequently appear on the upper balcony.   From one side they speak to Richard.   Then
they move to the other and address Richmond.   In
these few steps they must be supposed to have
traversed a considerable distance.   Only an unim-
aginative audience would be disturbed by their ability
to speak thus in one breath to two leaders so widely
separated in space.

V. iii. 236.   The oration to the soldiers.   Formal
declamations were very common in Elizabethan plays.
(See a further discussion of the subject in the chapter
devoted to *Henry the Fifth*.)

V. The Character of Buckingham

Suggestions have been made above relative to the
character of Richard.   On the whole, however, his
character is easily read, and, though it dominates the
play, can be understood with little or no difficulty.
The character of Buckingham, however, is altogether
different.   It is not easy to understand.   He does not

seem consistent. This defect, however, is not due so much to an intricate mingling of qualities as to Shakespeare's carelessness and crudeness of portrayal. So much attention is here given to a minor character for the purpose of illustrating the precepts regarding character study laid down in Chapter VIII.

After one is familiar with the text of the play it is well to review consecutively the passages in which a particular person appears.

I. iii. 288. Margaret addresses Buckingham as if he had not yet cast in his lot with Richard; perhaps he is as likely as the others to be misled but is better worth appealing to than they.

I. iii. 328. Richard refers to Buckingham as a gull. Attention is called below to several other disparaging remarks by Richard. They all hang together pretty well. But Richard's actions tell a different story. He would hardly trust the secrets of his mind and the execution of his dearest plans to a gull, or to one whose insurrection he considered of no moment. Yet he does throw Buckingham aside as if he were a nonentity.

Buckingham is often made up on the stage as very youthful, rather effeminate, and altogether like an innocent. Is this the proper way to represent him?

II. i. 29. Edward calls him " Princely Buckingham " and seems very intent upon winning his promise of subsequent support. Hence he must be considered by the former king as a man of much consequence.

II. i. 83. The significance of this line is discussed above.

II. ii. 151. Richard calls Buckingham " his other

self " and by many other trustful and endearing terms. There is the sound of hollow flattery in this speech; yet Richard so treats him, and a literal interpretation is quite in accordance with the facts.

II. iv. 44. A messenger calls him a mighty duke, and associates him on terms of equality with Gloucester.

III. i. 151-180. By these speeches we know that Buckingham is the partner of all Richard's plots, and certainly a much more considerable personage than the trusted henchman Catesby.

III. i. 193. Buckingham is not startled by Richard's suggestion of chopping off the refractory Hastings' head. He is also mercenary. He is promised the Earldom of Hereford. The refusal to grant it is the ostensible cause of his desertion.

III. iv. 12, 13. This is a point-blank lie to Buckingham's credit.

III. v. 5, etc. Buckingham orates most eloquently relative to his ability to play the hypocrite. And later he justifies the opinion. In his dealings with the mayor and citizens he is both liar and hypocrite.

IV. ii. 22. See above for a discussion of Buckingham's behavior at this point. He has suddenly become " all ice."

IV. ii. 42. Richard calls him the deep-revolving, witty Buckingham. This is the only place where Richard gives him credit in words for being a man of parts; yet the thoughtlessness with which he drops the duke implies that the king really thought of him as a gull.

IV. iii. 50. Richard considers Buckingham's rebellion as nothing in comparison with Richmond's.

IV. iv. 332. Richard calls him dull-brained. Compare this with " deep-revolving " alluded to above.

On the whole, I fancy Buckingham to be a great and powerful duke whose aid and support is necessary to Richard. He is a hypocrite, a liar, hesitates at nothing that is criminal so long as it tends to his own interest. When he sees the change of fortune coming he immediately deserts, but, overestimating his own power, is easily borne down to the ruin he deserves.

CHAPTER XI

RICHARD THE SECOND

I. Relation to "Edward the Second"

This play is often compared to Marlowe's *Edward the Second,* and it merits the comparison. Yet it is a question in my mind whether the usual implication of the comparison is correct. For to me, it is their differences rather than their similarities that are notable.

A rough outline of the two plots reveals similar situations: that is, a weak king, one who is unworthy of respect, deposed for inability, and succeeded by a more kingly monarch. But the treatment of the subject in the two plays is altogether different. In the introduction to *Richard the Third* it was pointed out how the series of York plays were objective, following Marlowe, that is, dealing with the narrative alone; and that the series of Lancaster plays were subjective, that is, more concerned with the inner and deeper meaning of historical events. This is Shakespeare's peculiarity in the latter part of the series. Now *Edward the Second* is of the former kind. So is *Richard the Third,* written when Shakespeare was still a close follower of Marlowe and his methods. But *Richard the Second* belongs to the latter class, and is a marked departure from the Marlowe method.

Nor is the characterization of the king in the Marlowe vein. Richard the Third was, like Edward the Second, essentially conceived along the lines of Tamburlaine and the Jew of Malta. Shakespeare's Richard the Second, however, is quite unlike these predecessors in the drama. He is not a type, but a man, well rounded out, with human qualities, and deserving of human sympathies.

There are many minor differences, however, that need not be referred to here. The above remarks are sufficient to suggest the true situation, and the actual difference. The similarity of the two plays is due to the accidental resemblance of plot and is essentially superficial. The differences are important and of vital significance.

Instead of being an additional illustration of Shakespeare's debt to Marlowe, I consider *Richard the Second* as an indication of Shakespeare's breaking away from early models, perhaps the first sounding note of his future independence. It is the first play written on his long voyage of independent travel.

II. NOTES ON THE TEXT

In the following notes a little more stress is laid than usual on structural points. This is due partly to the fact that this is the most symmetrically constructed of the three history plays here considered; and partly to the desire to illustrate promptly some of the suggestions contained in Chapter VII.

The theme of the play is very clearly defined. *Is it right to depose an unworthy king?* Note that Marlowe's *Edward the Second* is the story of how an unworthy king was deposed. This play goes deeper into things. Richard is an impossible king. He appears to much better advantage after his deposition, when he earns our sympathy as a mere man. Shakespeare, however, does not complete the situation which he has here begun to portray till the end of the series which involves both parts of *Henry the Fourth* and *Henry the Fifth.*

This play is of the two-hero type of construction, the most perfect example of which is *Othello.* Bolingbroke and King Richard are the two opposites. Richard is the action-producing element of the first half, Bolingbroke of the second. The absence of Bolingbroke from the time of his banishment till his triumphal return is a crudity of structure which Shakespeare corrected in his later plays modeled upon this style. (See *Hamlet, Othello,* and *Macbeth.* The last, however, contains an equally gross violation of the usual rules in the portions that relate to Macduff.)

The introduction to the play need not be recapitulated here. It is brought in naturally throughout the first act of the play, much of it in the second scene. The technical beginning, or exciting force, is Bolingbroke's charge against Mowbray. It is referred to at once in the opening lines; and is developed fully in the first and third scenes.

In weighing the relative merits of Bolingbroke and Mowbray in their controversy, and the character of Bolingbroke throughout, the modern reader, especially if he be an American, should bear in mind the following: King Henry the Fifth was to the Elizabethans their great national hero, either as statesman, general, or perfect man. He was a sort of English George Washington and Abraham Lincoln in one. So devoted were the people to his memory that Shakespeare thought it necessary to forestall adverse criticism of his portrait of Prince Hal in *Henry the Fourth* by a soliloquy which is altogether out of keeping with the character of the person who speaks it. Now, as the Bolingbroke of this play is the father of Henry the Fifth, it is easy to fancy that he appeared before an Elizabethan audience familiar with his history and prejudiced in his favor. Though it is suggested below that neither Bolingbroke nor Mowbray appeared to better advantage in the first act, it is probable that Shakespeare's audience instinctively sided with Bolingbroke and gave him the benefit of the doubt. It is probably due to this national prejudice that Shakespeare was not plainer-spoken regarding the right and wrong of Henry's motives on his return to England. His guilt or innocence in this respect is delicately answered, but in the later plays, and then only by implication.

I. i. What is King Richard like in this scene? This question is of greater importance here than elsewhere, for the character of the king is developed by a method used only once in a great while by Shakespeare. In fact there is no other example of such a great departure from his usual method. Shakespeare's usual method of developing character is to open with a correct but incomplete sketch which is later filled out in all its details. This is true of *Richard the Third*, and of *Hamlet*, *Macbeth*, and *Othello*.

Richard the Second, however, is a departure; or

should we say that Shakespeare had not yet fully developed his method? In the opening scene Richard appears to better advantage than elsewhere. Later his weaknesses are set forth more fully. Still later the wicked elements of his character appear. And, last of all, the good points of his character come into prominence after he has ceased to be king.

Which of the two, Bolingbroke or Mowbray, is right? Is there any possibility of their both being wrong? (See I. i. 25.) Does the king know which is right? Do the speeches of either man ring truer than those of the other? What motive could there be at this time to prompt Henry to bring a false accusation against Mowbray? Does he later desire to have Mowbray come before him to substantiate old charges as if he were himself troubled with a guilty conscience? The answer to the latter question depends largely upon the fact as to whether Henry knew of the death of Mowbray.

I. i. 100. The Duke of Gloucester's death. This charge is brought up emphatically several times in the play. Does it turn out to be a matter of any particular importance? Does not the degree of emphasis laid upon it foreshadow greater significance in the remainder of the play? Is the truth of the charge ever proved or disproved?

I. ii. Structurally, this is a division scene. Note also the emphasis laid again on Gloucester's death. The scene contains much of the introductory matter. And it serves also to introduce John of Gaunt.

Though Gaunt appears only in the early part, he is one of the great characters of the play. His is a splendid personality, perhaps the one man who deserves no ill feeling throughout. The great national awakening of the decade from 1585 to 1595 called into being first a national curiosity as to England's past, and then a true spirit of patriotism. The catering to the demand of the people for knowledge regarding the sources of these two widespread emotions brought into existence the history play. In this drama, Gaunt is the embodied spirit of patriotism, a figurative kind of character, almost allegorical, that finds its fullest development in Henry the Fifth.

I. iii. This is one of the most important scenes of the play. From a structural point of view it represents the completion of the exciting force. Note how the subsequent events are related to this. Bolingbroke's charge against Mowbray brings about the trial which is interrupted at the command of the king. As a result he banished Bolingbroke. Resulting grief and disappointment hastens the death of Bolingbroke's father, John of Gaunt. The absence of Gaunt's heir prompts Richard to seize the dead duke's property. As a result of this act, determination to win back his own causes Bolingbroke's return before the expiration of his period of banishment. The effort to establish himself as Duke of Lancaster leads him further, and ends in the overthrow of Richard.

The scene also contains a very important though partial presentation of the character of the king. As pointed out above, Shakespeare is here, contrary to his later method, developing Richard's character gradually. Here he appears to disadvantage through his weakness, but hardly as actually wicked. The character information is all bound up in the king's reason for stopping the combat. If we turn to the original

historical source we learn that Richard feared an outbreak from the adherents of Lancaster, and that he
took great precautions to police the lists. Fear lest
the precautions taken should prove insufficient probably caused him to stop the trial at the critical moment. And the lighter sentence on Bolingbroke, together with the reduction of his banishment from ten
years to six, is a sop to the faction of Gaunt. This
explanation is not emphasized in the text, though it
must have been in Shakespeare's mind, and he may
have assumed it as being taken for granted by the
audience.

Note the appearance of the following list of characteristics of the king:

1. *Lack of decision.*—He is almost unwilling to
pronounce the heavy sentence against Norfolk. The
timid king seems to lack the courage of his convictions.

2. *Lack of personal magnetism.*—We have already
noticed in scene i. that he has no control over Norfolk, and that he turns Bolingbroke over to his father's management as if quite beyond his own influence. Here he also fails utterly to dominate Norfolk,
and gives in to Gaunt merely as a result of his unspoken behavior.

3. *He does not know his own mind.*—So far as
we know the king has acquired no new information
since scene i. Any reason for not permitting the trial
to go on existed when he arranged it at first. It is
possible, however, that the king proceeded in the mere
hope that something accidental would turn up to stop
it without his own decided action.

4. *Insincerity.*—I. iii. 125. The reason the king

gives for stopping the combat is not the true one.   If
it were he would have urged it at the beginning as a
reason for not permitting the combat to take place at
all.   (See also I. iii. 184, where he commanded
Bolingbroke and Mowbray never to reconcile their
differences.)

5. *Cowardice.*—The king's reason for stopping the
combat is fear of the results.   In those days people
believed in the just and righteous outcome of such a
trial.   Physical powers had nothing to do with such a
result.   It makes no difference whether the king knew
which man was right.   If Mowbray won it might set
the dissatisfied party of Lancaster into active opposition against the crown.   If Bolingbroke won it would
reflect upon the past behavior of the king's party,
even upon the king himself.   No matter which prevailed, the king would be in a dangerous situation.

6. *Vacillating.*—Note the change in Bolingbroke's
sentence.

7. *Impracticable.*—Notwithstanding the fact that
the king has banished both combatants he lays strict
commands upon them to be obeyed in absence, as if
he were still able to control them by a mere word.
They must not communicate with each other or reconcile their differences.   In other words, the king ex-
pects them in absence, after a heavy and unjust penalty, to show to him a loyalty that he could not
command at home before this act of injustice.

8. *Unjust.*—So far as we know there is no reasonable proof that either is guilty.   There is no justice
for either sentence.   If, however, both be thought partially guilty of misbehavior, there is no reason for
discrimination.   And if Bolingbroke were worthy of

a banishment of ten years there is no justice in re-
ducing it to six.

Note that in this list of qualities the first seven
show Richard to be a weak man, and in no way a great
leader. Many a good man has been weak. The situation is to be lamented, but it need not necessarily be
interpreted to his moral discredit. The eighth quality
of injustice is a little more defamatory. Yet it would
be possible to fancy that his very weakness forced
him into this line of action against his will; or, at
least, not altogether of his own aggressive initiation.
In other words, this scene presents the disadvanta-
geous qualities of the king, leaving his most vicious
characteristics for later presentation.

II. i. 5. It was a common superstition of the time
that a person about to die, on the borderland, so to
speak, between life and death, could see forward into
the life to come. Hence the words of dying men were
listened to with peculiar respect and often regarded
as prophetic. The fact that Richard pays no attention to his uncle's words at this time is, therefore, more
indicative of his character than would be the case if
Gaunt were not at death's door.

II. i. 17. According to York, how fully Richard
seems to be given up to the influence of bad advisers.
(See also III. ii. 130.) Do not this outbreak of the
king against his favorites, and the hasty, erroneous
judgment shown, imply very plainly that the king
knew their bad qualities all along? If so he deserves
all the more blame for the national adversity they
have led him into countenancing.

Note also (line 31, etc.) the patriotic description
of England. As already pointed out, Gaunt repre-

sents figuratively the newly developing patriotism of the Elizabethans. Gaunt, who, throughout his whole life, has always subordinated the interests of his family to the interests of the king, is now near death. In the clearer vision of this moment he discovers that love and duty to England is a greater thing than even a blind devotion to the king and his interests. The king himself owes this devotion to England as well as the meanest subject in the land. And the upshot of it all is that a king who does not feel this patriotism has no right to continue being king.

II. i. 73-83. In Elizabethan times puns were not necessarily considered funny. There is no hint of wit or humor implied in this passage. (See a further discussion of this matter in the chapter on *Macbeth*.)

II. i. 115, 139. Shakespeare, having shown Richard to fair advantage at the start, then as weak and flighty, is now engaged in bringing out his most despicable characteristics. At no place in the play does he appear to worse advantage than here, with his brutal disrespect to the dying Gaunt, typified by the two lines cited above.

Richard might have shown some grief, or, at least, some outward respect, when he hears that his uncle, the greatest man in England, is dead. But he shows joy, rather than grief (II. i. 154), and absolutely no respect (II. i. 160).

Note how in keeping with his character is this seizure of Gaunt's property, and how inevitably the following events grow out of the seizure as a result of the law of cause and effect. This is a good example of the interplay of character and plot so necessary to dramatic effect. (See the chapter on Dramatic Structure.)

After the introduction and the exciting force were introduced in act I. we find a sort of pause in the general swing of forward motion preparatory to the great events of act III. In the second act, which has been spoken of as structurally transitional, we have the plot advanced, a good deal of foreshadowing, the return of Bolingbroke prepared for, and the bad side of the king's character further presented. The latter detail is completed in act III., scene ii. Note that no event in this act, save the death of Gaunt and the seizure of his property, which comes first, is of great spectacular importance. Yet all the remainder of the act taken together is preparation for what is coming in act III., and suggestions as to what it will be like.

The character of York should be noted carefully. He is a timeserver, one who wishes to be on the safe side from selfish motives. Yet he is not altogether bad. He is usually faithful enough for the time being, and often shows better impulses, though seldom able to live up to them. On the whole York fails to win our sympathy or admiration.

II. i. 163. It means a good deal for such a man to express himself as out of patience with the behavior of the king. Evidently it is the first time York has ever expressed himself thus. See the startled exclamation of the king, lines 169, 186. Note York's remarks to the king relative to the unjust treatment of Bolingbroke, and what will follow such a course of action; and compare these sentiments with what he says to Bolingbroke in II. iii. In this latter scene York is still a king's man.

II. i. 211. When the king reiterates his determination to seize the property of Gaunt, York replies, "I'll not be by the while." Thus quickly does his better impulse to opposition wear itself out, lest like treatment be accorded to him. (See line 151.)

II. i. 246, etc. The noblemen give a long list of Richard's misdeeds, many of them amounting to crimes. (See line 277, etc.) In their conversation the nobles say nothing of Bolingbroke's return to claim his own rights. On the other hand, line 292, it is very plain that their opposition is directed against the king. They deny this later. We should, however, take their denial, II. iii. 148, for no more than it is worth.

II. ii. 98-122. York here is much excited and muddled. His helplessness, however, is not so much due to lack of ability as to a lack of knowledge as to what it is best for him to do for himself in the long run. He acknowledges weighty ties both to the king and to Bolingbroke. It would be worth a good deal to him at this moment to know which side to espouse. He elects the king's, but changes as soon as a sight of the formidable following and backing of Bolingbroke convinces him of his error.

II. iii. 71. Bolingbroke asserts that he came to England only to reclaim his confiscated rights as Duke of Lancaster. It is interesting to determine whether he is here telling the truth. There can be no doubt but that the nobles rally to his support intending in their own minds to make him king. And it is barely possible that they have deceived Bolingbroke in this respect, and are trusting to the general drift of circumstances to embolden him to the seizure of the crown. As a matter of fact, Shakespeare leaves the honesty or dishonesty of Bolingbroke's original motives an open question.

II. iii. 88. York calls Bolingbroke a traitor. Compare with York's sentiments formerly spoken to the king, II. i. Does the use of the word traitor imply that York believes that Bolingbroke is in reality fighting for the crown? If so, what light does it shed on the character significance of York's desertion from the king's party?

II. iii. 113-171. Bolingbroke insists that he has come to England only to claim his own rights as Lancaster. Northumberland and the others support him in this assertion. York offers no objection save in line 152. Does he mean by " I see the issue of these arms," to say " Your intentions at this moment may be honest enough, but I see where this opposition will eventually lead you "?

Note, however, at the end of this passage, Bolingbroke's determination to attack Bushy, Bagot, and Green. Is this an act in the pursuit of his private interests? And in III. i. does he not order their execution as dictatorially as if he were already king? or counting confidently on becoming king?

We are now rapidly approaching the structural turning-point of the play—the point at which by abdication Richard gives place to Bolingbroke.

III. ii. The function of this scene is mainly to justify Bolingbroke's seizure of the crown. This justification is to be found mainly in the king's utter helplessness in an emergency. He has had every opportunity in the past. Now that the time and opportunity to do something has come his mismanagement of affairs has rendered him altogether incapable. Why should not a better man take the reins of government in hand? The answer to this question implies the total effect of the scene.

The wild and enthusiastic joy of the king when he sets foot on English ground does not redound much to his credit. One feels that there is a superficial sentimentality about the expression of such sentiments from the man who had loved England so little that he has brought it to the point of ruin through his selfishness and wickedness. The declamation is mere hollow insincerity. The exhibition of outward feeling here expressed is in no way in keeping with Richard's past actions. He has done his best to bring disaster upon England and to render it untenable, both for him and for others.

Even his own people condemn him. Carlisle and Aumerle consider him amiss in his dilatory dealing with Bolingbroke, line 33. Again, Aumerle comments on his cowardly pallor, line 75, and finds it necessary to remind the king that he is a king, line 82. A little later when Richard is wholly given up to his mournful wailing, Carlisle, his devoted friend, utters what is the strongest charge of inability brought against the king in the whole play: namely, " Wise men ne'er sit and wail their woes, But presently prevent the ways to wail."

III. ii. 97. The king apparently jumps to the conclusion that Bolingbroke is in reality aiming at the crown.

During all this scene the king appears to the greatest disadvantage. He is up and down in spirits, speaking grandiloquently at one moment when danger seems distant; utterly collapsing the next when it appears more near at hand. Not once, but several times, does he experience this transition from boastful hope to pallid fear. At the end we realize that he is incapable of offering any material opposition. All his strength lay in the wicked favorites who have been executed or in those lukewarm adherents who have deserted him. Bolingbroke has nothing more to fear. After this scene the result is a foregone conclusion.

III. iii. The complicated situation of this scene requires careful analysis. The king, having given up, practically in hiding, believes the end is near and that the all-powerful Bolingbroke has come to seize the crown. York, who has lately deserted the king, holds practically the same belief. Northumberland and the other peers are determined that Bolingbroke shall ascend the throne. However, they do not yet know the absolute weakness of the king. Hence they are not quite ready to come out into the open. So they pretend to support Bolingbroke only in his position of claiming his rights as the Duke of Lancaster. Bolingbroke's position, on the other hand, is not quite so clear. He may be at one with the barons, or he may be honestly desirous of regaining his own rights and no more.

At any rate, the move they have decided upon is to lay the claim for the full restoration of Bolingbroke, offering to disband their army if this is granted. They probably expected Richard to refuse point-blank. Their next move would be to depose Richard for this further act of injustice, and then proclaim Henry king.

But in a moment the king suddenly upsets all their plans. He agrees without the least hesitation to all terms.   Bolingbroke's apparently honest expression of satisfaction rather than of dismay may imply his innocence, or it may merely imply good acting.   To use a slang phrase, the king has called their bluff. They need time to devise a way out of the situation.

Note, however, that the king himself considers them all insincere.   He believes that he has really given up his crown, that he accompanies them to London in actual fact as a prisoner.   In the next scene the gardener not only takes this view but tells us that the king is generally considered to be deposed.   And in the scene next following Richard is called upon to acknowledge publicly what is assumed as already to have taken place.

So I should consider this scene as equivalent to the virtual abdication of the king, and place the structural turning-point here.

Notice how promptly in the next act Shakespeare begins to solicit our sympathy for the deposed monarch.   None of his good points appears till he is robbed of the position and the power which served to bring out only the worst elements of his character.

Structurally the fourth and fifth acts are less symmetrical than the first three.   The first 106 lines constitute an absolutely irrelevant scene.   From 106 to 160 attention is taken up with the tirade from Carlisle that results in nothing save his subsequent qualified forgiveness by Bolingbroke.   And the rest of the act is given up to a pitiful example of harsh treatment of the downfallen ruler which serves, however, to rouse the sympathy of the audience for him, but which has no plot significance.   And most of the fifth act is taken up with a comedy diversion.

It is well to note that in several cases Shakespeare's plays end more weakly than they begin.

IV. i. 1-106. See a former note relative to the frequent reference to Gloucester's death. The point is made very emphatic here. And nothing comes of it. Even the dilemma of Aumerle has nothing to do with the dilemma he finds himself in in the fifth act. The passage is dead weight to the progress of the play. Possibly it was meant to contrast Henry's behavior with Richard's in a similar situation at the opening of the play. But the effect, from this point of view, is wasted, for Henry immediately drops the whole matter. The day of trial, referred to in line 106, never comes.

IV. i. 107-161. Carlisle's brilliant speech on behalf of the king results only in his arrest for high treason by Northumberland, and his subsequent forgiveness by Bolingbroke.

Nowhere else has Shakespeare treated a character as he has treated the character of Richard. The dramatist has begun with an attractive glimpse, then the character of the king was gradually debased till our sympathy is entirely with his enemies. Then Richard is slowly but surely raised in our estimation. This latter phase is developed by the use of pathos.

The requisition that Richard announce publicly all the details of his downfall, even to the point of expatiating on his own deserts and praising his enemies, is certainly carrying the matter too far, now that Henry has gained all that he wants. Even he is at last shamed into bidding Northumberland to " urge it no more."

The next act opens with the queen upon the stage.

Her meeting with the king and their tender parting brings tears to the eyes of those who a moment before were willing to cry " Down with Richard." Our indignation is justly roused when we are told, V. ii., that the populace on the day of coronation " threw dust and rubbish on King Richard's head." There is no more pathetic touch in the play than Richard's injured pride at the news that Roan Barbary was proud to be beneath his new master.

V. v. 1-66. This wild rush of poetical but disconnected fancies, almost incoherent at times, represents the result of Richard's constant and lonely brooding over his change of fortune. It represents a mind on the very point of collapse. To a man in such a state we can render nothing but sympathy. Then he suddenly rises to a display of energy that would have made him a better king had it been rightly directed from the start. First one attendant and then another falls before his fierce onslaught. And, at our last view of Richard, we feel, with Exton, that he died " as full of valor as of royal blood."

The structural end of this play comes where it should come, at the end. It is the entrance of Exton with the coffin speaking the termination of the tale, " Great king, within this coffin I present thy buried fear." It is said above that before the end of the play all loose threads, etc., should be gathered up and disposed of. The opening lines of V. iii. are a reference to the escapades of Prince Hal, and serve to bind this play to *Henry the Fourth.* So also does the projected pilgrimage to the Holy Land, mentioned at the close. For *Henry the Fourth* opens with an explanation as to why this pilgrimage was not made.

In other words, these two details serve to link the play to the next in the series rather than to end it sharply and with finality.

III. THE CHARACTER OF BOLINGBROKE

It is hoped that in a subsequent edition of this volume room will be found for a treatment of both parts of *Henry the Fourth,* as they assist materially in understanding the character of Bolingbroke. It has been pointed out above that the interesting detail of Henry's character is in connection with the motives that actuated his return to England. Was he guilty of designs upon the crown from the very start, or was he forced upon the throne by the drift of circumstances? Shakespeare has left the question without an answer in *Richard the Second.* I think, however, that a careful consideration of the four plays of the series enables us to determine Shakespeare's position. In brief, it seems to be as follows:

Bolingbroke, in absence, was aware of the bad conditions at home, saw that the time was ripe for a rising against the crown, and awaited only a pretext that would permit him to place himself promptly in the limelight. This pretext came in the seizure of his rights and properties as Duke of Lancaster.

Consider for a moment the significance of the character of Gaunt as outlined earlier in the chapter. So long as only personal interests were at stake he did what seemed right, he remained subservient to the king. But when the good of England was at stake he turned against his monarch. This is Shakespeare's position as well as Gaunt's.

Now apply this to the situation of Bolingbroke. So far as he is actuated by selfish motives he is doing wrong and deserves punishment. But he was a good king and did well for England, and for this he deserves reward.

Shakespeare always observed the principle of nemesis with subtile justice. And he has applied it here with consummate skill. Henry is punished by remorse over the way in which Exton has misinterpreted his chance remark about the king,* by the inability to clear his conscience by a pilgrimage, by the rebellion of the north, and by the behavior of his unthrifty son. On the other hand, he is rewarded by eventual success, by peace and plenty brought to England during his administration, and, eventually, by the triumph of his house in the magnificent career of his son, Henry the Fifth.

IV. THE COMEDY ELEMENT

In the above notes on the text of the play the second and third scenes of act V. have been passed over almost without comment. If I am right, their proper interpretation has often been neglected. They furnish, in fact, the comedy element of the play.

Shakespeare's plays of this period are largely experimental. The age demanded a large admixture of the comedy element with the tragic. Shakespeare experimented as to the best place to put it. In *Richard the Third* it is practically omitted. In *Henry the Fourth* two stories, one serious, the other comic,

---

* It is interesting to note that this remorse is not hinted at in the chronicles. It is Shakespeare's addition.

are told, almost independently, and introduced in alternate scenes. In *Henry the Fifth* an effort is made to weave the comedy into the body of the story as an integral part of it. In *Richard the Second,* however, Shakespeare adopted still a different device. He waited till the serious part of the play was, to all intents and purposes, ended; then introduced a plentiful supply of comic diversion all at once.

In my classes I have frequently met students who, on a superficial examination, have failed to recognize the farcical nature of these two scenes. Hence a brief suggestion may not be out of place.

York, throughout the play, has been a timeserver. In these two scenes he is drawn as a caricature of himself. It is the willing reed bent by a sort of re-ductio-ad-absurdum method to the extreme limit. The very nature of what is coming is foretold, for the last line of act IV. promises us " a plot shall show us all a merry day." There is something ridiculous in the air of carelessness of an arch-conspirator who goes about with his bond exposed to view.

After the discovery we must imagine York storming about, " roaring as gently as any sucking dove " and completely overacting the part. Then appears the equally impetuous duchess, with the great conspirator standing by, doing nothing but twiddle his thumbs while his parents wrangle. And at regular recurring intervals comes York's imperious slogan, " Bring me my boots."

One who could manage to escape the humor of the next scene could easily fail to see its possibilities. The great Henry is placid in the face of danger. York, Aumerle, and the duchess are all on their knees before him. Both the elders are a bit too stiff in their knees to rise easily. So York continues to clamor for the conviction of the son who has already been forgiven; the duchess for his pardon, not knowing that he has been forgiven even before her entrance.

Through melodramatic overacting all this is made delightfully laughable. Throughout this play and both parts of *Henry the Fourth* the king is painted as a grim, stern potentate, quite unlike Prince Hal or Henry the Fifth. Yet even Bolingbroke is overcome by the humorous situation and exclaims, line 79, "Our scene is altered from a serious thing."

CHAPTER XII

HENRY THE FIFTH

I. RELATION TO OTHER PLAYS

THERE is a difference of opinion as to whether the four Lancaster plays, *Richard the Second*, the first and second parts of *Henry the Fourth*, and *Henry the Fifth*, should be considered separately or together. It has already been pointed out how the closing lines of *Richard the Second* link the play to *Henry the Fourth*. Both parts of the latter play are quite continuous. There are, however, reasons for looking upon *Henry the Fifth* as a separate venture, not as a continuation of the series.

Both *Richard the Second* and *Henry the Fifth* differ structurally from *Henry the Fourth*. Hence no structural unity in the series is to be discovered.

Richard the Second and *Henry the Fourth* conform to the description of a history play given in Chapter X. That is, they aim primarily at a dramatization of the chronicle in such a manner as to enlighten the audience regarding the historical events of the period under consideration. Now *Henry the Fifth* does not do this. It is little more than a spectacular dramatization of the Battle of Agincourt.

Furthermore, the first three plays mentioned above are thoroughly dramatic, full of action and interrelation of parts. *Henry the Fifth,* on the other hand, is much more epic in character, frequently delayed by long patriotic declamations, and requires a chorus before each act, a detail not appearing elsewhere among the plays of Shakespeare.

These differences are sufficient to support the contention that *Henry the Fifth,* in spite of its position in the historical sequence, is an entirely independent play. And to these facts may be added another of even greater significance.

Consider what the absence of Falstaff means. At the close of the second part of *Henry the Fourth* Shakespeare tells us that he already has the play of *Henry the Fifth* under consideration. He further tells us specifically that Falstaff is to be a character in it. And the implication is that the fat knight will be as important in the new play as he was in the old.

Shakespeare postponed the writing of *Henry the Fifth* long enough to produce the *Merry Wives of Windsor.* Then he wrote the play under consideration according to a plan, and of a tone, that precludes the presence of Falstaff. Evidently, in the interim, Shakespeare's conception of the play as a continuation of the series had undergone such a change that he could not keep the promise formerly made at the conclusion of *Henry the Fourth.*

The play also bears a special relation to Shakespeare's whole career. His early work was imitative. His middle work independent but experimental. This period and the next begins with *Henry the Fifth.* There follows the period of maturity in which he produced the great tragedies. In other words, *Henry the Fifth* looks back upon the history plays and for-

ward upon the tragedies. The sources of many of the
tragedies arc.to be found in Holinshed, whence came
the material for the history plays.

Now the history plays, as pointed out above, aimed
to instruct. The facts—that is, the plot—must be in
accordance with a ready found account and, if need be,
take precedence over a better arrangement from the
dramatic point of view. As Shakespeare matured, this
limitation became more and more irksome. When he
gave up history-play writing he gave up this limitation. He would henceforth be at liberty to change,
rearrange, omit, or invent at will. This change in
procedure is equivalent to an assertion of his complete independence of models, the beginning of the
full development of his own individual personality.

Henry the Fifth I consider to be the first play
produced in accordance with this change of method
and purpose.

Later, as another difference between this play and
the other three, will be pointed out the irreconcilable
inconsistency between the character of Prince Hal
and that of Henry the Fifth.

II. The Conception of the Play

So far as we know, Shakespeare did not stop writing history plays because the field had been covered.
Nor was it because the demand for them was waning
—witness his own popularity as a producer of this
kind of play. It was rather because, as has already
been pointed out, the type demanded a close adherence to facts already laid down. This condition ham-

pered his maturing genius, his developing dramatic powers began to demand a wider scope.

The generally experimental nature of the history plays is not always clearly enough recognized. Shakespeare appears in the three parts of *Henry the Sixth* merely as a reviser and polisher-up. In *Richard the Third* he is a follower of Marlowe. With *Richard the Second* he asserted his independence of Marlowe, but not of the history play as a type. The accidental plot symmetry of this play is due to the exceptionally dramatic nature of the original account. In *Henry the Fourth* the dramatist tried the experiment of the double plot, which, rather than adding to his prestige as a writer of history plays, made him famous as a comedy writer.

By this time, Shakespeare, as suggested above, must have decided to give up the writing of history plays. Of the four plays which constitute his notable contribution to the type, the first presents the picture of a weak and worthless king. Shakespeare resolved to say good-by to the type in a play presenting just the opposite kind of ruler.

The nature of the chronicle play and his experiments with it showed Shakespeare that dramatic unity was not the chief quality of the type. He therefore resolved to treat the whole thing in a new way. The new play was to be epic rather than dramatic (an experiment, however, which he did not repeat). He would sing the glory of his country. To do this he chose one man and one event.

Henry the Fifth was chosen not because he came after Henry the Fourth, whose reign had just been dramatized, but because of the peculiar attitude of the Elizabethans towards him and Agincourt. Henry the Fifth was their great national hero; and Agincourt was to them what Waterloo is to modern Englishmen, or Gettysburg to Americans.

Shakespeare's conception of the play is twofold. It involves the treatment of an ideal king, and also the glory of England. In the plan adopted, Henry becomes partly allegorical. At times he is a man, at other times he is England. Thus in I. ii. 275, etc., he is boasting to France as England. From 279 on he is speaking modestly to his own people as a man and their king.

Throughout the play it is necessary to bear in mind its twofold significance. It is constantly alternating between realism and allegory.

III. Notes on the Text

The Elizabethan dramatists made frequent use of the prologue, though its use was by no means universal. Shakespeare resorted to it sparingly; and in no other play inserted a prologue or chorus before every act.

The prologue was put to a number of uses. Sometimes it served merely as an introductory speech requesting the favor and patience of the audience. Again it would explain the special occasion for the production of the play. Thus some plays have a prologue for public presentation and another for production at the court. Again, the prologue was used to apologize for the inadequacy of the stage effects at the command of the presenters. Ben Jonson used it frequently to air his precepts regarding stagecraft and literary criticism. But perhaps the most common use of the prologue was to forecast the substance of the play or to give a synopsis of the parts omitted in the actual presentation. Several of these functions are illustrated by the choruses of this play. Their special significance, however, is discussed in a later section of this chapter.

Act I. Prologue. The Globe, Shakespeare's theater, was round, hence the allusion to it as a cockpit and a wooden O. The companies in that day were probably much smaller than theatrical troupes to-day, hence an army would be represented by a very limited number of actors. So this prologue is usually cited by critics as an apology for the crude and limited resources at Shakespeare's command for the presentation of stage effects.

I am inclined, however, to take a different view of the matter. Consider for a moment the actual conditions. The date of no other play of Shakespeare is generally accepted within such narrow limits as that of *Henry the Fifth*. If produced in the spring of 1599, as is generally supposed, the Globe playhouse was still too new for its novelty to have worn off. Shakespeare's company was the leading troupe of London, and the Globe the finest, most up-to-date theater. With such resources at his command is it likely that Shakespeare would take a humble and apologetic attitude, rather than one of ostentatious pride?

I think that there are two significations to this prologue. As pointed out in the section devoted to the Elizabethan staging of the play, it may be that a special effort is made to produce a great spectacular

effect as unusual on the London stage of that day
as the play itself.   In such a situation the opening
apology, soon to be put at naught, would be merely a
bit of rhetorical irony.

The other significance of the prologue may be
phrased something like this: " Here we are, the best
troupe in London, with the best playhouse in town,
making a special effort to do credit to our new theater
and to our theme.   But the theme is so great that
even our resources are utterly and absolutely inadequate to do justice to our subject."   In other words,
granted the unusual resources at command, every
word of disparagement is a word enhancing the glory
of Henry the Fifth.

I. i. 24.   Canterbury is here referring to the early
life of the king, fully set forth in the two parts of
Henry the Fourth.

I. i. 38.   Note this list of the characteristics and ac-
complishments of the king.

I. i. 64-69.   It is later pointed out that Prince
Hal is a different sort of man from the king.
Henry the Fifth is not merely a reformed Prince
Hal.   The ordinary way of accounting for the change
by those who see no difficulty in reconciling the difference, is a familiar, every-day occurrence known to
every one.   Yet Ely and Canterbury discuss the
change and give its explanation up as inexplicable.
In their opinion it can only be explained as the result of a miracle.   Remembering, as already pointed
out, Shakespeare's change of conception regarding
the play as a whole, is not this passage equivalent to
a direct hint from him to expect a different personality in the king?

I. ii. *33*, etc. This long and tedious exposition of the Salic law is a passage illustrative of the instructional element of the history play. The conception of *Henry the Fifth* as set forth above need not imply that Shakespeare broke away once and for all from every detail of the history-play type. It merely implies the peculiar qualities of the type have given place to something else. We even find reminiscences of the history-play habit very marked in *Julius Cæsar*.

Note how much of this scene is essentially undramatic. It is largely a patriotic recitation of the great deeds England has done and will do again.

II. i. Nym, Bardolph, Pistol, and Hostess were familiar to Elizabethan audiences as characters of *Henry the Fourth*.

II. ii. Note the undramatic quality of this whole scene. Nothing has led up to it. It produces no after effect, no new step in the action. It is a mere episode in Henry's journey to France.

It may be asked, Why is so much space given up to it? The answer is, To help portray the character of the king. Character description, so far as it is necessary to explain or account for action, *is* dramatic. But such disproportionate attention to the point here is the justification for calling the scene essentially undramatic. One reason why the play is so undramatic as a whole is that it is a character sketch presented on a large scale rather than a character protrayal by a continuous action produced in accordance with the law of cause and effect.

1. The scene contrasts the duplicity of the traitors with the honesty of the king.

2. Henry's leniency is shown in his dealing with the condemned soldier.

3. It illustrates the king's watchfulness, which has resulted in the discovery of the conspiracy.

4. It shows his just discrimination in forgiving the soldier and in punishing the conspirators to the full.

5. Henry's sorrowful pity for Lord Scroop reminds us of Lincoln's sympathy for his erring brothers of the South.

6. The contrition of the conspirators is a tribute to Henry's greatness of character.

7. Henry continues his journey absolutely undisturbed by such a momentous danger.

II. iv. 48, etc. Note throughout the play the contrast between Shakespeare's contempt of the French and the praise of Englishmen often put into the mouths of Frenchmen.

III. i. This is one of the finest declamations of the play. Inasmuch as it incites the soldiers to hearty action in the battle it may be looked upon as the only one of these well-known declamatory passages which is truly dramatic.

III. iv. This scene is translated in the Tudor Edition of Shakespeare's *Henry the Fifth*. The translation, however, is unnecessary to a comprehension of the effect. In fact, a literal knowledge of its meaning in a way destroys its purpose. The Elizabethans probably understood France no better than did King Henry himself. When Shakespeare wrote this scene he knew very well that the Globe audience would understand no more than the general drift, and that they would not clamor for an interlinear translation.

The active, energetic pantomime of the two French-women together with the strange words made it as funny to the Elizabethans as a similar scene in a French café is to an American to-day who knows French only through his Baedeker handbook.

III. vii. The purpose of this scene is to contrast the frivolous, over-confident behavior of the Frenchmen before the battle, with the sober, God-fearing preparation of Henry's army.

IV. i. 309-322. Note the bearing of this passage on the question raised in the discussion of *Richard the Second,* namely, the initial guilt of Bolingbroke's acquisition of the crown.

IV. DECLAMATIONS AND CHORUSES

The Elizabethan generation greatly loved declamations. Declamatory exhibitions and contests similar to modern oratorical contests and debates were popular. The drama, which was gradually superseding most forms of indoor entertainments, catered to this demand. It may almost be said that the drama without some sort of appeal to the declamatory instinct was exceptional. Irrelevant declamations were often introduced, much as popular songs are introduced into plays to-day. Shakespeare resorted to irrelevant, or, rather, to undramatic declamations at all periods of his career; but in no play so extensively as in *Henry the Fifth.*

A list of the more important declamations is as follows. If read over consecutively one will notice how little they have to do with the dramatic quality of the play.

I. ii. 183, etc. Canterbury's long oration about the state of man.

II. ii. 79. Henry, as outraged justice, reproves the traitors.

III. i. The only spectacular dramatic declamation of the play which has truly dramatic significance.

IV. i. 154. Note Henry's reply to Williams. It will help to explain Shakespeare's idea of a perfect king.

IV. i. 247. This splendid declamation is usually referred to as the " Sham of Ceremony " passage. Nowhere does Shakespeare reach a higher pitch in his poetry.

IV. iii. 118. Henry's reply to Westmoreland about Saint Crispin's Day.

V. ii. 23. Burgundy's long speech about the peace.

These declamations are nearly all epic or descriptive, and, except III. i., lead to no particular dramatic action, as is the case after Antony's speech in *Julius Cæsar*. This, like III. i. above, had direct dramatic significance. Except the choruses they seldom possess any value except that which attaches to pleasant declamation.

The use of the chorus is not characteristic of Shakespeare. It is interesting to raise the question as to why Shakespeare used the chorus here and nowhere else. In other words, What part do they play in *Henry the Fifth?*

Recall what is said above regarding prologues. One is instantly reminded of three points:

1. They serve slightly to apologize for the poverty of stage effects. This is especially true of the chorus

to act V., last five lines. (See the discussion above of the special significance of the chorus to act I.)

2. They serve to explain missing details and to bridge gaps.

3. All that is said above of declamations applies to them.

Yet it must be acknowledged that neither nor all of these uses accounts for the undue emphasis implied by their use.

A closer study reveals three other and far more significant qualities.

1. At the risk of repetition, note carefully the character of the first chorus. The tone of apology is not so much for the poverty of the Elizabethan stage as that any stage is inadequate to the presentation of so vast a theme. It enhances the value of the theme, and its magnitude, as employed in the conception of the whole play.

2. The very nature of the theme demands continuity. Now, continuity was not a quality of the Elizabethan drama. To-day, the most fitting selections of music for the orchestral intermissions would be patriotic airs between acts. The chorus takes the place of the modern but usually irrelevant musical interruption.

3. King Henry is the all and be-all of this play. His chief characteristic is modesty. A modest man cannot boast to advantage of the greatness for which he stands as a symbol. Yet the carrying out of the theme requires much of this kind of eulogy of the king. Most of it is put into the mouth of the chorus. In fact, it constitutes their principal value. They say what cannot well be said by others:—1. The theme is

too vast. 2. Eulogy of Henry. 3. Magnificent spectacle of Henry and his army. 4. Eulogy of Henry. 5. Eulogy of Henry expressed by the clamorous public joy at his home-coming.

V. The Character of Prince Hal and of King Henry

Many attempts have been made to make the change of character from Prince Hal to Henry the Fifth seem consistent. To my mind this is an impossible task. The serious side of Prince Hal is perfunctory and conventional—a mere bow on the part of Shakespeare to the contemporary feeling towards Henry the Fifth. The real character of the prince is to be found in the Falstaff scenes.

Most writers have tried to reconcile the two characters on the ground that the change is ethical. If this were all, they might have saved themselves the trouble. Every day we see about us sudden and complete reformation of morals. If this were the only characteristic of the change we should accept it as a mere fact and require no further explanation.

That this, however, is not the character of the change, is implied by the fact that Shakespeare essays an explanation but (through the mouth of Canterbury) gives it up, and falls back upon a miracle as the cause.

The change is one of intellect and temperament, not of morals.

Canterbury dwells upon the king's intellectual powers, a quality never displayed by Prince Hal. Henry's reasoning in divinity would have been doubted by Falstaff. Hal showed no love of state-craft, nor power to grasp it. Canterbury goes on to tell us that knowledge of war, familiarity and con-viction regarding a theory of life, were impossible to the prince but characteristic of the king. Consider-ing his past career it is impossible to imagine him possessed of even the rudiments of such things.

Indeed, between the intellect of Prince Hal and the intellect of the king there is an impassable gulf. But there is a greater ˉifference even than this. It is to be found in their relative sense of humor. Hal is full of humor, quick-witted. Henry, on the other hand, has a stolid, well-balanced mind, but no sense of humor. Imagine Prince Hal in the glove episode, or wooing Katharine in a foreign tongue, and com-pare with the behavior of King Henry. It is not that Henry suppresses his boisterous humor. He never had any. It is not a question of more or less of this or that. He is portrayed as an altogether different man.

VI. The Character of the King

On the whole the character of the king is so evi-dently and so simply set forth that one need call at-tention only to the principal points.

His simplicity of character is remarkable, amount-ing almost to naïveté. Though he is plain and out-spoken, and on terms of familiarity with his soldiers he always preserves his dignity. He ardently loves right and hates wrong. He is a good warrior and carefully solicitous as to the welfare of his soldiers. His persistency is of the bulldog type. He is modest

in triumph, and evinces a wholesome reverence, and
the fear of God is inbred in his whole nature.

Perhaps his most prominent characteristic is the
latter. At the close of Canterbury's harangue Henry
expresses his fear of God and his faith in Englishmen,
who in reality derive their only strength from the Al-
mighty.   He believes in the mediæval superstition
which preserves a sincere faith in penance. After the
Battle of Agincourt he insists that all the credit and
glory belong to God alone.

His homely modesty is shown in many ways.
Throughout he is boastful only to France, and that
when he is speaking rather as personified England
than as a man. But he is humble always to his own
people. He generously enlarges the soldier who rails
against him, excuses the fellow's conduct, and advises
mercy. Thus the king ever shows a desire to forgive
all injuries directed against himself. " Touching our
person," he says, " we seek no revenge." But he is
sternly just in regard to injuries against the state.
He claims no higher title than to be called a soldier.
Throughout we see his desire to put himself in the
position of his subjects; and he has the power to do so.

The following suggests his intellectual difference
from Prince Hal. Like Cæsar's Brutus he believes in
the efficacy of reasons, and requires a full explanation
of the Salic law, which he thoughtfully considers before acting. He evinces an instant recognition of the
stragetic importance of Scotland. Note the skill with
which he moralizes on the ingratitude of traitors; and
note also " the sham of ceremony passage " in which
he dwells in a masterly manner on a very trite idea.
Note also how he goes to the heart of the matter in

the passage beginning "So if a son that is by his father sent." How quickly he is able to see the justice of Williams' argument!

His lack of the sense of humor is referred to above and need not be emphasized here.

Take it all in all, Henry is the plain, simple, sympathetic man who as a king displays the same qualities in a larger field and on a grander scale. But the qualities do not alter. Modesty and humility increase in proportion to his exalted position. He is drawn both as a man and as a personification. As a personification of the perfect king he represents all good, manly qualities turned in a true Christian spirit wholly to the service of his people.

VII. ELIZABETHAN STAGE CONDITIONS

The student should refer to Chapter III. before examining the following notes regarding the Elizabethan staging of the play.

In the first place, consider the following list of scenes. The stage directions are taken from the Tudor, not the original edition.

Prologue—Chorus	. . . .	1
I. i.	London, Ante-chamber, Palace . . .	2
I. ii.	The Presence Chamber	2
Prologue	. . . .	1
II. i.	London, a street	3
II. ii.	Southampton, Council chamber . . .	2
II. iii.	London, before a tavern	3
II. iv.	France, the King's palace	2
Prologue	. . . .	1
III. i.	France, before Harfleur	4
III. ii.	The same	4

No modern presentation of the play could very well afford to provide for twenty-nine changes of scene. The task of the stage manager would be to reduce this number as far as possible. The same task appeared before the stage manager in Elizabethan times. Let us apply our knowledge of the stage conditions of that time and see what could have been done with the situation.

At the beginning of the play the transverse curtains would be drawn between the columns supporting the heavens. At the moment of the third sounding of the bugle the curtains would be parted and the prologue appear. This would happen at the beginning of each act; and also at the end of the play there are two scenes where this arrangement could be conveniently used. Let us call this setting 1.

Doubtless every theater possessed the necessary

paraphernalia for setting up a stock interior before the play began. This would doubtless be pressed into service; in the background a drop representing paneling. What is perhaps more likely is that the back of the stage was so decorated that in its normal condition it represented and looked much like the interior of a room. Then any trifling change of properties would easily suggest "another room." The illusion, however, would depend much upon movable properties in the form of furniture and hangings. Any one who has had anything to do with staging amateur theatricals knows that it is a comparatively simple task to make a perfectly satisfactory representation of a room without resorting to much scenery or carpentry. Let us call this interior setting 2.

After speaking the prologue the traverse is withdrawn disclosing the interior. Ely and Canterbury enter. During their conversation they get well in front of the traverse and to one side. At the end of the scene, at the words "Then go we in, to know his embassy," they turn and start towards the king and his followers, who are just entering. Ely and Canterbury slip out to re-enter a moment later. This brief change of position, together with the words cited above, would be sufficient to suggest that they had passed from the ante-chamber to the presence chamber.

Next to an interior I fancy that the most usual possession of a theater in the way of scenic material was a painted cloth representing a street. This would be let down from a roller not far behind the traverse. Call it setting 3.

To return: at the end of scene ii. the traverse is

again drawn. While the prologue is speaking, the street scene alluded to above is let down. At the end of the prologue the traverse is drawn. Act II., scene i., is performed before the street drop. It is then raised, disclosing the original interior used for scene ii. Though it is the same interior used in act I., the prologue emphatically says that it represents a room at Southampton. Then the street drop is again let down for scene iii. and raised for scene iv. Possibly a few articles of French furniture have been introduced slightly to alter the general appearance of things. The drawing the traverse marks the end of the act.

Trivial as they may seem, the next three scenes, virtually, however, but one scene, are difficult to account for. It is hardly possible that they were acted on the inner stage, for this would require the removal of the interior setting. This is hardly likely, as this set is needed again. The upper gallery might be pressed into service. They, might have been acted before the traverse, as the prologue. Or another painted cloth may have been let down representing some sort of general landscape. Let us accept the latter suggestion for a moment and call it setting 4. At the end we return to 2 for two scenes. Then the traverse is drawn. The next two scenes could easily be spoken before the traverse.

These two scenes, together with the chorus, give plenty of time for any change of scenery on the inner stage. The interior, which is not needed again, is taken away, and preparations made for the great spectacular scene of the play. My interpretation of the first chorus, the newness of the Globe playhouse, and the theatrical prestige Shakespeare's company was bound to maintain, leads me to infer—I admit that it is an inference—that at this point a special effort was made to produce a grand spectacular result. I can see no reason to believe that the Elizabethaus never made capital out of something dramatically new. Note also that the scene suggested below is practically in continuous use till the end of the play.

In the earlier production of Elizabethan plays a multiple setting was frequently resorted to. In this method of presentation one portion of the stage represented one locality, another part another, etc. The position of the actors on the stage determined the location of the scene, all being visible to the audience all the time.

Let us see how Shakespeare's manager could have carried out this idea in designing a single scene on a large spectacular scale that would practically furnish the stage for the remainder of the play.

Imagine a painted cloth let down at the back on which is represented the open country of France, with numerous tents on either side, disappearing gradually in the diminishing distance. These are the camps of the two armies. On one side of the stage proper are several tents and groups of soldiers. Flags etc., indicate that they are English. Entrance from that side indicates an entrance from the English camp. Action on that side takes place in the English camp. A similar representation of the French camp is arranged on the other side of the stage. The space between represents the general battleground between the two camps. Call this setting 5.

At the end of V. i. the traverse is drawn. V. ii. and the epilogue are spoken before it.

The question naturally arises as to the reliability of this suggested setting. To those who require documentary evidence for every detail accepted regarding Elizabethan stagecraft it will not appeal. But to those who possess a flavor of imagination I suggest the following:

1. Every theater must have possessed something in the way of stage paraphernalia.

2. The mode of presentation suggested above requires two painted cloths, the usual representation of an interior, the use of the traverse, and one spectacular scene designed to bear out the newly augmented reputation of the company's theater.

3. Of the two settings of the inner stage, one remains undisturbed during the first half of the play. Then it is removed and the other put into place, in turn remaining undisturbed throughout the remainder of the play.

4. Any one to-day who has any skill in the adaptation of a crudely constructed stage could do this and more with only amateur help at his command. Is it possible that the ingenious Elizabethans did not do as much? My only feeling is that I have underestimated the scenic attractiveness of the Elizabethan production of *Henry the Fifth*.

CHAPTER XIII

ROMEO AND JULIET

I. Introductory

In the Tudor Edition of this play the editor discusses the date of its origin, finally assigning it tentatively, or timidly, perhaps, to 1594 or 1595. Many critics, however, believe that the present text of the play is the result of a revision of an earlier version much of which still remains. In connection with this point of view two dates are thought of, one earlier and the other later than that suggested above.

At any rate, parts of the play closely resemble in style the known early efforts of Shakespeare; and the stylistic qualities of other parts more nearly resemble the poet's style of a later date.

There are several other points to be considered. Though a beautiful love story it does not conform to the rules of dramatic tragedy. This may be due to the fact that it is an early play, written before Shakespeare acquired that technical skill which characterizes his later work. In the following notes another possibility is hinted at; namely, that the play was originally written as a tragi-comedy and at a later date hastily reconstructed into a tragedy.

It will also be noticed that in many of the parts of the play which show evidences of early style, Romeo is

155

trivial and not over-manly in his behavior; and in the parts whose style resembles that of a later date Romeo is a far worthier lover of a heroine like Juliet. I venture as a mere suggestion that in the revision of the play the character of Juliet was completely rewritten. This necessitated the rewriting of many of the Romeo parts but permitted others to remain unchanged.

II. Notes on the Text

Act I. Prologue. This is a sonnet, a characteristic of Shakespeare's early style in which he resorted to many forms of verse and stanzas. Note, however, that the Elizabethans seldom made use of the familiar rhyme-scheme of the sonnet. The sonnet prologue appears again before the second act. But there are no more prologues to the play.

I. i. The first 70 lines of this scene are merely low comedy. Such continuous word-play is characteristic of Shakespeare's early style. Find other similar passages throughout the play.

I. i. 72. Enter Tybalt. Though Ben Jonson frequently named characters after their personal qualities, Shakespeare soon gave up the practice. Tybalt means tom-cat; Benvolio, good-fellow or peacemaker; Mercutio, one of a mercurial disposition.

I. i. 90, etc. Earlier blank verse was more conventional, more sing-song, fuller of pauses at the end of the line than later blank verse. Compare this passage, written in the earlier style, with the blank verse of the balcony scene. Find other passages that illustrate both the earlier and the later forms of verse.

I. i. 121, 122. Repetition of words and phrases is

resorted to oftener in this play than in any other. Find illustrations throughout. They occur from first to last, but usually in passages that have other ear-marks of early style.

I. i. 177. Note that Romeo is much of a punster in those scenes which are written in the earlier style. This quality disappears in the more serious portrayal of the hero.

I. i. 182, etc. This coupling of opposites, heavy lightness, cold fire, etc., is another early trait.

By the end of this scene we learn that Romeo is already suffering from the effects of unrequited love. We are told by critics that this is the most likely condition as a preliminary to love at first sight, and that Shakespeare here displays his keen knowledge of human nature. However, he overlooked the situation in regard to Juliet, who fell in love with equal celerity. It is just barely possible that Shakespeare introduced this detail of Romeo's past merely because it was in the original version of the story, and also afforded an excellent opportunity for getting started.

I. ii. Compare Capulet's attitude towards Juliet, as displayed in his conversation with Paris early in this scene, with his actual behavior later. How is the contrast to be explained? Is he insincere at either time?

I. iii. Juliet is said by the nurse to be fourteen years of age. Even after making due allowance for the earlier maturity of southern girls in olden times Juliet seems to be more than fourteen years old. This allusion is probably a remnant of the earlier version. In the revision, Shakespeare must have had in mind a woman, not a girl.

I. iv. 2. Apology in this line, Cupid in line 4, without-book prologue in line 7, etc., are references to masking, a popular form of Elizabethan entertainment.

I. iv. 53. This fairy speech by Mercutio may be looked upon as one of the formal declamations so popular in Elizabethan times. Though beautiful poetry it has no dramatic significance.

I. iv. 106-113. Evidences or indications of a tragic conclusion are very scarce in the first four acts of the play. Most of these few are like the passage cited above; that is, they could have easily been inserted bodily at the time of revision. The tragic element of this play is accidental, not ingrained.

II. i. In the setting on the Elizabethan stage some provision must have been made by which the audience could see both Benvolio and Mercutio on one side, and Romeo on the other. Yet Romeo, who was near enough to hear what the others said, was invisible to them.

II. ii. 1. The antecedent of " he " is " Mercutio." The line refers to his jesting of a previous scene.

II. i. This so-called " balcony scene " is not only one of the most beautifully poetic passages of the play but of all English literature. The sentiment is deep and rings true, without the least approach to sentimentality. It is sufficient, one might almost say, to wipe out of existence all memory of the crude touches and inconsistent details that appear elsewhere.

But there is more to the balcony scene than just this. Heretofore, love-scenes and love-making on the Elizabethan stage had been conventional and sentimental to a high degree. No such genuine passage as this had appeared before the advent of *Romeo and Juliet.* It is easy to imagine, perhaps it would be more truthful to say it is difficult to imagine, the enthusiasm of the contemporary audience at the first reception of this brilliant scene, which, as after events showed, was but an earnest of what was to come.

II. ii. 63. Recall the deadly feud between the two families. Do not overlook the nerve it required on the part of Romeo to make this dangerous entry into the garden of his family enemies. Later he appears as a nerveless, puling nonentity whom even the nurse compares to a foolish woman. This scene is written in Shakespeare's later style. III. iii. is written in his earlier style.

II. iii. Friar Laurence is a purely conventional character. It is not necessary to study his personality analytically or to take too seriously his copy-book phrases of philosophy.

II. iii. 90. Note that Friar Laurence agrees to marry Romeo and Juliet because he thinks that it will bring about a reconciliation between the two families. Perhaps this reconciliation was intended to come about in the earlier version of the play. There are other evidences of it that will be later pointed out. The actual conclusion of the present play shows that it could easily have been accomplished.

II. iv. 222. " The dog's name." That is a growl, the R in Romeo. In Elizabethan pronunciation it was common to roll the r.

III. i. 65. Note the peaceful rejoinder of Romeo. The audience understands the ironical significance of his remarks. But none of the others possess this clue. What ought to be the effect upon his companions of Romeo's peaceful demeanor? Ought they not all to be surprised, and his partisans chagrined? Yet Mercutio is the only one who shows such emotion. Is there any indication in this reception of his attitude that this is the kind of behavior to expect from Romeo?

III. i. 127. Compare Romeo's behavior here with his behavior earlier in the scene, in the balcony scene, and in the friar's cell.

III. ii. The opening speech of Juliet certainly emanates from a woman older than fourteen. And the smooth pliability of the blank verse is similar to the style of Shakespeare's verse of a date later than that usually assigned to the first draft of the play.

III. ii. 45-50. Note the repetition of I, ay, eye, all pronounced alike. Note throughout the play the numerous examples of excessive repetition.

III. ii. 73. Is it natural for Juliet to turn so suddenly against Romeo? What recalls Juliet's loyalty? (See line 90.)

III. iii. Note the repetition of banished and banishment.

Romeo's behavior in this scene gives no evidence of the nerve that first led him into Capulet's orchard, or inspired him in the fight with Tybalt. The friar upbraids him for his weakness, and even the nurse upbraids him for his pusillanimity.

III. iii. 108. Stage direction. Imagine the situation of the play at this point. The nurse is the typical comic character throughout. There is an element of the ludicrous in her attempt to stop Romeo from stabbing himself. One can in this situation hardly be

seriously affected by Romeo's anguish. In his rant-
ing behavior he out-nurses the nurse herself. The
two of them together would be able to make a capital
comic scene.

On the other hand, this vein is quite inconsistent
with the tone and tenor of a serious tragedy. Is the
true explanation to be found in Shakespeare's inability to portray Romeo here to the same excellent standard reached in some other parts of the play?

There is a third suggestion that is worth a moment's consideration. Mercutio and Tybalt, it is true,
have both been killed. Yet they are minor characters who, though attractive, have not been sufficiently prominent to thoroughly grip our sympathy.
Their deaths, Romeo's banishment, and the situation
of Juliet constitute just the sort of complication characteristic of a tragi-comedy. Were the earlier play of
this type, just here is where the resolution would be
likely to begin. That it is expected seems to be very
plainly hinted at in lines 150-155. And what more
likely than the insertion of a scene in a lighter vein
just at the turning-point!

The play preserves all the characteristics of a
tragi-comedy until the middle of the last act. Later,
allusion will be made to the sudden and artless manner
by which it is wrested into the path of a tragic conclusion.

III. v. Contrast the general tone of the scene with
that of III. iii. Is it similar or different? Is the
opening similar to the rest in this respect?

On the whole I find this a very puzzling scene. In
the first place, look at it seriously for a moment as
a step in the serious development of a tragedy. Ju-

liet is secretly married to the banished Romeo. Her
parents wish to force her into a marriage which can
be prevented only by the disclosure of her secret.
Now, is this situation as essentially tragic as usually
represented? In the first place, Romeo is now out
of the Capulet reach. No harm can come to him by
the disclosure. And Juliet could hardly be subjected
to worse treatment than is threatened by her father
for crossing his will. Furthermore, in case she will
not marry Paris she is to be turned into the streets
and left to her own devices. What more could she
desire with a husband waiting, and a willing friar,
for a go-between, who is confident that it will all turn
out well in the end! In other words, the high-spirited
Juliet could have acknowledged her lover without
injuring him, with hardly a risk of making her own
situation worse than it would be if she persisted in
her refusal to marry Paris without making a full
acknowledgment, and the possibility of righting the
whole situation in the end. And in addition, the reconciliation at the end of the play is due wholly to the
fact that the parents discovered that the two were
lovers and married. The situation in all of its details
is certainly not to the credit of Shakespeare's powers
of invention if we consider it seriously! nor does it
show any of the skill displayed by him a few years
later as naturally as if it were second nature. However, it must be remembered, on the other hand, that
a few years makes a great difference, and this play
was written before the culmination of Shakespeare's
preparatory period.

On the other hand, suppose this to be a scene left
over from, or a part of, an original tragi-comedy.

From the former scene the audience has learned through the words of the friar that a reconciliation is not unlikely to take place when the truth is known. With this cue the audience is prepared to take pleasantly details which are but complications on the surface. The earlier part of the scene contains several remarks from Juliet that have a double meaning. Their wrong interpretation by Lady Capulet must have caused a smile, to say the least. Then comes Capulet, who, through his overexertion in the matter of abuse becomes almost comic. And last, the ridiculously impossible solution of the whole matter suggested by the nurse. And the scene ends by Juliet's promise to return to Friar Laurence, the one who formerly gave the pointed intimation that the play would end happily. As a scene of this intent it is much better conceived and carried out than as a tragic scene.

Though I do not wish to insist on the inference here suggested relative to the character of the early draft, I should like to point out that parts, like this scene, indicate on the part of the writer greater skill in the lighter vein than in the tragic vein; and that it was not till years later that Shakespeare excelled in the writing of tragedies. The question remains, if such were the original draft, why did Shakespeare change it. Perhaps the play was a failure. It must have been both written and rewritten during Shakespeare's period of experimentation. Perhaps he was just experimenting with tragedy, which he had not attempted since his passable but not excellent *Titus Andronicus*. And the carelessness of the revision is quite consistent with his methods displayed in his earlier plays.

IV. iii. The apparent comedy outcome is carried on in this scene. The friar suggests a perfectly feasible plan which will solve the present difficulty, dependent only upon Juliet's will and courage to carry it out. She has both, and departs in good spirits. By all customary standards the preparation and foreshadowing of the scene can suggest to the audience nothing but a happy resolution at the end.

IV. iii. 10. Note that Capulet's stormy scene and Juliet's refusal to marry Paris has caused no interruption in Capulet's plans for the wedding.

IV. iii. 14. There has been nothing said or done to arouse on the part of the audience any distrust of the friar. Nor has anything occurred to justify such a thought in the mind of Juliet. Her present thoughts are due entirely to the exigencies of the present moment. The audience would certainly share her fears and terrors, for it is a courageous and mysterious act she is about to perform. But the sympathy of the audience would be tempered by the certainty that her fears were groundless.

As the act closes, everything seems to be carrying out the friar's plot to a satisfactory conclusion. There is as yet no sign of the coming tragedy.

At the opening of act V. we find that Romeo hears the news of Juliet's death before he gets the friar's letter explaining that it is a sham. Trouble may come of this, but the audience does not expect it:— for two reasons: 1. The passage is preceded by a bit of happy foreshadowing. 2. Romeo postpones killing himself out of misery till he gets to Juliet's grave. There is every chance for him to be disillusioned at this point. This looks very like a device to make his happiness the more complete as it is the more unexpected.

There are two conditions universally acknowledged as necessary to a tragic development of the plot:—1. The story and its development should be incapable from the beginning of straying from the path that leads to a tragic conclusion. 2. That the tragic ending should depend upon events related to each other by the law of cause and effect. If the story is plotted in defiance of either of these rules it lacks excellence to just that extent.

V. ii. 4. Here we find the first step or detail of the tragic conclusion. The fact that so much of this play could be discussed as above, as if it were a tragicomedy, is a gross violation of rule 1.

The failure of the friar's letter to reach its destination is an equally gross violation of rule 2. In the first place, the miscarriage of the letter is due to the merest accident. Why did not Brother John deliver the letter at once instead of getting himself quarantined on the way? If one explains this on the ground that friars had to travel in pairs, and that Brother John perforce had to find a companion, and was as likely as not to pick up one with a contagious disease, matters are not much bettered. Why did Laurence send John at all? The letter by all indications should have gone by Balthasar. At III. iii. 170 the friar, when sending Romeo to Mantua, says that he will use Balthasar to carry letters to Romeo. And when Balthasar enters (V. i. 11) Romeo is surprised that his man does not bring a letter from Friar Laurence.

In other words, in order to bring about a tragic

conclusion, Shakespeare made the friar drop his customary channel of communication, which would inevitably have prevented the final catastrophe, and select another messenger, which device by the merest accident turns a good comedy ending into a poor tragic end.

As I said above, it is a mere inference, a mere guess, that the first draft of this play was in reality a tragi-comedy, converted by a hasty revision into a tragedy. Whether this is true or not is a matter of no considerable importance. I have used this idea merely to illustrate the fact that four acts of *Romeo and Juliet* constitute part of a splendid tragi-comedy, light-hearted, joyous in spite of the early deaths of Tybalt and Mercutio. The effect of the play with its beautiful poetry would have been, had the end prepared for been written, as delightfully pleasant as *Cymbeline* or *The Tempest*. But if, from the nature of its end, we are compelled to examine it as a tragedy, we find its structure bad, the invention poor, and in no way deserving to rank with the great series of tragedies that began with *Julius Cæsar*.

Scene iii. contains the tragic conclusion. In this scene the audience experiences three painful and unexpected shocks.

1. The audience, it seems to me, is fully prepared by numerous hints for a happy conclusion, the resolution which does not come. With the example of a fake drug administered to Juliet, and a knowledge that Friar John is on his way to the tomb, or soon will be, and that Juliet is about to awake—all this taken together renders the actual death of Romeo like a bolt out of a clear sky.

2. The second shock is due to the death of Juliet, emphasized by the fact that she overslept herself by just a moment, and that the friar was also late by just a moment. Had Romeo been subjected to any little delay, accidental in nature, such as seems to have overtaken all the others, the day would still have been saved.

3. The third shock is the fact that Friar Laurenee's prophecy of a peaceable reconciliation (III. iii. 151) was true, but delayed till after the death of Romeo and Juliet. What after all reconciled the two houses of Capulet and Montague? It was not the murder of Paris, nor the death of the lovers, nor even the command of the prince which had been ineffective before, but a knowledge of the fact that Romeo and Juliet loved each other, and were man and wife.

Does it not seem as if the final result would have come about had Juliet courageously disclosed her marriage when Paris was first urged upon her?

CHAPTER XIV

THE TAMING OF THE SHREW

I. Introduction

In the selection of plays for this volume I have been guided by the student and his needs. There are some teachers and students as well who believe that every word Shakespeare wrote or uttered was inspired, that his mere ejaculation of Tweedledum is capable of subtile psychological analysis. *The Taming of the Shrew* as a play was, easy as it is to read now, still easier to the Elizabethans; but it is easily misunderstood to-day. The play has been misconstrued both by critics and by actors. So I shall suggest with the utmost brevity a few points explanatory of the text; and then explain the real significance of the play, which with such facility escapes the attention of a modern reader unused to Elizabethan conditions.

II. Notes on the Text

Title.—Only female hawks were used in hunting. They were proverbially cross, perverse, and stubborn, that is, curst. The word "taming" in the title refers to the process of training the shrewish hawks into a condition of obedience suitable for the chase.

The induction.—This framework serves to introduce the play. For the players who arrive in scene i.

are supposed to perform *The Taming of the Shrew* for the benefit of Sly. In scene ii. he appears aloft, that is, in the upper balcony above the stage. From this vantage point he views the start of the play, and makes some comments at the end of scene i. Later, however, he simply drops out of consideration by disappearance. This fact implies that the cutting off of the upper balcony from the view of the audience by means of a curtain or some similar device was possible. Otherwise there would be the need of some outward means of ridding the stage of Sly.

I. i. This scene and the next introduce the elements of a somewhat complicated plot. Most students find it difficult at first reading to avoid some confusion. Note how rapidly, almost simultaneously, the threads of the story are introduced; and compare with *The Merchant of Venice,* where the threads of the story are introduced gradually, one at a time. However, on the stage, where one is assisted by the eye, the confusion encountered in reading the early part of the play nearly disappears.

It will be a help to the student to analyze the plot carefully. See the chapter on *The Tempest* for an example.

In anticipation of the third section of this chapter —one should not take the character of Katharine or of Petruchio seriously. Their actions should not be analyzed. No human beings ever acted like this. At any rate, no Elizabethan would have looked at them from this point of view, or have been distressed by the unnatural excesses of their behavior.

II. i. 278. See the note on the title relative to the word taming.

IV. i. 191-210. This passage is full of the technical allusions to the process of training a hawk for the chase. In the first place, there was but one thing to be done to a wild hawk, namely, to break her wilful spirit; but there were many ways in which it could be done. One was to keep her hungry to the verge of starvation, tantalizing her with the sight of food. This is one of the methods resorted to at a later time by Petruchio. Another common mode of training was to keep the hawk awake till exhausted for want of sleep. The Elizabethan word for waking was watching. The word is used in this sense in the passage cited above—he will watch (keep her awake) as we watch these kites. The word is similarly used in *Othello,* where Desdemona says, " I'll watch him tame." She means that she will keep Othello awake, give him no peace, till he is more tractable. Another even more cruel procedure consisted in sewing up the eyelids of the hawk for a time. This was called seeling. It suggested the line in *Othello,*

" To seel her father's eyes up close as oak."

This kind of cruelty can almost be forgiven as sometimes a necessary step in the training of a falcon; but it is painful to record that seeling was sometimes performed by Elizabethans on harmless doves for the mere sport of witnessing their frantic and helpless efforts in misery. We are told in Sidney's *Arcadia,* " Now she brought them to see a seeled dove, who, the blinder she was, the higher she strove to reach." We have, however, not exhausted the allusions to falconry in Petruchio's speech. " I have a way to man

my haggard," he says. " To man " was the technical
term for gaining the mastery. An unmanned, that is,
an untrained hawk, was called a haggard.

> " If I do prove her haggard,
> Though that her jesses were my dear heart strings,
> I'd whistle her off and let her down the wind
> To prey at fortune."

Thus, in his suspicious moment, Othello compares
his wife to a haggard hawk. Oftentimes a hawk that
had not been properly trained would turn aside while
in pursuit of prey in order to follow something else.
This turning aside of a haggard was called checking,
and is referred to in Marmion's motto, " Who checks
at me to death is dight." And in the words of Viola:

> " To do that well craves a kind of wit:
> He must observe their moods on whom he jests,
> The quality of the persons and the time,
> And, like the haggard, check at every feather
> That comes before his eye."

Until the hawk had learned to fly properly at the
game she was constantly reclaimed, that is, drawn
back by a long string after she had been started.
The falcons were cared for and trained by the falconer and his assistants, the falconer's boys. When
the falcon was injured in the hunt it was the falconer who proceeded to imp the wing. This process
of mending required the broken wing to be carefully
trimmed, and the feather of another bird matched to
the broken one. The hawk, when not following the
game, was kept covered by a hood that completely
blinded her. This headdress was made of silk or of
leather, often exceedingly dainty and ornamental. It

bore upon its top a tuft of feathers by which it could be easily and quickly removed when it was desirable to start the falcon after game.

It is interesting to note how closely Petruchio in this speech has outlined the process of taming, not a wife, but a hawk, and how closely he follows out the suggestion in practice.

Note how this process is carried out. In IV. iii. 3, etc., Katharine alludes to the fact that she is being famished. In the conversation that follows, Grumio, evidently at the command of his master, is tantalizing Katharine with the idea of delicious food just as an untrained hawk was tantalized. And Petruchio continues the idea by sending away the food just as Katharine is about to eat it. The same tantalizing methods are kept up in the dealings with the tailor, the haberdasher, etc.

Such treatment of a hawk was kept up till the hawk was absolutely tractable. So IV. v. portrays Katharine as entirely docile. In other words, The Taming of the Shrew is complete, and there remains nothing but to give an exhibition of the effect at the end of the play.

III. The Significance of the Play

In section one I suggested that, but for one point, this play is so easy to read as to render its study almost unnecessary. And in the few notes above I have referred practically to only such points as refer to this one point.

It is a mistake to take the play seriously, to fancy that Petruchio has developed a scheme by which a cross woman may be brought into a docile state of obedience. Neither his method nor the results are at all to be desired in this world. And he who goes at the play from this point of view, who tries to imagine such characters, and to justify the acts of Petruchio and the results as exemplified by the final behavior of Katharine is but laying himself open to ridicule.

In reality Shakespeare is telling a sort of fairy story. His audience were as familiar with all the details of falconry as we are with the details of football or of baseball. He knew that his people would catch the cue from the very title. They would understand that there was here a mere translation into facetious human terms of the process of training a hawk. One who is altogether unfamiliar with the game of chess misses the delightful adventures of Alice with the White Knight. So one who is unfamiliar with the game of falconry misses the whole point of *The Taming of the Shrew*. Petruchio and Katharine are not human beings; they are the falconer and his haggard hawk. In a fairy-story way they represent the process of training that was so familiar to all the Elizabethans in the audience. It was far from them, or from Shakespeare's conception—this analysis of the principal characters from the human standpoint. One would as soon present a medical explanation of the crooked gait of Alice's White Knight.

CHAPTER XV

THE MERCHANT OF VENICE

I. Notes on the Text

READ the play rapidly, noting in a general way the complicated story, and the interlinking of the threads of the plot. Also the supplementary nature of the fifth act. Make an outline scene by scene of the narrative.

Read the play again more carefully, performing such tasks as are suggested in Chapter VIII. Also attend to the following points in the text.

At the opening of the play Antonio appears depressed in spirits without a knowledge of why or wherefore. This is a literary device used in order to strike at the outset the tone of the story of Antonio, which is serious almost to the point of tragedy, but not beyond the possibility of a happy ending. Antonio is unaware of the cause of his depression, because nothing has really happened to account for it. This absence of a cause suggests that the result will not be so serious in the end. Shakespeare is careful to keep the attention of the audience forward towards later developments. Lest the audience should infer too serious an outcome, the light-heartedness of Antonio's companions serves as a corrective, at the same time leading up to the delightfully care-free

174

beginning of the Portia story in scene ii. Her thread of the story is all joyous. The audience must be far from the serious suggestion at the beginning. Note that both scenes begin with similar expressions. Portia is also weary of the world, but her body is not little. The whole speech is belied by her manner of acting, hence the heightened contrast with the words of Antonio, who is sincere.

Try to place the best positions on the stage for those who enter throughout the act.

In scene i. Salarino speaks much more than Salanio. Is this relative importance kept up throughout the play? Which part requires the better actor?

At the entrance of Antonio's friends their names are all mentioned. This serves to introduce them to the audience. How frequently is this device used? Is it used more in the earlier parts of the play?

Notice the long speech of Gratiano beginning, " Let me play the fool." It serves to describe his character. It is also a defense of frivolity. This passage needs some accounting for. It would hardly be considered dramatic unless Gratiano's character is important enough to demand it. Is it? But there is a more important use for it. It is a formal piece of declamation. The Elizabethans were very fond of declamations to be spoken from the front of the stage irrespective of their lack of dramatic significance— speeches with which we associate The Seven Ages of Man, The Death of Ophelia, Cleopatra's Barge, etc. (See the chapter on *Henry the Fifth*.)

Note how much the remainder of the scene contains that is useful in subsequent portions of the play: 1. The beginning of the story to raise money; 2. The character of Bassanio; 3. The friendship of Bassanio and Antonio; 4. Description of Portia.

In scene ii. we are introduced to Portia and Nerissa. The parts should be taken by actresses of very different personalities. Why? What hints are contained in the text that would help one to cast these parts?

This scene is illustrative of a kind of passage that has to a great extent lost its interest to people of our day and generation. Many of the remarks of Portia are allusions better understood then than now. Many of the most popular Elizabethan horses were of Neapolitan breed; hence there is point in comparing the Neapolitan prince to a colt. The satires of the time abound in slurs upon the Elizabethan habit of aping French customs, and Falconbridge is ridiculed therefor. Indeed, the aptness of such hits must have made this scene very sparkling to the Elizabethan wits.

From this point on, try to keep the Antonio story and the Portia story separate. As the play goes on, several new threads appear. The difficulty of keeping them separate will suggest how skilfully they are interwoven.

Shylock is the great character of the play. His first appearance shows him to be covetous, untruthful, and an usurer. For all that, he is very different from the other great Elizabethan picture of a Jew contained in Marlowe's *Jew of Malta*. A comparison of the two plays shows the latter to be a repulsive monster of cruelty and wickedness. Shylock, on the other hand, is a human being from whom our sympathies are not wholly alienated. Later in the play, though we blame we also pity him. It seems as if Shakespeare were trying to make out the best case he could for the Jew in a time when public sympathy was all against the race.

With very few exceptions, Shakespeare first presents a bold outline sketch of a character. As the play goes on, this first sketch is filled out and completed, but the character does not change. Macbeth is one of the exceptions. Is Shylock?

It would be well at this point to read in succession all the scenes in which Shylock appears. Question the motive of each act. Formulate your estimate of his character at the end of the first act, at the end of the third, at the end of the play. Note carefully whether the character changes, and also whether your feeling towards him changes.

In II. i. we have another glimpse of Portia's room. Note how gradually and how carefully Shakespeare is leading up to the culmination of the casket story. This breaking the story into bits enhances the familiarity of the audience, gives opportunity to introduce the other characters, and the remaining threads of the story.

In modern presentation some of the casket scenes are thrown together and abridged. Does this imply that Shakespeare's account is too long drawn out? Has the Elizabethan love of declamation anything to do with the question?

II. ii. To the average reader this scene is anything but amusing, though it is delightfully funny on the stage. In fact, the amusement depends almost wholly on the stage business introduced. It is well to remember that oftentimes the text of the play is the smallest part of the actual presentation. And Shakespeare wrote always with the actual presentation in his mind, as all successful dramatists do. Many so-called difficult passages are easily made clear by the attempt actually to imagine the stage picture.

II. ii. 157. Stage direction. "To his followers." When did Leonardo and the others come upon the stage? What have they been doing in the meantime?

Except for the allusions to the coming dinner, the first 175 lines of this scene are wholly a comedy diversion. They serve no purpose in the plot, nor do they add to our knowledge of the important characters. Does one often find in Shakespeare so long a passage with no dramatic value? Such passages were in common use with the other Elizabethan dramatists. They are not so common to-day.

Beginning with line 183 is another picture of Gratiano, but it is not altogether like the first, it supplements it. Note what was said above relative to Shakespeare's method of drawing character. Richard II is an exception to this method, but not in the same way as Macbeth.

II. ii. 198, etc. Should Gratiano act as if he were speaking seriously or in mockery? The student can answer this question by taking into consideration: 1. Bassanio's next lines. How does he take it? 2. Why does Gratiano want to go? 3. How serious is his intention? 4. Would one behavior or another be more likely to gain Bassanio's permission? 5. How does he actually behave himself when he gets to Belmont?

With scene iii. we have the beginning of another thread of the story, which must be thought of both by itself and as a part of the whole. Like the story of the caskets, the story of Lorenzo and Jessica is introduced piecemeal. One advantage of this method is that it produces the effect of passing time.

II. iv. What does this scene add to the play? Note the minor plot details; also the touches that add to the character of Jessica. On the Elizabethan stage the change of scene was probably not indicated except by the momentary clearing of the stage. Doubtless the characters of scene iii. went off one side of the stage to be followed immediately by another set entering opposite.

II. vi. There were no women among the Elizabethan actors. Their parts were taken by boys young enough to have unbroken voices. Though they were thoroughly trained professionally they were still boys. Their immaturity accounts for the absence of complex characters among the women of Shakespeare's plays. (Cleopatra and Lady Macbeth are two possible exceptions.)

It is easy to imagine how much more at home a boy on the stage would be in his own clothes. Hence the frequent disguising of the heroine in male attire. How often does Shakespeare make use of this device?

Note that the scene ends with a suggestion regarding the journey to Belmont—and the next scene opens at Belmont. Such little connective touches add much to the impression of continuity throughout the play.

II. viii. This is a very important scene. It tells the outcome of what happened in scene vi. It adds a few touches to Shylock's character. It serves as a division scene between the one before and the one after, both laid in Portia's room. Such division scenes were very common in the Elizabethan drama. If they served no other purpose they could be omitted in modern presentation, their place being taken by a momentary drop of the curtain. But Shakespeare, almost alone among Elizabethan play-writers, seldom failed to make them serve other purposes as well. He was very economical of space.

Note also that the lovers are grouped with those in whom Antonio is interested, so their flight serves to whet Shylock's enmity against Antonio. This is an added motive for his malignity. And there immediately follows a hint as to the possibility of financial disaster before Antonio, which will give Shylock his chance.

II. ix. The gold and silver caskets are now disposed of, leaving only one for Bassanio to choose. So we are prepared for the outcome in advance. He cannot choose wrong. Shakespeare always takes his audience fully into his confidence. This is in contrast to the practice of his great contemporary Jonson.

Though Portia says nothing during Bassanio's speech, she is the most important figure on the stage. The audience should be watching her. Where is she? What does she do? Does she act as if she knew the outcome? Should the other persons on the stage be watching her or Bassanio? Or should one be watching her and the others Bassanio? Which one, and why?

III. ii. As the structure of a comedy is looser than that of a tragedy, it is not always possible to discover all the structural points in a comedy that we expect to find in a tragedy. However, this scene may be looked upon as the turning-point. It marks the culmination of Bassanio's successful suit. Almost at the same moment comes the news of the distressing turn in Antonio's fortune. Henceforth the success of Bassanio is made the means of relieving Antonio.

Recall the allusions to lapsing time in the preceding scene. Bassanio seems very impatient to make his choice and to be done with it. Does not this imply that but little time has elapsed? Is Bassanio a mere fortune-hunter? Do we at any time feel as if he were not good enough for Portia? Or has he changed from a fortune-hunter to a true lover since he came to Belmont? In such a case, however, would he not have been impatient from the first? and prone to delay later? just the reverse of what he does.

IV. i. Note that Shylock has done nothing illegal. He is a hard man, but the case is with him. Has Antonio's haughty behavior justified the Jew's hatred? Antonio has shown no wisdom in allowing himself to fall into such a trap. Had Shakespeare been trying to illustrate the proverb, " Pride goeth before destruction," could he have done better?

Note also how the scene, like a play in miniature, rises to a climax and falls away. Shylock steadily grows more confident till Portia's fanciful interpretation of the bond. Then, by degrees, he is crushed more and more almost to the point of annihilation.

Shylock claimed his bond justly. The Christians outwit him by a quibble, then rob him. Is there not a good deal to be said on Shylock's side? Is he any more devilish than his enemies? Do they not really kill him? If a Jew were holding Christian practice up to ridicule, would he write differently? We are glad of Antonio's escape, but are we proud of the method? Did Shakespeare mean to produce the impression implied by the above questions?

A play usually advances in rapidity towards the end. In the fifth act of this play there is a great cessation in the action. In 125 lines nothing happens except the arrival of Portia and Nerissa. The ring episode is started as a new interest after the play is practically finished. (Compare with the fifth act of *The Midsummer Night's Dream* and Canto 6 of Scott's *The Lay of the Last Minstrel.*) By trifling alterations, mainly omissions, this play could be reduced to four acts. This is probably an attempt to make the jig an integral part of the play.

The fifth act, however, is interesting from another point of view, to be discussed in connection with the Elizabethan staging of the play.

II. The Plot

Make an analysis of the plot, employing the following suggestions:

1. How many different threads to the story?

2. Note how difficult it is to tell any thread without telling parts of the others.

3. Note how they are interwoven.

4. Does each story have a separate climax, or do they come to a climax together?

5. Note the order in which the stories are introduced, and the order in which they are disposed of. Has this order anything to do with their relative importance?

6. Is there anything that could be omitted?

7. Would you suggest any change in the arrangement of the scenes?

III. The Characters

It is supposed that the student has been following through his study the suggestions contained in Chapter VIII. In paying especial attention to character, it is well to read through in succession the scenes in which the characters appear.

Formulate your impressions of Shylock, Antonio, Bassanio, and Portia.

IV. The Elizabethan Staging of the Play

The notes on the Elizabethan staging of this play are fuller than elsewhere in the present volume in order to serve as an example to the student who should consider each play from this point of view.

Below is a list of the stage settings as derived from the Tudor Edition of the play.

1. Venice, a street.   I. i.; II. ii.; II. iv.; II. viii.; III. i.; III. iii.; IV. ii.
2. Room in Portia's house.   I. ii.; II. i.; II. vii.; II. ix.; III. ii.; III. iv.
3. Venice, a public place.   I. iii.
4. A room in Shylock's house.   II. iii.
5. Before Shylock's house.   II. v.; II. vi.
6. Portia's garden.   III. v.
7. Venice, a courtroom.   IV. i.
8. Avenue to Portia's house.   V. i.

The probable average duration of an Elizabethan performance was two hours and a half, a period of time that does not allow much time for intermissions or scene shifting. At any rate, it is hardly conceivable that the Elizabethans allowed for eight different

scenes, or for the frequent tearing down of one scene
and replacing it after another had been used as is
implied by the above list.

Let us examine it.   Note that seven scenes occur
on a street in Venice and six in a room in Portia's
house.   The other scenes are used but once.   (II. v.
and II. vi. were probably acted as one continuous
scene.)

Examine the list further.   3, a public place, might
be the same as 1, a street.   This street might also
contain Shylock's house, 5.   Notice the list with these
slight alterations made.

1. Venice, a street.   I. i.; I. iii.; II. ii.; II. iv.;
II. v.; II. vi.; II. viii.; III. i.; III. iii.; IV. ii.

2. A room in Portia's house.   I. ii.; II. i.; II. iii.;
II. vii.; II. ix.; III. iv.

3. Portia's garden.   III. v.

4. A courtroom.   IV. i.

5. Avenue to Portia's house.   V. i.

Notice that the setting for the first three acts
(except III. v.) alternates between a Venetian street
and a room in Portia's house, and that *neither of
them is used again*.   Glance over the scenes enu-
merated above, and it will be seen that all of those on
the street could be easily acted in a smaller space than
the others, and with less paraphernalia in the way
of properties, etc.   We may suppose them a series
of outer scenes, and the Portia house scenes to be
the inner scenes.   So it would be easy to provide
practically for the first three acts of the play by
means of one interior setting and one or more painted
cloths let down from rollers overhead.

Let us fancy the setting of the room in Portia's

house. There would be all the necessary properties in the way of furniture, etc., placed upon the middle stage. At the beginning of the play the table upon which rest the caskets would probably be on the inner stage concealed from the audience by a curtain, to be drawn in the casket scenes. Doubtless there were painted cloths at the back, representing the walls of an interior, a stock set which it may be supposed was already in the possession of the playhouse. All this material could be in place before the play began, and not materially disturbed till the end of the third act. Most of it, however, would be concealed from the audience by the drawn curtains between the posts supporting the heavens.

At the beginning of the play these curtains are drawn apart, showing a painted cloth that has been let down in front of the articles that furnish the material. This cloth would represent a street for the street scenes, and a house to serve as Shylock's house, probably to one side, so that the balcony above could be used as the second story of this house. At the end of the scene the cloth is rolled up, disclosing Portia's room. At the end of the next scene it is dropped for I. iii., raised for I. iv., and so on. Note that up to this point one painted cloth on a roller and the stock furnishing for an interior have provided for all the scenes.

It would be well for the student to go through the play looking for every suggestion both in stage directions and in the lines themselves that will help make out a list of the properties needed. This, however, is merely an exercise for practice. It should be remembered that many of the stage directions have been introduced by modern editors. If the student wishes to include only such items as are mentioned in contemporary texts he should consult the " First Folio Edition," Crowell & Co.

A second painted cloth representing a garden could now be let down for III. v. This would doubtless already be in possession of the company that had produced *Romeo and Juliet*. While the scene is being acted a slight rearrangement of properties would convert Portia's room into a courtroom. When the painted cloth is raised the audience would see the court of justice, a seat for the duke, tables, etc., and a portion of the audience on either side of the stage, dressed in clothes similar to those worn by most of the actors. This portion of the audience would eke out the handful of spectators witnessing the trial.

At the end of the scene the original painted cloth is let down, and the preparations made for act V. As the last scene of act IV. is very brief, there may have been a short intermission here, for the next scene may well have been the great scene of the play. In fact, act V. affords plenty of scope for the fancy to rove.

As I read through the succession of Shakespeare's plays I find that a few stock sets and half a dozen drops will furnish the stage effects of most of them. Every now and then, however, I am driven to the conclusion that some play demands an extensive new setting, just such as would to-day be advertised under the heading of extensive and elaborate scenery. The camp scenes of *Henry the Fifth* are an example. It is my feeling, a mere inference, I confess, that the playhouse owners of that day frequently made an effort to produce some new effect which could be introduced to enliven a play that was staged for the most part with scenery already in possession of the company. In the present case I have suggested that four acts of this play could easily and effectively have been staged by material already in possession of the house. And I imagine that the special efforts were put upon the setting for the last act.

I shall not attempt to describe it. That would be a mere exercise of invention as to what could be done with the resources we know the Elizabethans had at their command. What I wish to call attention to is this: the scene is so much more effective when acted upon a stage that can be darkened, that I believe the Elizabethans would do so if they could. No other act in Shakespeare affords so many indications that the scene was acted upon a partially darkened stage. I wish to point out these facts and then show how the Elizabethans could have accomplished the effect readily with the resources at their command.

Let us consider the situation in detail. The scene is before Portia's palace at night. There are many places in Shakespeare's plays where a descriptive passage seems to serve the purpose of suggesting surroundings not visible to the audience. There is no contradicting the fact that such suggestions may be serviceable, and were frequently made use of, and that an audience could take advantage of them to supply the absence of a tangible setting. On the other hand, if such suggestions be carried to the extreme, they defeat their own end. A suggestion must be lightly touched, not driven in with a sledgehammer.   Nothing would be easier or more disastrous than to overdo the matter of suggestion.

Now what is the situation in this regard of the last act?   The fact that it is night is referred to no less than thirteen times.   Is not this a little too emphatic for mere suggestion?   Would not the constant repetition seem ridiculous rather than suggestive?   But this is not all.   The presence of a visible moon and stars is referred to six times.   Of even greater significance are some of the situations.   Stephano enters, but is not recognized till he tells who he is. Launcelot enters.   Several phrases are spoken before the persons on the stage can properly locate each other.   Portia and Nerissa appear.   They neither see the others on the stage nor are seen by them.   Portia is at last recognized by her voice.

Even after granting a vivid imagination to Elizabethan audiences, far more vivid than ours in dramatic affairs, I cannot help but feel that this scene would not carry itself on a fully lighted stage such as we imagine in connection with a daylight performance.   Though it is but an inference, it seems a justifiable one, that during this scene the Elizabethan stage was actually darkened.

Two points add somewhat to the plausibility of the suggestion.   If the playhouse and the stage were flooded with daylight fewer references and slight alterations would add to the effect of mere suggestion, were that all that was desired.   The fact that Shakespeare, who by this time was a master of stagecraft, took a different course, implies different conditions.

Second.   It would be easy to darken the stage.   The distance across the top of the playhouse was not too great to be easily spanned by wires, or ropes. Canvas could be easily drawn backward and forth upon such cables and manipulated as easily as the shades which control the light in a modern photographic studio. Could the inventive Elizabethans have failed to resort to such an easy and inexpensive means of adding effectiveness to many scenes that seem to have been written to take advantage of a darkened stage?

The stage could also have been darkened in another way. The middle stage was shadowed by the heavens. It would have been easy to draw curtains from the supporting posts to the rear of the stage upon either side. This would have materially lessened the amount of light falling upon the middle stage. The inner stage would have appeared almost like a cave for darkness. And the contrast would have been increased inasmuch as the audience would then have been in the full light. The total effect would be that of one in the full light looking into a cavern.

It might be suggested that this method would cut off the view of that part of the audience seated upon the stage itself. But not necessarily. If the side curtains did not come to within four feet of the stage floor seated spectators could look under them, and the curtains would have been equally effective. The spectators themselves would fill the gap made by the shortened drapery.

(As an example, let the student search for other examples throughout the plays that seem to cry out for a darkened stage. Note also the slightly different method of working out the setting of scenes as suggested in the chapter on *Henry the Fifth*.)

CHAPTER XVI

JULIUS CÆSAR

ONE who assumes that an Elizabethan play is named after the principal personage is easily led into error regarding *Julius Cæsar*. It is a fact that the Elizabethans did not consider it necessary to follow the practice of closely relating the title of a play to the subject-matter. Shakespeare evidently considered it a matter of no importance to give a play an irrelevant title, or a title that suggested a minor part:— for instance, *Twelfth Night, As You Like It, The Merchant of Venice, Cymbeline,* etc. This play, in reality, is the play of *Brutus.*

Structurally, the play appears more symmetrical when viewed from the standpoint of Brutus. Like *Hamlet*, it is a study of the disastrous results of a man's attempt to perform a task for which he is wholly incompetent. Brutus at the beginning is innocent but disturbed in mind. He is won over to the conspirators largely because he considers them to be as high-minded in their motives as himself. He then attempts the impossible task of running a political conspiracy on moral principles. Because he does not understand the wicked passions and motives of the men he has to deal with, he makes one blunder after

190

another, till he brings ruin upon himself and his followers.

In this plot design Brutus is opposed to imperialism, to the office of Cæsar, represented in the play by three persons: Julius Cæsar, Antony, and Octavius. The first of the three is, therefore, not to be thought of in any way as the most important character of the play.

The theme of this play is identical with that of *Hamlet*. There is, however, this important difference between the two plays. In *Hamlet* the working out of the idea is the dominating element. Everything is made subservient to it. In *Cæsar* this is but partly true. Shakespeare had just emerged from his history-writing period. The habit was still strong upon him. Habits are difficult things to drop, and we find in places that the mere dramatization of Plutarch's story seems to take the precedence. For all that, the play illustrates a considerable progress on the part of Shakespeare along the road of dramatic independence.

I. i. This scene shows primarily that there is already in existence a considerable party opposed to Cæsar. Perhaps this party was secretly incited by Cassius. Is there anything in the play to confirm or disprove this notion? Brutus may have known of it. It may have been the existence of this faction that set him to thinking along new lines. But at the opening of the play he is still uninfluenced by it. His actions are due wholly to his own reasoning out of the situation.

This scene also implies that important use is eventually to be made out of the Roman mob. The

behavior of the mob, however, need not be taken
to represent Shakespeare's conception of the common
people and their characteristics. Compare with *Henry
the Sixth,* where such persons are introduced wholly
for comic effect; and with *Henry the Fifth,* where
the commonalty is the chief justification for the existence of a king, as well as his mainstay and support. Note also the characteristics of the common people in *Coriolanus.* If one of these plays represents
the personal feelings of Shakespeare more than another I fancy that it is *Henry the Fifth.*

I. i. 69. Is this fact referred to again in the play?

I. ii. Examine this scene carefully. Note all the
references to the character of Cæsar and to his physical personality. Note how many of them are unat-
tractive and uncomplimentary. Later, supplement
this list with material drawn from the remainder of
the play. We find Cæsar superstitious, pompous,
vain, and boastful. How is this unfavorable view of
Cæsar to be accounted for? Does Shakespeare mean
to imply that the position of Cæsar, that is, imperialism, is independent of the particular man who for
the moment represents it? That because he is
Cæsar he can carry these defects as if they were no
load to speak of?

I. ii. 29. Note how Brutus and Antony are contrasted from the very beginning of the play.

I. ii. 46. It must be remembered that at the moment Cassius approached Brutus the latter was, as
we learn later, much disturbed over the very matter
that Cassius has come to broach.

I. ii. 79. Brutus says, " I do fear the people choose
Cæsar for their king." He here uses the word fear in

the same loose way in which we now use it colloquially in such expressions as " I fear it will rain to-morrow." Cassius, however, pretending to understand Brutus to mean the word in its literal sense, so uses it himself, thus forcing Brutus into an acknowledgment which he did not intend to make. This quick-witted attention to details is very characteristic of Cassius. Find other illustrations in the play of his quick and keen observation of details.

I. ii. 162-175. Though Brutus has already been thinking along the very lines suggested to him by Cassius, he is cautious and unwilling to act without sufficient thought. Cassius realizes that it will be difficult to win the support of Brutus. But Cassius also knows that if Brutus is once won over he will became a staunch adherent. This slow reasoning to a permanent conclusion is the prime characteristic of Brutus.

I. ii. 200-212. This passage is a very accurate estimate of the character of Cassius. Does it in reality emanate from Shakespeare or from Cæsar? Consider the character of Cæsar throughout the play. If he knew all this, and believes all he says to Antony about Cassius, would he be likely to take no precautions to protect himself?

Notice also how this scene suggests the importance of Cassius in relation to Cæsar.

I. ii. 267. Casca refers to Cæsar's doublet. In Elizabethan times there was practically no serious attempt at costuming as we now understand the word. It is true that one of the largest expenses of the Elizabethan actors was for clothes. But the clothes they wore were Elizabethan clothes, not costumes representative of the parts enacted. A warrior wore armor, but Elizabethan not Roman armor. Cæsar here wears an Elizabethan doublet, not a Roman garment.

I. ii. 312, etc. (See the remarks concerning soliloquies in the chapter on *Richard the Third*.) This soliloquy is accurate so far as the character of Brutus is concerned. It is also quite in keeping with the character of Cassius. It calls attention to the "honorable metal" of Brutus, but hints that he is gullible and easily deceived. It suggests in line 315 the pitfall into which Brutus eventually falls. It also implies the crafty nature of Cassius, a rather low view of human kind (316) and that he is a trifle vain (319). It shows him, here as elsewhere, a good judge of men and utterly unscrupulous. Find other examples in the play of these characteristics of Cassius.

I. iii. The Elizabethans believed in the widespread superstition which held that abnormal physical conditions, especially great storms, preceded or accompanied great crimes. Therefore, the effect of such a tremendous display of omens and portents is to enhance the magnitude of the crime that follows.

With this fact in mind, one feels that the scene, acted in the broad daylight, would be almost ridiculous. See elsewhere the discussion of a darkened stage in Elizabethan times and the method of accomplishing it in the contemporary theater.

Note how cleverly Cassius sounds Casca and wins him to his side. We may imagine this typical, not as a single occurrence, but as an example of how Cassius is working upon all the likely people with whom he comes in contact. His success here also fore-shadows his future success with Brutus.

II. i. 10-34. This passage is a genuine soliloquy. It shows Brutus in the act of making up his mind. He is the apostle of reason. That is the character-istic which made him one of the conspirators, and it is also the characteristic which eventually brings about his downfall. Is this assertion supported by the re-mainder of the play? Or should we say that Brutus is a poor reasoner, and that that is what brings about his final ruin?

Brutus reads the paper that is thrown in at his window. The audience has already been informed about this paper. How does Brutus take it? Does the way in which it influences him show whether he is or is not a practical man of the world? How do we usually feel towards people who act as the result of, or are influenced by, anonymous communications?

II. i. 61. Note how seriously Brutus is taking the matter. He does not cast in his lot with the con-spirators heedlessly. If he makes a mistake it is because he is unable to judge the situation more ac-curately.

II. i. 90. Cassius is a very skilful flatterer. Ob-serve how often he gives evidence of this character-istic.

II. i. 101-111. No importance attaches to this scrap of conversation. It is merely put in to occupy the time while Brutus and Cassius are whispering. It would be very awkward for the other actors on the stage to be doing nothing for a moment or two.

II. i. 114. Why does not Brutus want them to take an oath? 1. What he says is quite true of himself.

2. Is it true of the others?   3. Should he have thought it true of all the others, or should he have known better?   4. Does the situation not show that Brutus is unacquainted with the general run of men? In other words, that he is not a practical man of the world?

Note also that this first act of Brutus after he has decided to join the conspirators is to object to one of their plans.   This happens several times in the play. As a rule we find that the opposition of Brutus is due to high-mindedness, but, as a rule, it is ill-timed.

II. i. 150. Again, in regard to Cicero, Brutus raises an objection to what all the other conspirators seem agreed upon. They have very earnestly desired the co-operation of Brutus; and the ready way in which Cassius permits himself to be overruled by his new recruit shows the advantage he hoped would be derived from the accession of Brutus to the ranks of the conspirators. Yet Cassius must have begun to repent very soon. In fact, his misjudging the character and the advantage of Brutus is the blunder that in the end wrecks the conspiracy.

Note that generally throughout Shakespeare's plays the men who deserve punishment bring it upon themselves.

II. i. 162, etc. Still again Brutus opposes the suggestion of Cassius,—this time in regard to their attitude toward Antony. This is the third time Brutus has manifested his opposition. And, as events turn out, it proves to be the fatal mistake. For it is Antony's permission to speak at Cæsar's funeral, granted by Brutus but opposed by Cassius, which eventually overthrows the conspiracy.

In all this Brutus shows himself to be a poor judge
of present conditions. He is acting in accordance with
his theories. He is trying to run a conspiracy on
paper. He does not know what is likely to happen in
real life. He misjudges the behavior of the mob and
underestimates the power of a man who possesses a
persuasive tongue like Antony's.

How does the failure of Brutus to act to the best
practical advantage of the conspirators affect our
estimation of the character of Cassius? Should he not
have known Brutus better?

II. i. 183. Cassius is not so subservient to Brutus
as before. He expresses some opposition himself.
But he has been so urgent to the other conspirators
regarding the advantage of Brutus' assistance that he
finds his hands in a way tied at the present moment.

II. i. 219. Brutus will give Ligarius reasons. The
key to the character of Brutus, and to his failure, is to
be found in the fact that he does not know that most
men are swayed by their passions rather than by their
minds. Indeed, this fact is one of the principal details brought out in the play.

II. i. 229. The return to Lucius for a moment, with
whom the scene began, serves to round up this portion
of the scene as a kind of unit. It is now ended and we
are ready for other things.

The closing portion of the scene, in which Brutus
talks with Portia, serves several purposes: 1. It recalls us to the every-day world about us which we left
at the entrance of the conspirators, much as the knocking on the gate does in *Macbeth*. 2. It also emphasizes the deliberate, thoughtful way in which Brutus
has made up his mind. 3. It further serves to give us

a little touch of the more human side of the man who
has just been caught up by the current of great public events.   Nowhere in the play does Portia rise
above the position of a mere minor character.

II. ii. Note how the opening conversation between
Cæsar and Calpurnia recalls the closing situation of
the preceding scene, the conversation between Brutus
and Portia. By such little devices are the portions of
a play linked together and made to seem more continuous.

Does this scene bring out the constancy of Cæsar
of which he boasted?—or the reverse?   Do selfish
motives figure in Cæsar's final decision to go to the
Senate House?

Scenes iii. and iv. were probably acted continuously
on the outer stage, and the time of their enactment
occupied in setting the scene which follows, on the
inner stage.

III. Scenes i. and ii. of this act, which practically constitute the whole act, have to all intents and
purposes the same setting. We may, therefore, think
of them as constituting a continuous scene. Note,
then, how much significant matter is contained in this
great central scene of the play. 1. There is the
outbreak of the conspiracy culminating in the murder
of Cæsar. 2. Next comes the sudden rise of Antony.
3. The scene contains what is, to all intents and purposes, the overthrow of the conspiracy. 4. It makes
very evident the fact that Brutus, after all, was the
real cause of failure on the part of the conspirators.

III. i. 8. Is this phrase of Cæsar's a noble sentiment, or mere grandiloquence?

Note the care with which Antony is drawn aside.

Brutus formerly made light of the pretense that Antony might turn out to be an enemy with whom they need seriously to reckon. But the conspirators seem to have known better.

III. i. 35, etc. Cæsar speaks a good deal of bombast in this scene. Is its effect on the audience prejudicial to the character of Cæsar? Throughout the play, does Cæsar act with the consistency of which he brags in this scene?

III. i. 95. Note that Antony's name appears again at the most critical moment of the play.

III. i. 104. Brutus acts as spokesman as if he were the actual leader of the insurrection. Yet Cassius has really been the heart and soul of it up to this moment. How important a part does Brutus think he himself has played?

III. i. 124. The servant's speech is a masterpiece. It must have been planned in every detail by the clever Antony. It plays upon Brutus' weakness, it is thoroughly non-committal, and every safeguard is taken for eventually jumping either way.

III. i. 141. Brutus has been quickly caught by Antony's bait of an opportunity to give reasons.

III. i. 147. One of the most skilfully managed passages of the play follows the entrance of Antony. He is acting every moment of the time. He pretends to be loyal to Cæsar lest the conspirators will not trust him if he seems to desert too easily. Yet he wants them to believe that in the end he is to be won over. Of course, at heart, he is loyal to Cæsar throughout.

III. i. 177, 178. This is an odd speech for Cassins to make. Does he mean it?

III. i. 205. This expression of praise required splendid courage on the part of Antony, and shows his far-sighted intuition. It is a true representation of his feelings, but it is not a spontaneous outbreak. Every detail has been planned in advance and carried out with the skill of a consummate actor. His motive is to make the conspirators feel that if he could be so loyal to Cæsar under such dangerous circumstances, just so loyal will he be to them if he is once won over. Antony took a great risk when he made this speech, but he triumphed.

III. i. 232. Cassius knows men far better than Brutus does. He instantly sees the danger of allowing Antony to speak, and seeks to restrain Brutus from giving permission. Brutus, however, insists on having his own way. And it is the result of this insistence that turns the tide against him. Thus Brutus is really the cause of the overthrow of the conspiracy. And his cause fails because of his own unswerving devotion to his own high motives.

III. i. 245. Brutus' belief that Antony will obey his commands argues very little worldly knowledge on the part of Brutus—it is almost childlike. This incident also reflects somewhat on the character of Cassius, who should have gauged Brutus to better advantage before he made him the leader of the conspiracy.

III. i. 254. Up to this point the audience has not been quite sure whether Antony is playing fast and loose with the faction, or whether he is really meditating an advantageous desertion to its ranks. At this point he throws off the mask of his acting. This soliloquy represents the real Antony, and sets the audience right.

Note how the sympathy of the audience swings like a pendulum. Cæsar's arrogance turns this sympathy towards Brutus. Brutus is so easily taken in by Antony that he now loses some of the sympathy that has been aroused for him as a conscientious leader. Meantime, the attention of the audience is becoming centered upon the rising genius of Antony. In other words, the sympathy of the audience is again swinging towards Cæsar and the successor of Cæsar.

III. i. 276. Notice here the allusion to Octavius. It was Shakespeare's habit to introduce an allusion to the force that is going to resolve the action at the very moment at which that action reaches the height of its first culmination.

III. ii. 7. Brutus is going to give the public reasons. He is the philosopher, the exceptional man, who regulates his actions entirely by his mind. He knows mankind so slightly that he fancies all men like himself. He cannot understand how a man can fail to side with him if sufficient reasons are given for so doing.

On the other hand, Antony is the man of the hour. He knows that men are swayed at important moments by their passions, not by their minds. He is willing to risk all on a half-hour incendiary oration.

As the sequence shows he is right. The much purer, higher-minded Brutus is all wrong. And so Antony wins and Brutus loses because the former is familiar with his tools and the latter is not.

III. ii. 78. This wonderful speech of Antony will bear careful analysis. It is a masterpiece of eloquence. Its proper delivery requires the exercise of marvelous acting ability.

Antony is the friend of Cæsar, speaking at the moment of the triumph of his enemies, at their victim's funeral, by their sufferance, and before a hostile crowd. It is his intention to turn that crowd against the very men they are now adoring, and to win them entirely to his own side. And he essays the task without fear, and with no doubt as to the outcome.

III. ii. 87. Antony speaks of Brutus as an honorable man. There is here not the least hint of sarcasm in Antony's voice. His first step towards winning the crowd is to adopt their point of view and make them believe that he is one of them. Later he uses the same words sarcastically. In the meantime he gradually, but very gradually, changes his tone. All the while he is on the outlook for indications that the crowd has begun to come to him. Perhaps the first touch, the slightest touch, however, of sarcasm, appears in line 104.

III. ii. 112. In reality Antony pauses, not because he is overcome by emotion, but in order to catch some audible hint of the change of feeling on the part of his hearers. He needs a cue as to how to continue. He is richly rewarded by the scrap of conversation which he overhears among the citizens, and begins again to speak with renewed confidence.

III. ii. 129. The increased sarcasm of this line is soon to develop into an open sneer.

III. ii. 145. Now that he is sure of success, Antony begins to tease his audience with delay.

III. ii. 219. Fancy the contempt Antony puts into the word, " reasons "!

III. ii. 225. Note the splendid irony of this line and in what follows.

III. ii. 265. With the exit of the citizens the conspiracy, if not over, is at least foredoomed to failure. At this point one can easily fancy the outcome. From here on the play consists of:—1. The mere continuation of the story to the end. 2. A picture of Brutus in defeat. And, as often elsewhere in Shakespeare, the play ends more weakly than it began. *Hamlet* and *Othello* are the two most notable exceptions to this reflection.

IV. i. At the opening of this scene we meet the triumvirs, all of whom figure in *Antony and Cleopatra*. The suggestion contained in line 9 is quite unworthy of the Antony of the latter play. In fact, throughout this scene Antony's attitude towards Lepidus is not at all to his credit. It must be remembered, however, that Lepidus was generally considered to be the nonentity of the triumvirate.

IV. ii. Note how quickly dissension has got among the conspirators. In line 19 Brutus refers to Cassius as "a hot friend cooling." Is this charge true? Is it due to the fact that Cassius is well aware of the blundering of Brutus? Does Cassius think he could make better progress without Brutus? Does Brutus have any idea as to what causes the present behavior of Cassius? Is their reconciliation in the next scene genuine?

IV. iii. Doubtless Shakespeare thought that the news of Portia's death would cause even the philosophic Brutus to act in an unusual manner. But the testy wrangling with Cassius in the early part of the scene is quite unworthy of Brutus. It does not belittle the greatness of Shakespeare to acknowledge that once in a while he is at fault in the presentation of a character—especially in his earlier years, a period that may be said to close with *Julius Cæsar*.

IV. iii. 31. Cassius here asserts that he is an abler soldier than Brutus. From the standpoint of the practical management of a revolution he is certainly right. But note that he denies the word abler in line 56.

IV. iii. 76. In a way Brutus is helpless and acknowledges his dependence on Cassius for everything in the way of practical details.

IV. iii. 104. Is Cassius sincere? At the opening of the scene we get the impression that Cassius is trying to pick a quarrel. If this speech is sincere, we must attribute the change in Cassius to the effect of Brutus' noble personality.

On the other hand, if it is a hollow piece of flattery spoken for the purpose of mollifying Brutus we must discover why Cassius, who a moment before wished to quarrel, now desires a reconciliation. This is a difficult discovery to make.

In the latter part of this scene we have in Brutus' tender consideration of Lucius one of those little touches which show how much brighter Brutus shone in private than in public life.

Act V. The fifth act is merely the working out of a foregone conclusion. It contains practically nothing but a description of the battle. It is not often that the last act of one of Shakespeare's plays contains so little vital material.

V. i. 45-47. Cassius prepares himself for death protesting against the policy of Brutus.

V. iii. 5. The last fatal slip of the battle is set down to the long list of blunders on the part of Brutus.

V. v. 68-81. Note the final estimate of the character of Brutus put into the mouths of Antony and Octavius.

In the view of Brutus' character set forth above he is conceived as one unused to public life, unskilled in the very kind of work he is called upon to do. This view, however, does not imply anything derogatory to his character. Antony was right when he called Brutus the noblest Roman of them all.

There are critics who see in all of Shakespeare's plays Sunday-school morals of the conventional sort. Though this view is usually obscured to me, there can be no doubt about the fact that underlying each of the great tragedies of Shakespeare there is some great human truth. And this play is no exception.

The situation may thus be phrased: it is of one who has high ideals, a noble nature, called upon to execute some great task. The tools at his service are such as he cannot use with justification to his own conscience. Shall he use them and succeed, or shall he refuse them, live up to his ideals, and fail nobly?

Shakespeare does not answer the question. But he shows that the latter course will inevitably bring worldly ruin.

It is interesting to note that the play which involves the reappearance of so many of the characters of *Antony and Cleopatra,* is very closely associated with that play in its general idea. In the later play Antony appears as a hero of gigantic proportions. Again, throughout the play, public duty and personal desire are placed in opposition. Everything, so far as Antony is concerned, is sacrificed to his personal devotion to the Egyptian queen. In one way it is an ignoble passion, in another it is the opposite. He goes down grandly, dragging the queen and his followers with him. But our sympathy is with him to the very end. Shakespeare has hardly achieved so much in the case of Brutus.

CHAPTER XVII

HAMLET

I. OUTLINE OF THE EARLY HISTORY OF THE PLAY

THERE are, or were, several versions of the story of Hamlet in Elizabethan times. In the first place, there was a long prose account known as *The Hystorie of Hamblet*. Though no longer extant, it is generally supposed that a play setting forth the same story was in existence as early as 1589. This is frequently referred to as the *lost-Hamlet*, and many suppose it to have been written by Thomas Kyd, author of *The Spanish Tragedy*. In 1603, the year after the probable appearance of *Hamlet* on the stage, the first quarto edition of the play was published. This differs in many respects from the second quarto of 1604. And the text of the Folio, 1623, differs in a few respects from that of the second quarto. The texts of the second quarto and of the Folio are evidently but slightly differing versions of the same play, and they are combined to produce the currently accepted text of to-day.

The extraordinary differences between the first and the second quarto, appearing as they did from the press so close together, has given rise to endless critical discussion. There are three possible suppositions: 1. The first quarto may be Kyd's supposedly lost play or a version of it. 2. It may be an earlier play of the same subject by Shakespeare himself. 3. It may be a pirated edition of Shakespeare's play which called into existence quarto two, the true version, as a mere matter of financial protection. I incline to a firm belief in the latter hypothesis.

I do not think that it can be Kyd's play. So far as we know, there are extant but two of his plays. One of them, *The Spanish Tragedy,* is, when judged by contemporary standards, remarkable for its excellence. The other, *Soliman and Perseda,* judged by the same standards is as remarkable for its lack of excellence. At any rate, neither one resembles the other, or shows any evidence of self-imitation.

Later I shall try to show that the resemblance between *The Spanish Tragedy* of Kyd and the *Hamlet* of Shakespeare is so close that we are driven to the conclusion that the former served as a model to the latter. And the main points of this resemblance are visible even in the first quarto. It does not seem to me likely that Kyd would thus copy his own earlier effort—for four reasons: 1. There is no confirmatory evidence of the fact. 2. The two extant plays suggest diversity of work rather than close self-imitation. 3. The copying of an earlier skeleton plot is not unlike the practice of Shakespeare. 4. It is a mere matter of personal taste, but to me the bad points of the quarto are unworthy of Kyd, and the good points more suggestive of Shakespeare than of the earlier playwright.

Nor do I think the play to be an earlier play by Shakespeare. Its crudeness in parts is so great that it must have been written by Shakespeare, if at all, at a very early date. Yet *Titus Andronicus,* Shakespeare's earliest tragedy, is so superior to it as to suggest a wide difference in their dates. Yet *Titus Andronicus* must have been written very early in Shakespeare's career.

On the other hand, the contemporary conditions of literary piracy seem to account plausibly for all, or practically all, of the essential differences between the first and the second quarto. It was the usual custom of that day to keep popular plays unpublished till the temporary stage popularity had waned. Then, if a further penny could be turned by publication, the companies did not scruple to do so. On the other hand, the crooked practices that obtained among publishers prompted them to resort to all sorts of underhand means in order to procure a copy of the text. They would bribe the players, doubtless resort to theft if necessary, or send stenographers to take down the play while it was being acted.

There was no adequate system of shorthand writing in vogue at that time. Hence one, in taking down the play, would perforce leave many gaps to be filled in later from memory. As this is a student handbook, I shall not go into the case thoroughly. But in my opinion a close comparison of the two quartos suggests that the former in the main could very easily be the result of the work of such an imperfect stenographer and hack-writer's attempt to take down and subsequently fill out the play as represented by the second quarto.

Of course, this theory does not explain everything. If it did, there would be no case left for believers in the other hypothesis. And a student who would go into the case more thoroughly should study both the quartos carefully and all the attendant conditions of contemporary theatrical life and practice. It is sufficient to say here that in my opinion such an examination not only gives to this explanation far greater validity than to either of the other two, but it also gives sufficient validity to it to warrant its acceptance despite a few unexplained details that appear to me on the whole as trifling in comparison.

If this explanation be the right one there remains no difficulty in explaining the appearance of the second quarto. In accordance with current practice Shakespeare's company refused to publish the play. A publisher got hold of the garbled copy issued from the press as the first quarto. As the play, though in a mutilated condition, was now on the book market the theatrical company who owned the play naturally desired to reap whatever advantage was due to publication. Hence they came forward promptly with the true text.

II. "The Spanish Tragedy" and "Hamlet" *

The attribution of the lost play of *Hamlet* to Thomas Kyd lends additional interest to the relations between Kyd and Shakespeare. Resemblances of many kinds are noticeable among the works of the two writers. Such a coincidence as the following can hardly be accidental:

* This note and most of what is said subsequently regarding the "Mouse-trap" have appeared in "The Sewanee Review."

"I had not thought that Alezandro's heart
Had been envenomed with such extreme hate:
But now I see that words have several works,
And there's no credit in the countenance."
—*Sp. Tr.*, III. i.

"There's no art
To find the mind's construction in the face,"

are the words of Duncan. It is, however, not in such
verbal similarities that we find a resemblance between
the dramatists of remarkable degree; it is rather in
the similarity of treatment and conception between
the great play of Kyd and the masterpiece of his successor.

The motive of both plays is revenge, in each for a
murder. In *Hamlet* the murder is committed before
the beginning of the play and is revealed by supernatural means. In *The Spanish Tragedy* the murder,
which forms a part of the action, is revealed by means
of a mysterious letter. None will forget the burst of
human grief that almost vanquishes Hamlet at the moment he hears the details of his beloved father's
death. Though there is no attempt to portray Hieronimo fully as a human character of many sides, he
experiences sufficient grief and sorrow to cause him to
lose his mental balance temporarily.

I hope to show that there is reason to believe that
Shakespeare had *The Spanish Tragedy* in mind while
writing *Hamlet* and that, though he followed it as a
model, he improved it at many points. It is noteworthy as an illustration that at the point in *Hamlet*,
corresponding with the above suggestion from Hieronimo's behavior, Hamlet makes the speech which
contains the phrase "To put an antic disposition on."

Shakespeare, however, was, I think, too shrewd a judge of human nature to imagine that Hamlet, who had just been startled out of sane behavior by the terrible revelation of the ghost, could in the same moment, like Hieronimo, be so self-possessed as to plan in a moment the ruse of assuming a future cloak of madness. The "antic disposition" is doubtless a reference to the "wild, whirling words" that his fellows could not understand, the general incoherent behavior that has preceded the utterance of the line, and which Hamlet fears may occur again under a similar strain.

The author of the crime is revealed to Hamlet by the ghost—to Hieronimo by a letter. Both persons instantly suspect the trustworthiness of their information. Hamlet's doubt is due to his belief in a well-known Elizabethan superstition: namely, that the devil possessed the power to appear in the likeness of a dead person in order to tempt a living. This is a doubt shared likewise by Horatio and may well bid Hamlet pause till he has better proof. Hieronimo, however, suspects from no cause. The detail is unmotived.

However, both men suspect and both of them resolve to test the truth of the information which they have received. Hamlet most carefully plans the "Mouse-trap" which, though it turns out in an unexpected way, convinces him of his uncle's guilt. Hieronimo asserts that he must take time for investigation, but in reality does nothing. He merely waits till a second more convincing letter comes to him by accident. Just why this letter should be written is not quite clear. It is intended by Kyd to convey information to Heironimo, but it is intended by its writer, Pedringano, to convey an appeal for relief to Lorenzo. Yet the substance of the letter is that most calculated to harden Lorenzo's heart. Hieronimo, who before was so ready to doubt the revealing letter, accepts this as true in every respect and considers his doubts as completely set at rest. Both Hamlet and Hieronimo are now ready to act upon their original information —and both allow their revenge to be delayed till the end of the play.

How can we account for this delay? The answer to the former case is evident. Hamlet has planned to sit quietly by till the " Mouse-trap " is finished and then compare notes with Horatio on his uncle's behavior. But he is himself affected by the scene beyond the limits of endurance. By interrupting the proceedings too soon, Hamlet causes the court to disperse with the impression that Hamlet, not Claudius, has made an exhibition of himself. Though Hamlet is himself convinced of his uncle's guilt, he realizes that he has so bungled the affair that he will be unable to convince others of anything but his own inability to act with reason. In the reaction of despondency he allows himself to be drawn away from Denmark; but the moment his spirit returns he hastens back to accomplish his revenge.

Why Hieronimo delays is not quite so evident, yet a similar scene to the above appears in the corresponding portion of *The Spanish Tragedy*. Immediately upon the completion of his self-conviction, Hieronimo resolves to appeal to the king. He has every reason to believe his appeal will be successful. Yet, when he comes to the point, he is so wrought up by his emotion

that he cannot say what he intended to say, and at
last dashes off the stage hysterically mad. As in
Hamlet, the impression left upon the court is exactly
opposite to that intended by Hieronimo. In consequence, however, Hieronimo merely remains quiescent
till the end of the play. He has no excuse for inaction. When Bel-Imperia upbraids him for his delay
he requests her to wait and to expect great things,
but he offers no defense.

These two scenes cannot be dismissed without a
word concerning the wild behavior that occasionally
characterizes both Hamlet and Hieronimo. This is
not the place to consider in detail the question of Hamlet's madness. He is certainly not insane in the sense
that Lear is insane; nor is he believed insane by any
of the shrewder intellects of the play—nor is Hieronimo. The key to their wild behavior is the same.
Both have exceptionally passionate natures. The revelation of the ghost, the " Mouse-trap," and the burial
of Ophelia act so powerfully upon Hamlet's nature
that he temporarily loses self-control—control, however, which he immediately regains. The same is true
of the character of Hieronimo.

There are a few other similarities between the
two characters. Immediately after the failure of the
" Mouse-trap " during a conversation with the queen,
Hamlet conjures up a vision of his father come to
chide him for his long delay.

" Do you come," says Hamlet, " your tardy son to
chide, That, lapsed in time and passion, lets go by
The important acting of your dread command? " Immediately after his failure to convey his appeal to the
king, Hieronimo conjures up a vision of his son come

to chide him for his delay. "And art thou come, Horatio," says Hieronimo, "from the depth To ask for justice on this upper earth, to tell thy father thou art unrevenged?"

Hamlet is spurred back to activity from the period of despondency following the failure of the "Mousetrap" by the accidental sight of a company of Fortinbras's soldiers who remind him of his own unfinished task of revenge. Similarly Hieronimo is spurred back into action by the sight of a handkerchief dyed in his son's blood which he accidentally draws from his pocket.

When the end of the play is reached and the offenders are killed, both Hamlet and Hieronimo recognize the necessity of some public justification of their actions. Hieronimo delivers his own plea. For this, however, Hamlet's span of life is insufficient. Yet he dies, begging Horatio do the office for him:

"Absent thee from felicity awhile,
And in this harsh world draw thy breath in pain,
To tell my story."

With this close parallelism in mind is one not likely to hazard the inference that Shakespeare's play bears less resemblance to the lost *Hamlet* than to *The Spanish Tragedy?*

It is hard to believe that the first quarto, which in all its larger and broader qualities so closely resembles the second, bears any close resemblance to the play by Kyd. This, if considered in the light of the above list of parallels, implies an almost inconceivable degree of self-imitation. On the other hand, one can easily imagine that Shakespeare, who borrowed not only plots, but other dramatic details that proved successful, would take for his model the most popular tragedy of the time, and adhere to it in the main with the same fidelity illustrated, for instance, in *Romeo and Juliet*. Yet he did in *Hamlet* what he had already done in *Romeo and Juliet*. He transferred the unpoetic dross of the original into the poetic ore associated in our minds only with Shakespearian genius.

III. Notes on the Text

I. i. 23. Note that Horatio is introduced as skeptical regarding the story he has heard of the ghost. Yet his subsequent behavior (see I. iv. 70) shows that he believes in ghosts. The convincing of the skeptic Horatio contributes to the vividness and reality of the situation here. (See note at the end of the chapter relative to the Elizabethan staging of the play, and the article of Mr. Baker therein cited. This scene was probably acted on a darkened stage.)

I. i. 42. "Thou art a scholar." Critics have cited the fact that an old superstition implies that a ghost should be conversed with in Latin; therefore Horatio, who was a scholar, was urged forward as spokesman. But the critics seem to have overlooked the fact that Horatio does not address the ghost in Latin when the time comes to speak. In fact, there is probably no allusion whatever to this superstition here. The others are slightly frightened, a good deal terrified, if we are to believe the account given by Horatio to Hamlet later. He then says that they were almost distilled to jelly by the act of fear. Horatio, however, is of superior education, has boasted of his skepticism.

His companions urge him forward just as a child will say, "You are the biggest. You go first."

I. i. 79, etc. How easily the correlative information needed as an introduction is inserted. Fortinbras, though a minor figure, plays a very important part in the drama.

I. i. 126-139. One must understand this passage in order to read it correctly. There was a superstition of the time which held that a ghost, though endowed with supernatural powers, was limited in many directions. For instance, it was necessary, perhaps, to address him by the proper name in order that he be able to speak. This is why Hamlet (I. iv. 44), says, "I'll call thee Hamlet, King, father, royal Dane." We must imagine a sufficient pause after each name for Hamlet to discover whether he has used the right epithet.

Again, it was believed that a ghost could not speak till he was addressed relative to the subject uppermost in his mind. This is the superstition involved in the passage cited above. The ghost refuses to speak, line 129. So Horatio guesses. He asks if the ghost wishes to talk regarding anything advantageous to himself, Horatio. Then there is a pause. The silence of the ghost shows that this is not that regarding which he wishes to speak. Horatio tries again. "Is it relative to the welfare of your country?" he asks. There is another pause. This is not it. Does the ghost wish to speak of hidden treasure? Continned silence answers no. And so the phantom disappears.

There was still another superstition which held that a ghost would remain silent unless addressed by the proper person. As the ghost has failed to answer Horatio, the latter thought comes into his mind. The ghost would not speak to the others. He would not speak to him. Who is the person who ought to address him? Probably his son, the younger Hamlet. So they decide to ask the prince to share their watch with them.

I. ii. We may look upon this as the first formal, public gathering of the court since the death of the king and the marriage of his widow to his brother Claudius.

We are told in this scene much of the introductory material, are introduced to most of the remaining characters. Laertes is given permission to depart. He is kept in mind by several touches hereafter, but does not appear as an important character till act IV.

In the structure of this play we find the two-hero type exemplified in its perfection by *Othello*. Claudins and Hamlet are the two opposites. The character of the former should be scanned carefully throughout the play.

I. ii. 65. This is the first line spoken by Hamlet. It should be examined carefully. Its literal meaning is: A little more than kin (uncle by blood, stepfather by marriage) and less than kind (unnatural; a reference to the indecent haste with which he has married his brother's widow). In the Tudor Edition this line is marked " aside." Some critics do not so mark it. I do not think it matters much. In either case the implication is the same. Shakespeare's first line attributed to Hamlet shows: 1. That he is out of harmony with his uncle, the present king. 2. That something is preying deeply on his mind. In the conversation that follows the king shows that he is either ignorant of the former condition or that he pretends to neglect it. His words, however, the queen's, and Hamlet's all emphasize the second. Something extraordinary is preying upon his mind. It is not fully accounted for by outward circumstances. It is not yet fully understood even by Hamlet himself. It is only cleared up later.

I. ii. 129, etc. This soliloquy shows, but not yet quite fully, what is preying upon Hamlet's mind. It is his mother's hasty marriage. He idolized her, and her over-hasty marriage shattered his mind's image of a superior woman.

I. ii. 226, etc. There is nothing impossible to Hamlet about what Horatio says. Yet the former, who can imagine easily the appearance of the ghost, wishes to make sure. He has been told that the others were terribly frightened by the appearance of the apparition (I. ii. 205). So, as I said, he wishes to make sure. The only significance to the rapid fire of questions that follows is Hamlet's desire by cross-examination to test the coherence of their story. The clue to Hamlet's character throughout is justice, the desire to go slow and to be sure of himself and his cause. This is the first example of it.

I. ii. 256. Doubt in Elizabethan times usually meant suspect.

I. iii. Note that Laertes does not take the idea of Hamlet's courtship of Ophelia seriously. Yet it is serious and honest.

The Elizabethans not only enjoyed but demanded a fair admixture of comedy with their tragedy. In some plays, as in *Othello*, Shakespeare ignored this de-

mand. In *Macbeth* and in *Hamlet* he catered to it
only slightly. In the latter play the grave-diggers of
act V. and Polonius afford the comic element.

We must fancy Polonius as an old man who has in
the past been a worthy and trusted councilor. But he
has now passed the zenith of his intellectual career,
becoming a little childish. His mind is most occupied
over trivial matters. There is a ludicrous element in
this scene about his urging Laertes forward in haste
for the waiting ship while he simultaneously detains
him to hear a long-winded declamation full of copy-
book precepts relative to good behavior. And later
Polonius goes to the king with an altogether erroneous
interpretation of Hamlet's behavior, upon the truth
of which he is willing to stake his life and reputation.

Polonius takes almost the same view of Hamlet's
courtship of Ophelia as that taken by Laertes. Does
Ophelia believe what her father and brother say?

I. iv. 69-78. There was a belief in that day and
generation that the devil possessed the power of appearing to living persons in the semblance of some
deceased loved one. It is to this detail that Horatio
refers. Note how quickly he grasps the situation.
This apparition may be the spirit of the dead king.
On the other hand it may be an evil spirit come to do
harm to Hamlet. This doubt figures largely in what
follows. Hamlet has no thought of it in scene v. of
the first act. By the opening of act II. he has begun
to share Horatio's doubts. It is to test the truth of
the ghost's story, incidentally to discover whether it
is a true ghost or an evil spirit, that he plans the
" Mouse-trap."

I. v. 40. "Oh my prophetic soul! My uncle!"

This exclamation has been explained as indicative of the fact that Hamlet had already suspected his uncle's guilt. I do not, however, find any justification for this interpretation. In the first place, I conceive it to be an exclamation of surprise. If, however, Hamlet has not suspected his uncle, to what does he refer?

Now, Hamlet is overwhelmingly depressed in spirits and he hates his uncle viciously. The excuse for the low state of his spirits is to be found partly in the grief due to his father's death. But, as Claudius aptly remarks, strong men do not collapse under such circumstances; and Hamlet knows that the king is right. Furthermore, Hamlet is much distressed over his mother's hasty marriage. In a way, it has shattered one of his ideals of womanhood. Yet Hamlet knows that under ordinary circumstances he could have borne even this with a fair degree of equanimity.

And why does he hate Claudius? Partly because Claudius has usurped the throne, and partly because he has married the queen. Yet these motives hardly justify Hamlet's extreme aversion to the king.

In other words, Claudius, the queen, and Hamlet himself all feel that the extremity of his emotion is not fully accounted for by the known facts. And now, at the ghost's revelation, Hamlet suddenly realizes that there is a reason sufficient to account for all his feelings; and, inasmuch as he had had no previous knowledge or suspicion of the fact, the feeling itself was in a way prophetic.

The line should be read as two distinct exclamations, not as one, as is implied by the punctuation of some texts of the play.

At the end of scene iv. Hamlet departs with the

ghost against Horatio's will. We must fancy that his lingering companions on the ramparts of the castle wait a reasonable time for his return; then decide to hunt Hamlet up. They find him towards the end of scene v. Hamlet has just heard the astonishing revelation of the details of his father's murder. For a moment he is completely overcome. His high-strung nature is unable to retain its calm self-control. He talks nonsense (the "wild and whirling words" of line 133). And he acts ridiculously. He desires an oath against which the others protest. However, when Hamlet holds up the cross-shaped hilt of his sword for them to take oath upon they agree to his whim. Just at the critical moment Hamlet changes his mind and drags them off to some more likely position for the oath (line 156). And still again when they are willing to humor him with an oath he drags them to still another place of vantage (line 163).

During the next few lines Hamlet begins to recover his self-control. He realizes how he has been acting. He recalls Horatio's fears at their last parting. He knows that Horatio must be saying to himself, " This is just what I expected." Yet Hamlet is greatly wrought. He has no plans for the future. He has not had time even to conjecture what will be the sequel to all this. He has not yet decided whether or not he will relate the whole affair in confidence to Horatio. But there is one thing he is sure of. The present meeting with the ghost has momentarily thrown him off his balance. It may happen again in the future. If so, he hopes his friends and companions will not betray him by referring to the incidents of to-night. In other words: " If at any time in the future you see me act as strangely (put an antic disposition on, line 172) as you have seen me act in the last five minutes, do not shrug your shoulders, look wise, and say, ' That is just the way he behaved himself one night after meeting his father's ghost upon the ramparts.' "

Many critics have assumed that in the excitement of the moment Hamlet has found time to formulate definite plans for the future which involve the assumption of madness. They quote this line as a reference to the intention of assuming insanity in the future as a cloak to his plans. To me, however, it is perfectly clear that the exclamation does not point forward, but backward to the antic behavior that has just been acted out on the stage. It would at least be fresh in the mind of the audience, and it is hard to conceive how the audience would fail to connect the two.

II. i. One of the cleverest dramatic devices of the play involves the prominence of Laertes in the fourth act. It is needful that we do not forget him during his absence throughout the first three acts. The opening portion of this scene is largely for the purpose of keeping Laertes in the mind of the audience.

II. i. 75-100. This passage should be studied in connection with III. i. 90-158. One may profitably return to this discussion after reading the section devoted to Hamlet's madness. The result of these two meetings of Hamlet and Ophelia is: 1. Ophelia is convinced of Hamlet's madness. 2. Polonius is confirmed in his belief of Hamlet's madness. Yet Hamlet is acting quite rationally.

Let us for a moment try to fancy what has been passing recently in the mind of Hamlet relative to Ophelia. There can be no doubt that Hamlet is honestly in love with her. Yet the gross-minded Laertes doubts the fact. Polonius, while not taking quite so low a view of the matter as that taken by his son, considers marriage as out of the question because of the social difference in rank between his daughter and the prince. It is to prevent Ophelia from falling hopelessly in love that Polonius commands her to return Hamlet's presents and letters and otherwise cause a break in his attentions which can only result in harm.

Now look at this situation and its results through the eyes of Hamlet. It must be remembered that he has received no explanation of Ophelia's conduct. He is honestly in love with her. She seemed to be so with him. He was heir-apparent to the throne. His father died. His uncle seized the crown. Immediately he is jilted by Ophelia. And very shortly before this his mother's hasty marriage has shattered his belief in womanhood. What more likely than that Hamlet should conceive Ophelia to be a mere fortune-hunter who thrust him aside when he lost the throne? And much of the pathos lies in the fact that he is so completely mistaken. However, under this belief he approaches Ophelia (II. i. 75). But he still loves her. He cannot trust himself to speak, departing in distressed silence. On the second meeting, however (III. i. 90), he speaks his mind plainly. Though there is down deep in his heart left some of that former love, to come to the surface violently at the scene by Ophelia's grave in act V., Hamlet feels now only contempt for the woman who could treat him as she has done. Claudius, who secretly overhears the whole conversation, sees no sign of love or affection. When Hamlet tells Ophelia over and over again to go to a nunnery he means just what he says. Penance and a monastic life are necessary to purge her of her sinful nature.

II. ii. In this scene Polonius proposes his theory of madness. Had Shakespeare desired the audience to believe in this explanation would he have originated it in the foolish mind of Polonius? or would he have propounded it with so much in the way of amusing accompaniment? In the conversation that follows even Polonius can see some method. It is hardly likely that an Elizabethan audience would fail of the matter altogether.

Pursuant to the commands of the king and queen given at the beginning of the scene, Rosencrantz and Guildenstern here approach Hamlet to discover if possible the cause of his distress. They have probably been informed of the madness proposition suggested by Polonius. Hamlet immediately sees through them. Line 305, so shall my anticipation, etc., may be paraphrased as followed: You have been sent by the king and queen to worm something out of me. If I tell you of my own accord you have certainly not got it out of me. You may tell them so, thus befriending me and saving your own conscience.

II. ii. 396, 397. There is nothing irrational about this speech. Handsaw means heronshaw. The allusion to the wind would be understood by any one familiar with the out-of-door sport of falconry. The sentence means: I am not mad at all, but so possessed of my reason that I can distinguish the trifling difference between a hawk and a heron in mid-air a long way off.*

* A description of the point in falconry referred to here is to be found in my *Elizabethan People*, page 117.

II. ii. 361. The Elizabethan plays are full of anachronisms to which the audience of that day had no
objection.   Notwithstanding the fact that the setting
of this play is Denmark of an earlier time the conversation in which the above line occurs is relative to
the Elizabethan companies of boy actors who for a
time proved such formidable rivals to the older companies of men actors.

II. ii. 454-634. This passage is so intimately connected with the treatment of the " Mouse-trap " that
it is difficult to determine which should be considered
first.   I think, on the whole, that it is best to point out
the significance of each scene first, returning later to
point out some technical matters in relation to this
passage.

Note, however, this situation.   At the end of act
I. Hamlet firmly believed in the honesty of the ghost.
During the interval between acts I. and II. he has begun to share Horatio's doubts.   At least, if he does not
share them, he is not so positive in his conviction as
to discard them altogether.   He admits a possibility of
their truth.   One of the keys to Hamlet's character is
absolute justice.   He will not proceed till he *knows*
the truth.   How shall he find out?   He cannot tell.
So far he has thought much but done nothing.   The
good acting and the declamation of the players affect
him powerfully.   They can *do* as a mere matter of
hire and pay.   But he himself has been able to do
nothing, notwithstanding the fact that his motive is
stronger than theirs by a thousand-fold.   So he is
shamed into action, immediately planning the " Mouse-
trap."

This passage will be returned to in order to point

out the significance of the form of verse spoken here by the players and that spoken by them while enacting the " Mouse-trap."

III. i. 53. This is the first hint that the audience has received relative to the truth or the falsehood of the ghost's revelation. Up to this point the audience would be as doubtful as Horatio or Hamlet as to whether the apparition was a true ghost or a dishonest devil. And so easily might the qualified hint here given be overlooked, Shakespeare has repeated the information later with more emphasis at a most critical moment (III. iii. 37).

III. i. 28-195. In this passage the king overhears all. The eavesdropping device was planned when Polonius came to the king with the explanation of Hamlet's behavior based upon madness. It is notable that at the end of the incident the very shrewd Claudius, instead of being convinced that Hamlet is mad, is convinced of the contrary.

THE MOUSE-TRAP

At the risk of monotonous repetition I shall repeat one or two of the details already mentioned. For I consider this the most important passage in the play.

The usual interpretation of this part of the third act of *Hamlet* renders some of the protagonist's subsequent actions difficult if not impossible to explain. If Hamlet, as is so often supposed, was completely successful in the plot by which he put his uncle's integrity to the test, it is hard to understand why he made no immediate use of it, or why he gave himself up so easily to the diversion caused by the projected journey to England. He could not have set out in ignorance of his companions' character, for Hamlet acknowledges to the queen that he would trust them as he would adders fanged, an assertion indicative of his complete distrust of Rosencrantz and Guildenstern. Hamlet has set out upon a course of revenge, and he had held back from its accomplishment for certain reasons that the " Mouse-trap " was intended to remove. If they were removed by the complete success of the plot, why did he not continue as he had planned in advance? He does not, however, but gently, without opposition consents to his own removal from the scene of action at the very moment which most demands his presence, in company of men set over him by his enemy the king, men whom he suspects capable of foul play of the foulest kind. The suggestion that Shakespeare winked at this apparent inconsistency in the character of Hamlet for the purpose of ridding the plot of him at the time of the reappearance of Laertes is hardly worth consideration in a play that shows elsewhere the most careful construction even to the minutest details. In order to show that Hamlet's inaction is due to the utter failure and collapse of his plan to compromise the king during the performance of the " Mouse-trap," it is necessary to go back for a moment to the beginning of the play.

The Elizabethans as a class were implicit believers in the ghost-lore of the time, and Shakespeare, in relying upon a supernatural revelation, is appealing to one of the strongest sympathies of his audience. To them, no thought of weakness was introduced by the idea that a man of Hamlet's character was swayed

in his actions by the promptings of a shadowy apparition. It was also a part of the contemporary ghost-
lore that a spirit had the power of becoming invisible
to whom it pleased, to one or more of many as the
case might be; hence there is no necessity of providing
an explanation that assumes a difference between the
ghost seen by all who are present on the platform
at the beginning of the play and the ghost seen later
by Hamlet and not by the queen.

There was, however, another tradition equally believed at the time that introduced an element of un-
certainty as to the identity of the ghost: namely, that
the devil (for the Elizabethans believed in a personal
devil) had the power of appearing in the likeness of a
departed friend for the purpose of tempting one to a
crime for which he would suffer eternal punishment.
It should be borne in mind that this idea is not introduced subsequently by Hamlet as an excuse for inaction; on the other hand, it not only occurs at once to
Horatio but also prompts him to oppose Hamlet's retirement with the ghost to a different place alone.
Never till the " Mouse-trap " is over does Hamlet lose
hold of the idea of the danger to his soul if he re-
venges a crime that was never actually committed. It
is in order to discover by the king's behavior whether
the ghost of the elder Hamlet has appeared with a
true tale upon its lips, or whether the devil in a
pleasing shape has appeared with a tale of falsehood,
that Hamlet plans the " Mouse-trap."

Note the plan in all its details. Hamlet believes
that no man who had committed the crime attributed
to Claudius could sit through the visible reproduction
of that crime without displaying unusual emotion.

Such an exhibition on the part of the king will at once settle the question of the ghost's identity, and thus determine Hamlet's future line of action. Hamlet, however, with the full intention of doing complete justice, fears that his own bias may influence him to a wrong judgment, so he imparts his plan to Horatio, who is also to note what happens, and they are to compare notes on the king's behavior *after* the play is over. Note that it is Hamlet's full intention to sit idly by till the play is finished before he arrives at a final conclusion.

In this clever scheme Hamlet has forgotten one important detail. He has forgotten to think what may be the effect of this scene upon himself. In the sequel it turns out that Hamlet is far more deeply moved than his uncle, and at last completely collapses under the strain. The play proceeds. Both Hamlet and Horatio watch the king like a pair of hawks. Hamlet, however, is the first to give evidence that he is suffering extreme emotion at the sight of what is meant to be a reproduction of the murder of his father. This seems to be the motive of the exclamation "Wormwood, wormwood!" equivalent to "Bitter as gall," which is not marked as an aside in the early editions. Doubtless the king is struck with the similarity of the love-making of the actors to his own situation, for he turns to Hamlet to ask whether he has seen the play, and whether there is any offense in it. Whatever emotion Claudius may have shown up to this point, it has not taken shape in words. This anxiety to know what is coming tells Hamlet beyond peradventure that he is on the road to the coveted proof. He is madly joyous over this fact and impetuously

makes the fatal blunder of the play. In his reply to
the king he, as it were, shows his hand completely.

> *Hamlet.* No, no, they do but jest, poison in jest: no
> offence i' the world.
> *King.* What do you call the play?
> *Hamlet.* The Mouse-trap. Marry, how? Tropically.
> This play is the image of a murder done in
> Vienna: Gonzago is the duke's name; his wife
> Baptista: you shall see anon. 'Tis a knavish
> piece of work: but what o' that? your
> majesty and we have free souls, it touches
> us not: let the galled jade wince, our withers
> are unwrung.

The word tropically, which means figuratively, and
the last phrases, tell the king the whole situation. He
realizes that Hamlet has either discovered or suspected the secret crime, and is now trying to entrap
its author. A less accomplished villain than the man
who could say with so much dignity at such a dangerous moment—

> "Let him go, Gertrude: do not fear our person:
> There's such divinity doth hedge a king,
> That treason can but peep at what it would,
> Acts little of his will. Tell me, Laertes,
> Why thou art thus incensed. Let him go, Gertrude.
> Speak, man——"

is indeed far too accomplished in self-control not to be
able to meet the coming shock when he is so fully
aware of what is expected of him.

Hamlet immediately discovers the mistake that he
has made when he appreciates the fact that the only
effect of his words is to steady the king. It is exas-

peration at his own failure that causes Hamlet to violate his original plan of waiting to the end in order to compare notes with Horatio. It is the exasperation due to a coming sense of failure, because the players cannot accomplish it, that prompts Hamlet's attempt to force the king into an outward display of unusual emotion, by himself springing up and taking the words out of the actors' mouths.

Yet, wherein lies the failure? Has not Hamlet convinced himself of the ghost's integrity? Remember Hamlet's desire for justice. To kill Claudius in a way that will appeal to the public as a murder without setting the story in a true light is far from Hamlet's plan. He desires to be an avenging judge, not an implicated murderer. And thus he is bound to appear if he acts upon the information derived from the " Mouse-trap."

Hamlet has already won a reputation for madness about the court. He has jumped up in the midst of a play before the king, interrupted the players in an important part of the narrative, talked fiercely to the king himself; in other words, he has done much to strengthen the belief in his madness. It would be easy for Claudius to turn this impression to his advantage, as he actually does shortly afterwards. The unusual situation, however, is first mentioned by others. It is Ophelia who first speaks. It is Polonius who first suggests that the play be given over. And the king, though greatly wrought, is able to get away, almost unnoticed, leaving Hamlet in undisputed possession of the courtiers' thoughts. Almost immediately Rosencrantz and Guildenstern return to tell Hamlet that his mother has been struck with his mad behavior, struck into "amazement and admiration." And so his behavior must appear to every one who has seem him at the play, except Horatio and the king.

Hamlet voices this idea in his utterance beginning, "Now might I do it pat." Claudius would be sent to heaven, not because killed upon his knees, which is the usual interpretation, but because he would be canonized in the popular mind through having lost his life at the hands of a disappointed insane claimant to the throne. And this view of the situation is still in Hamlet's mind at the end of the play when he begs Horatio to preserve his life a little longer, saying,

"O good Horatio, what a wounded name,
Things standing thus unknown, shall live behind me!"

So Hamlet's "Mouse-trap" has not turned out as he expected it. He has made a mistake that has virtually convinced him of the truthfulness of the ghost and at the same time robbed him of the power of acting effectively as a result of the fact. A fit of despondency ensues. He feels that he has bungled the whole matter. He has once before regretted that he has been chosen to set things right; now he feels as if his own weakness makes the attempt utterly useless. In this frame of mind he is willing to depart far from Denmark, even to England, in company with men whom he distrusts as "adders fanged," rather than to remain where duty cries him on while his futility cries impossible. But this mood is of short duration. He is soon spurred into his true self again at sight of the soldiers of Fortinbras. He seizes the first opportunity, comes back to Denmark, is trapped into a fencing match ignorantly and against his will, and kills the king only when the evidence of his own poisoned cup and Laertes' dying confession leaves a record that tells posterity the truth.

II. ii. 454-634. Now, for a moment, let us return to this passage, and examine it jointly with a consideration of the staging of the " Mouse-trap." The difference that first catches our attention is the form of the verse. Here the players speak in vigorous, stirring blank verse. In the " Mouse-trap " they utter in sing-song couplets that unaided would soon put the audience asleep. Why this difference? In this scene Hamlet is thoroughly affected by the players. To sympathize with him the audience must be likewise affected. In other words, our attention is upon the players, shifted suddenly at the end of their speech to Hamlet. So they must declaim and act to the best of their ability.

In the " Mouse-trap " scene, however, our attention is on Claudius. Anything that diverts our attention from Claudius first, later from Claudius and Hamlet, will mar the scene.

Now Hamlet and Horatio should be placed as far apart as possible on the stage, provided their positions enable them both to watch the king to advantage. And Hamlet should be so placed that the audience is not likely to see him and Claudius at the same time without an effort. For our attention, as is that of Hamlet and Horatio, should be fixed upon the king and upon him alone.

The players of the " Mouse-trap " are in the upper balcony. If the audience looks up at them it will not be able to watch easily what is going on below on the

stage proper. So Shakespeare has taken every pre-
caution to render this diversion of eye and attention
unlikely.

1. After the first entrance of the players, Hamlet
has outlined in a general way what the "Mouse-trap"
is to be about. This serves partly to allay the curiosity of the audience.

2. At the moment of presentation Shakespeare
makes use of a monotonous insipid verse that would
hardly attract attention for itself.

3. A dumb-show is introduced which enables us
to see the whole thing in advance. We must not imagine that Claudius received any hint from this silent
presentation. The dumb-show is merely a device to
inform the audience and to satisfy its curiosity, so
that attention will not be diverted to the players during the critical time when we should be watching
Claudius. So we watch the king intently for some
sign of blenching. Hamlet, for the time being, should
be so placed on the stage as to be out of the direct
line of vision.

Suddenly the cry "Wormwood, wormwood!" diverts our eyes to a new part of the stage. This is
the most important point of dramatic effect in the
whole play. We suddenly realize that we have been
watching the wrong man. The scene is working more
powerfully upon Hamlet than upon Claudius. The
"Mouse-trap" is closing upon the prince rather than
upon the king. After the revelation by the ghost
Hamlet grew hysterical for a few moments, that is,
he acted in a way that inspired the phrases "wild
and whirling words" and "an antic disposition."
Now the same situation is happening again. Hamlet

feels that he is losing command of himself. And then he suddenly goes to pieces, as outlined above.

The " Mouse-trap " has disclosed the whole truth to Claudius. He is aware now that Hamlet possesses the secret of the murder. And Claudius, who well knows Hamlet to be a man of prompt action, knows also that he will strike fearlessly. Claudius can fore⁻see protection only in striking back first. This he determines to do. He plans the trip to England with secret instructions to put Hamlet out of the way.

III. iii. 36. Note that, but for one slight and dis-guised allusion, this is the first full open information which the audience receives that Claudius is guilty. And the insertion of this material here implies that the behavior of Claudius at the " Mouse-trap " was not such as to attract the attention of one who was not made alert by knowing what to look for. In fact, Horatio nowhere expresses himself as positive of the king's guilt. And I think that Hamlet himself is convinced more by the effect of Claudius' tremendous effort not to betray himself than by any outward action of moment.

III. iv. 24. Hamlet kills Polonius under the im-pression that it is the king who is behind the arras.

During the following conversation Hamlet con-vinces himself that the queen has had no part in or knowledge of the murder of her husband.

It has already been suggested that in the fit of desperation due to his bungling management of the " Mouse-trap," Hamlet simply gives up, permitting himself to be drawn away to England without opposi-tion. But moods seldom are of long duration. Hamlet soon comes to himself again. With startling energy he grasps the first opportunity to come back to work out his revenge.

In the structural scheme of this play there are "two mighty opposites," Hamlet, and Claudius. Hamlet is the motive power in the first half. It is he who receives the information from the ghost, he meditates revenge, he engages the players, he plans and carries out the "Mouse-trap." The latter may be considered the turning-point of the drama. Henceforth it is Claudius who furnishes the motive power. He meditates revenge also. He plans the English trip. He mollifies Laertes. He plans the duel and prepares the poisoned cup.

Act IV. One should not fail to recognize the great dramatic skill displayed in the management of the material contained in this act. During most of the act Hamlet, the principal actor of the play, is absent. It would be a difficult task to prevent a let-down in the interest under such circumstances, to prevent the impression of an interruption during the progress of the act. Yet Hamlet must be away in order to bring about the climax.

Shakespeare has managed the difficulty by skilfully relating the character of Laertes to that of Hamlet. Note the similarity of situation. Laertes appears. His father has been murdered. He does not know all the details, but he is bent on revenge. And so we may say that in many respects his situation is like Hamlet's. At any rate there is enough to suggest Hamlet and his story even while we are listening to the story of Laertes. And this helps us to keep Hamlet in mind while he is really absent.

Furthermore, the character of Laertes is in many

respects the exact opposite to Hamlet's. Laertes goes headlong without sufficiently making sure of his ground. He will act first and consider later, just the opposite of Hamlet's mode of procedure. Laertes is prompt to act, to take whatever turns up and use it to his advantage without stopping to think of the consequences. But in Claudius he has found a shrewder man than himself, one who is able to pull the wool over his eyes. Instead of similarity Shakespeare is here making use of contrast. Laertes is in more ways than one contrasted with Hamlet. The more we analyze the characters of the two men the more firmly convinced we feel that if Hamlet had had Laertes' characteristics combined with his own he would have made a better success; or, had Laertes the characteristics of Hamlet combined with his own he would have succeeded. In other words, as we contemplate Laertes and his career we are constantly thinking of how it would be if Hamlet had gone about it in this way, or how Hamlet would have acted under such circumstances, or how different this is from the way in which Hamlet acted, etc., etc. In other words, Hamlet is kept vividly in our minds all through the act, notwithstanding the fact that he is not present during the greater part of it.

The usual reader and critic of *Hamlet* fails to attach the proper significance to the character of the king. To be sure, he is not made so prominent as Hamlet. On the other hand, he is not such an insignificant figure as is implied by the popular proverb, " Hamlet with Hamlet left out." Hamlet speaks of himself and the king as two mighty opposites. The phrase is apt. The king is a formidable antagonist, one of keen intellect and ripe judgment. And the more we study his behavior the more thoroughly we understand how carefully Shakespeare has worked out every detail of his character.

IV. iii. 4. Claudius cites the love of the common people as a reason for not taking an open course against Hamlet. Note in the conduct of Laertes how helpful this resource might have been to Hamlet had he availed himself of it.

IV. iv. The Fortinbras thread of the story, though very slender and inconspicuous, has, however, a very important mission to fulfil. In the opening scenes of the play it helps to give an opportunity for the insertion of some of the correlative material of the introduction. Here its value is a little greater. Hamlet is on his way to England while still under the sway of the fit of despondency that followed the failure of the " Mouse-trap." Here, however, he sees a group of common people willing to fight to the last moment, lay down their lives if need be, fighting for a mere point of honor rather than for a mere plot of ground that has no intrinsic value. Hamlet falls to self-comparison. As a result of this he is spurred back to his earlier mood and swiftly emerges from the despondency that has lately overtaken him.

And, again, in the last act, Fortinbras and his army appear. Their value at the end is merely mechanical. There are several dead bodies on the stage. There was no drop curtain in those days, so far as we know, by which this closing scene could be immediately screened from the audience. Shakespeare cleverly disposes of the dead bodies by introducing Fortinbras and his army. His soldiers convert their shields into stretchers, thrust their spears through the rings in the sides, and walk off with the corpses to the stately strains of a funeral march. Critics have been known to object to these last lines of *Hamlet* on the score that the play is already finished, and that they therefore constitute an anti-climax. To be sure, the play is actually finished. In a modern presentation the curtain could very easily be dropped and the closing passage effectively omitted. But, to the Elizabethans, this clever device for overcoming one of the stage difficulties at the end must have appealed as an element of merit.

IV. v. 121, etc. Note the calm, dignified behavior of the king. There is not an atom of fear in his make-up. He is thoroughly self-possessed. This is another instance of his firm behavior very like that which followed the presentation of the " Mouse-trap " where he showed such marvelous self-control. The king displays his skill in managing Laertes in the conversation that follows.

IV. vi. 12. From the letter received by Horatio we learn what has happened to Hamlet after his meeting with the army of Fortinbras. How much more smoothly the story proceeds with this information conveyed in this way than would have been the case had a scene been written in which the events regarding the pirate attack had been actually dramatized! Furthermore, it would have interrupted the general effect of Laertes as a contrast to Hamlet, as suggested above. Note that this letter shows that Hamlet was quick to act when he was convinced that action was the proper thing. If one were to make out a list of all the places in the play where Hamlet evinces

the power of sudden action there would be little likelihood of believing even for a moment that the key
to his character is inaction and procrastination.

IV. vii. The fact that in this scene Laertes is hand
and glove with Claudius is a vivid testimonial of the
latter's cleverness in dealing with the hot-headed
young man.

IV. vii. 65. Claudius has already murdered his
brother in a secret manner so skilfully planned that
it was suspected by no one till revealed to Hamlet by
supernatural means. In the suggestion here he is
merely falling back upon the weapon with which he
is most familiar.

IV. vii. 143. The Italians were very skilful in ad-
ministering poison, and invented many ingenious ways
for its conveyance. In fact, secret poisoning was
called, in England, the Italian crime. And Englishmen abhorred it as the worst. To murder a man in
cold blood with a sword was to them a less heinous
crime than to murder a man by poison. Hence there
is point in portraying Laertes as a man who not only
would resort to such means but who would also actually carry the means with him habitually against a
chance opportunity to use it. At this point, or, rather,
before this point, there would be a little danger of too
great sympathy on the part of the audience for
Laertes, whose father has been murdered and whose
sister has gone mad. But this attributing to him of
a facility in the practice of the Italian crime robs
him immediately of all such sympathy at the very
moment when our feelings should surge back in favor
of Hamlet.

V. i. More than once I have called attention to

the fact that the Elizabethans often interjected into their plays passages that referred to contemporary conditions, even though the play had a foreign and ancient setting. Part of the dialogue of this scene between the grave-diggers has reference to a contemporary lawsuit that was quite familiar to the Elizabethan audience. Not all the references are now understood, but it is quite generally admitted that this is a comic scene much more palatable to a contemporary audience than to one of to-day.

V. i. 280. Notwithstanding what was said above relative to Hamlet's two meetings with Ophelia, we must imagine that his affection was too deep-rooted to be entirely canceled. Hamlet is here upset by the hollowness of Laertes' shallow sentiments. Remorse, too, for Ophelia's death may have been born on the instant, for the rites and ceremonies indicated that this was the funeral of a suicide even before anything was said. The situation so works upon Hamlet that for the third time in the play he suffers a momentary loss of self-control. It is while in this state of mind that he leaps into the grave to grapple with Laertes.

V. ii. The last scene is a mere carrying to a conclusion of the narrative of the end. Hamlet has fully recovered himself. He fights an honorable match and is as innocent of Laertes' death as of the fact that Laertes is plotting foully against his life. But when the truth is told him he instantly realizes that the king is back of it all. This is the situation Hamlet has been working towards since the beginning of the play. He has cornered the king at last hot-handed in crime. The poisoned sword and the cup of deadly drink are damning evidence. Hamlet does not hesitate to act a moment. And his last words to Horatio imply that one need but tell his story now with the circumstances at hand to convince posterity that his act was an act of judgment, not a murder. And this will put Claudius in the light he deserves.

(The entrance of Fortinbras at the end of the play has been commented on above.)

IV. STAGE SETTING

Until comparatively recent times the idea prevailed that the Elizabethan plays were acted upon a bare and structureless stage practically devoid of all scenic effect save that produced by the use of simple properties. By degrees this idea has vanished before a mass of inference so plausible as to be considered to all intents and purposes equivalent to proof. There is danger, however, of going too far in the opposite direction, of permitting the fancy to build a picture which is heightened beyond the limits due to justifiable inference. Let us see whether we can review within the extremes the Elizabethan presentation of Hamlet.

Consider first the following assignment of the individual scenes.

I. i. The platform without the castle.
I. ii. A room of state.
I. iii. A room in Polonius' house.
I. iv. The platform without the castle.
I. v. Another part of same.
II. i. Room in Polonius' house.
II. ii. Room in the castle.
III. i. Room in the castle.
III. ii. Hall in the castle.
III. iii. Room in the castle.

What at first sight seems to be a succession of twenty scenes is in reality but a few. The platform (1) is used three times. There is a plain in Denmark (2). And there is a churchyard scene (3). All the others, fifteen in number, are rooms, now the queen's closet, now a hall of state, in Polonius' house or in the castle. For all that, every one is an interior (4), varied, perhaps, from time to time, but essentially the same. In other words, from the standpoint of staging the twenty scenes reduce to four.

There is another point to bear in mind before we consider the staging in detail. The platform may have been provided in the form of two painted cloths, one let down at the front of the inner stage, another continuing the picture at the rear of the upper gallery. A similar painted cloth let down at the front of the inner stage would provide the plain in Denmark. Doubtless the theaters then, as to-day, possessed the materials for the general setting of an interior which with little difficulty could be adjusted to the need of the moment by a variation in the movable properties. Thus three painted cloths on rollers and one stock interior is all that is necessary in addition to movable properties to make a very good setting for *Hamlet*.

The production of the graveyard scene will be alluded to later.

If the inference suggested by the last act of *The Merchant of Venice* be correct, we may imagine that the canvas covering of the theater, or the side curtains, were drawn at the time the audience assembled. The semi-darkness would have a quieting effect, and would serve to put the spectators on the proper road to a mood suitable for the opening of the play. The curtains between the pillars supporting the heavens would be also closed. At the beginning of the play they were drawn, disclosing Francisco at his post on guard. Beyond him, on the painted cloth, is the masonry of the castle platform, and above, at the rear of the upper gallery, more walls and parapets appear.

At the end of the scene the means for producing darkness are drawn back, flooding the stage with light. Meantime the upper gallery has been closed by curtains, and the lower cloth raised. The scene that now presents itself has been set up before the play began. It is a hall of state. The stock interior has been used, elaborated as much as possible for the occasion by the introduction of properties, among which would be a throne. Inner, middle, and outer stages are all open for the accommodation of the court. At the end of this scene a painted cloth representing the wall of a simpler room might be let down, cutting off the view of the throne at the back of the stage. By the simple and easy manipulation of painted cloths the room could be easily changed from a room of state to another room, etc. And then back to the castle ramparts again. As easily would a cloth provide at the proper time for the plain in Denmark. And

another, used in V. i., would represent a graveyard.
Previous to this scene, however, the curtains would be
drawn, shutting off the inner and middle stages. A
few solid properties, such as tombstones, are brought
in, the trap in the stage floor is opened, and the grave-
diggers are ready to begin their work. At the end the
curtains are drawn again. The last-named properties
immediately removed, and the stage restored to " A
hall in the castle."

Thus it will be seen that the most elaborate setting
of the play can be put in place before the play begins
and remain practically intact during the whole performance.

V. Hamlet's Madness

This question has never had for me the interest
or importance that has so often been attached to it.
However, for form's sake it cannot be altogether
neglected. Some critics have held that Hamlet is
mad, or loses his mind during the play. Others believe that he is perfectly sane, but pretends to be
mad. While others believe that he is neither mad nor
pretending to be mad.

In the notes on the text I have tried to make it
appear that the " antic disposition " passage points
backward to the recent behavior of Hamlet and does
not imply the use of an intentional cloak of madness
in the future. And we may search in vain throughout
the remainder of the play to find an illustration of
his assumption of madness to further his own ends.
There is, however, one trivial passage where he is
trifling with Polonius by making unintelligible remarks. The remarks, however, are unintelligible

only to Polonius. The amusement of the passage lies in the fact that Hamlet plays with the idea of Polonius as to his madness, the audience being at the same time perfectly aware of the contrary. It is also interesting to note that in the earlier version of Hamlet's story which Shakespeare is supposed to have had before him, the assumption of madness on the part of Hamlet is made very plain. All this has been cut out of the present play. This is in itself evidence to me that Shakespeare did not wish it to remain.

It also seems equally plain to me that there is not the least evidence of actual madness in the play. And I shall merely suggest the principal points without discussing the matter at length.

At no place in the play does Hamlet act like a madman. After the revelation by the ghost, after the " Mouse-trap," and at Ophelia's grave Hamlet momentarily loses his self-control and acts without reason. But he soon recovers himself and realizes perfectly what he has done. His ultra excitement borders on hysterics, but no more deserves the term of madness than the weird behavior so often attributed to persons in the excitement of a fire when feather beds are carried downstairs and mirrors thrown out the window. Hamlet is guilty of no other kind of irrational action.

And what do the people in the play itself think of the matter? The idea that Hamlet is mad never seems to have occurred to Horatio, notwithstanding the fact that he feared the ghost, if it should turn out an evil spirit, might rob Hamlet of his reason. In other words, Horatio, who feared that such a thing might be, never seems to think that it actually happened. Rosencrantz and Guildenstern approach Hamlet, having been informed of and perhaps believing in his madness. They seem to leave him convinced of the contrary. Claudius, for the sole purpose of confirming Polonius' belief in the madness of Hamlet, plays the part of an eavesdropper in order to get the proof. But the only effect of the scene is to convince the king that Hamlet is not mad. Ophelia and the queen both believe him to be mad; but, as pointed out above, they base their belief upon a misapprehension of the very circumstance that gives rise to this belief.

Polonius, who misunderstands Hamlet's treatment of Ophelia, jumps to the conclusion that he must be mad. Yet Polonius is never more humorously foolish himself than when he is urging Hamlet's madness. And even he is constrained to see a little method in it.

And, as evidence from the opposite point of view, Hamlet throughout the play is extremely shrewd, giving evidence again and again of a mind under control that would be the envy of many a person who has escaped the charge altogether.

VI. The Character of Hamlet

So much has been said above relative to the character of Hamlet that there is need of no more than a few notes binding the suggestions together. It is often suggested that Hamlet is the man of inaction put into a place or situation that demands a man of action; or that he is a deliberative philosopher losing his opportunity in the procrastination of his deliberation. I cannot bring myself fully to accept either of these suggestions.

In the first place, Hamlet is to me, though a scholar,

not a philosopher. He breaks down hysterically three times. He argues about his own cowardice in a way that is evidently false. He is easily put up and down in spirits. These are not characteristics of a philosopher.

Furthermore, he is a man of prompt action who acts quickly as a result of his convictions. He accepts at once the invitation to meet the ghost. And he undertakes without a moment's hesitation the dangerous task of following it alone. He instantly seizes the opportunity to use the players in the " Mouse-trap." He sees through, or thinks he does, the treatment of Ophelia, and acts accordingly, though in violation of his inmost feelings. There is not a moment's hesitation in the murder of Polonius, whom, however, Hamlet mistakes for the king. Hamlet is quick-acting in the pirate attack. He is prompt to return to Denmark. He leaps into Ophelia's grave. He accepts the challenge of Laertes without delay. And he kills the king at last with a celerity unequaled elsewhere in the play.

What, then, is the key to Hamlet's behavior? I think that it is to be found in an adherence to the principles of absolute justice. He acts only upon a firm conviction that what he is going to do is right. He delays the main act during the first half of the play because he, like Horatio, is not fully convinced that his uncle is the murderer of his father. He fails to kill the king after the " Mouse-trap " because he is as fully convinced that to do it then will produce a wrong impression. And he kills Claudius at last because the time has come when he can do it with full justice to himself and in the eyes of all men.

CHAPTER XVIII

KING LEAR

In the preface to this volume I have called attention to the fact that it is not only impossible but also inadvisable to attempt to devise a uniform scheme according to which all of Shakespeare's plays can be studied. *Lear* does not lend itself conveniently to the method made use of, with wide variations, however, in other parts of the present volume. In taking up the study of *Lear* in the manner here set forth, I have in mind the task of offering to the student or the teacher a plan that may with advantage be followed elsewhere. It implies, however, a slightly different method of preliminary study. In the discussion of many of the other plays I have assumed a single preliminary reading of the play. Then the drama is gone through with again, with emphasis laid upon details that come up for discussion in the order in which they appear in the text. After a familiarity with the play has been gained in this way, general questions have been discussed that require for their comprehension a pretty familiar knowledge of the whole composition. Such a knowledge should in the present case be obtained before the beginning of the study of the play according to this plan.

It may not be amiss as a suggestion either to students or to teachers, to hint a little as to preliminary work necessary to the successful study of the play along the lines here set down. Let the whole play be assigned as reading for the first recitation. In the class-room the play is talked over in a miscellaneous sort of way. Perhaps it would be well to ask a student to begin by telling the story of the first scene. In my own experience I have always found that, once a start is made, there is no difficulty in keeping the class asking and answering questions. Nor do I think it makes much difference, for a time at least, what they ask about, so long as the questions are such as to show that the students have actually read the lines and have honestly been puzzled for an answer.

A general reading of the play may then be assigned a second time for the next recitation. And I should require each student to hand in a list of selected questions that involve difficult or unanswered points in the play. The questioning during this recitation may well be guided more definitely by the instructor than in the first recitation. At any rate, he can easily manage to fill up any gaps left in the first preliminary survey. Thenceforth, I should assign two or three acts to be read carefully at each recitation till the consideration of the play is ended. The whole purpose that is to be constantly borne in mind during the preliminary study is the familiarizing the student with the contents of the play as a whole.

As for the questions handed in by the students, I always study them with care at home. In fact, the questions suggested in the following chapter are the result of such lists presented in my classes in successive years. Every one of them is a question

actually asked by a student, most of them many
times.

1. *What has happened before the beginning of the
play?*—In the discussion of this question it would be
well to point out the fact that the preliminary portion
of this play has not been worked out by the author
with anything like the care that the preliminary portion of, for instance, *Macbeth,* has been worked out.
For instance, Lear is eccentric to the point of madness. Do we know how long this has been true of
him? How many people in the play know of it? The
sisters seem to be the only persons who are familiar
with the fact and take advantage of it. How came
it that no one else shared their attitude?

What is the situation of Edmund? He has been
"out" nine years. Yet he seems to be perfectly
familiar with every detail of British court life. Was
he kept well-informed during his absence? If so, by
whom? Do his father, and others, behave themselves
towards Edmund as they should, considering his origin
and his absence from the country? Is he made sufficiently attractive to account for his affair with the
princess later in the play?

In the opening lines Kent says that he always
thought the king to be partial to Albany. How,
then, account for his equal division of the kingdom?
Does the remainder of the play bear out Kent's
suggestion? How about the impression that seems
natural, to wit, that Lear is really partial to Cordelia?

Gloucester has often in the past blushed to acknowledge the origin of Edmund, yet in this play he
seems to give credence to what he says even against

Edgar. And in this respect there seems to be not the least hesitation on the part of Gloucester.

Towards the end of the first scene Cordelia expresses her perfect familiarity with the wolfish character of her sisters. Yet Kent, who seems to understand Cordelia and Lear so well, gives no evidence of knowing the truth about the other two sisters. Have they ever before given evidence of such characteristics? If not, is it possible for them to have become such accomplished villains on the spur of the moment? If they were always thus, would it be possible for them to keep the knowledge of their characters away from every one but their sister Cordelia? And if she actually knew what was in store for her father as a result of putting himself completely under their dominion, would she, if she really loved her father, have taken a course that in the end was bound to remove herself, his only protector, entirely from the scene of action?

The discussion of these and similar questions will reveal the fact that Shakespeare has not worked over the material concerned in the preliminary details of the play with his customary care.

2. *Tell the Lear Story.*—Also tell the Gloucester story. Try to pick out the essential points of each. Show how one is the reflection of the other. The latter serves to break up the strain of continuous attention to such a terrible tale, at the same time preventing too great an interruption, too great an impression of the lack of continuity.

Note that the sub-plot is very like the main plot in many respects, and sufficiently different in others to enable the author to make use of the effect of

constrast. (Refer to the discussion of the fourth act
of *Hamlet* for a note on the dramatic effect of
contrast.) Note the suspicious quality of both Lear
and Gloucester. Compare in this respect with the
unsuspicious character of Othello. Note also that
there is a deliberate attempt to maltreat Lear by his
daughters for selfish motives. The same attempt is
made against Gloucester by his son. Lear is partly
culpable because he is so unjustly headstrong.
Gloucester is partly culpable because of his unsus-
piciousness, which leads him to give credence to what
Edmund says against Edgar. Lear's suffering is mental and more terrible than Gloucester's, which is
mainly physical.

3. *Work out the idea of nemesis.*—1. Upon Lear
for his treatment of Cordelia. This is in a measure
justified, for he has treated her with great injustice.
The means of punishing him for this treatment of his
daughter is the combined attack upon his liberties by
Goneril and Regan. They, however, visit him with
so much more punishment than he deserves that we
find: 2. Nemesis deserved by Goneril and Regan.
3. Punishment also falls upon Gloucester because of
his treatment of Edgar. His son Edmund is the
means of effecting this. But he also wreaks far
greater punishment than Gloucester deserves, which
in turn lays him open to punishment. 4. Therefore nemesis falls upon Edmund.

4. *Discuss the character of Lear.*—The following
suggestions may prove helpful:

Regarding his mental condition at the beginning
of the play: In the opening situation we find Lear's
insistence upon trifles emphasized. The speeches re-

quired by his daughters are mere forms. He had already definitely made the division of the kingdom. Kent and Gloucester both seem to know this quality of the king. We find, also, that he is getting old and tired of ruling. Is there also evidence that he is getting incapable of ruling? He wants the pleasure of the title without the responsibility. He really loves all three of his daughters in his own tempestuous way. He is shrewd enough to divide his kingdom equally lest one gobble up another's share. Yet he is slowly losing his mind and knows it, therefore he would put his kingdom into better hands.

As proof of the latter assertion one might say:—

Lear is absurdly fond of childish display, and magnifies trifles, as in the requiring of his daughters' praise, and the following treatment of Cordelia.

His inability to fully comprehend the situation when Kent puts it to him.

He does not realize that he has given away all his power, but immediately exercises the royal prerogative which he has discarded, in the banishment of Kent, and later threatens to take back what he has given away. (It should not be forgotten that the Elizabethan audience was familiar with a model of the correct kind of abdication in the action of Charles the Fifth of Spain.)

The surprise of France that Lear has gone to such an extreme over so small a matter.

The attitude of Goneril and Regan. " How full of changes his life is." " 'Tis the infirmity of his age." " The unruly waywardness that infirm and choleric years bring with them." Gloucester speaks of

Lear's dotage, and treats him generally as if he were in his second childhood.

Lear seems to realize the fact himself. "Oh, let me not be mad, not mad," he exclaims.

His erratic behavior lends countenance to the charge.

What is the character of Lear in act II.? In act I. he has cursed Goneril and her issue, and threatens to assume again the shape that she thinks he has cast off forever. Then he arrives, bent on seeing Regan. He abuses Gloucester because he brings the message that the duke and the duchess cannot see him. In the next breath, however, Lear tries to apologize for them, but he is hardly able to excuse their conduct.

As a matter of fact, this act has brought the king to the verge of distraction. He makes an effort to control himself, but breaks down at the end and leaves wildly in a rage. He has sworn that he will never go back to Goneril, yet he does soon go unheroically back to her as the lesser of two evils, because Regan has cut his following down to twenty-five retainers. It is pathetic to note that when Lear is charged with dotage he does not deny the charge.

The student should ponder carefully the meaning of every detail of Lear's behavior in this act. Does he act like a hero, or like a weakling, or like a strong man going to pieces?

One may say that the development of Lear's character ends with the heath scene. For a while he is mad. Then he merely recovers his mind sufficiently at the end to enable him to die in peace.

5. Study the characters of Goneril and Regan.—
Are they real people or merely types of wickedness?
Are the sisters essentially different? that is, are they
really individuals? The student may help himself to
answer these questions by canvassing his mind and
memory to see whether he has had difficulty in keeping the sisters and their acts apart. For instance, is
it Goneril or Regan who makes the first cut in the
number of Lear's followers? Was this or that cruel
remark made by one or the other?

6. Study the character of Cordelia.—What does
she know of Goneril and Regan at the start? What
does she know of her father's condition? How does she
behave herself in act I.? What does Kent think of her
behavior? What does France think of it? What does
Lear think of it? What do you think of it? Had
there been any real kindness in her heart would she
have taken a course knowingly that turned her doting
father over to the clutches of a pair of wolves, and, at
the same time, removed herself, the only one on whom
he could depend for help? And yet she virtually acknowledges that this is what she does. At the end
of the play she appears as a saint come to rescue her
father. How do you account for the change? Is there
any evidence that Shakespeare appreciated the fact
that Cordelia at the end is merely trying to make an
effort to deliver her father from the terrible situation
into which he has been thrust as a result of her own
pig-headedness in the first act?

These questions imply a view of Cordelia's character
that is not usually taken. To be sure, she is one of the
minor characters, introduced for the mere sake of the
plot, and not carefully worked out. Such characters

should never be scanned too carefully. Under such circumstances we should not be impelled to scrutinize her character with the same seriousness that one would analyze the actions of a main character. Yet she is, on the other hand, important enough to justify one's looking at her character with a sufficient degree of care.

It is hard to escape the conclusion that Cordelia is brutally perverse in the maintenance of her pride in act I. Nor can she be excused on the score of ignorance. She says plainly that she understands her father's condition and the likely future attitude of her sisters. Rather than speak a little harmless flattery to please her old and failing parent she submits to banishment, disappoints him, contributes to the triumph of her sisters, brings her husband no dower, turns her sisters loose upon her father, and puts it out of her own power to help him. Nor is it possible to reconcile this behavior with the loveliness of her character in act V. Had she behaved herself in the beginning as she does at the end there would have been no tragedy in the life of Lear. Cordelia is what we might call a thoroughly plot-ridden character.

7. *What of the character of Albany?*—Is he another plot-ridden character? Early in the play he is utterly unable to assert himself in the presence of his wife. Later he manifests the opposite quality. What has occasioned the change? What would have been the result had he displayed the characteristics at the beginning that he is able to display at the end? Is it fair to say that, had he asserted himself at the beginning of the play, there would have been no tragedy, and that there is no sufficient reason for his not doing so?

8. *The character of Kent.*—Find passages to show that he is shrewd, courageous, foolish. Is he a help or a hindrance to Lear? Kent's character, on the whole, seems inconsistent, as is implied by the above questions relative to his being both shrewd and foolish. He comprehends the foibles of the king and acts upon them. Yet he is himself just as erratic as the king he criticises so adversely. He brings trouble upon Lear by his own actions when all indications point to the fact that he is a shrewd enough man to know better.

9. *The character of Gloucester* introduces some difficulties. How does he really feel towards Edmund and towards Edgar? Why does he place such implicit trust in Edmund? What becomes of the plot he overhears to kill the king? Does he deserve his punishment?

10. *The character of Edmund.*—Why do not others know him better? What motives prompt his wickedness? Has he been a villain before, or has he become an accomplished villain all at once, without training? Yet, if he had had plenty of training how happens it that no one suspects him of being otherwise than he seems? In the main, he is rather blundering in his plotting, and succeeds rather by accident. Compare in this respect with the skilful plots laid by Iago.

11. *The fool.*—Before one attempts to make up his mind as to the character of the fool one should consider just what an Elizabethan fool was and what privileges his station implied. The fools were household servants whose purpose was to make fun for their masters. In order to give them free rein they were considered immune from punishment under ordinary

circumstances, and at liberty to speak their minds freely without fear of consequences. Hence, Lear's threat to have the fool whipped is equivalent to saying that the king has almost forgotten what is due to a fool. And it will be noted throughout that the fool makes remarks, without the least hesitation, that no one else would have dared to make in the presence of the tempestuous king.

The question arises as to whether this fool is like other fools. He is, indeed, much like the other fools of Shakespeare; but note that he only speaks, as a rule, to Lear himself, and his words are generally of a nature to " rub in " the mistakes of Lear.

Do the moments at which he acts produce a peculiar effect? Why does he drop out in the middle of the play? Does the fool stand for anything in particular?

The answer to the last question involves the enigma of the fool—that is, if there be any enigma of the fool. It has been ingeniously suggested that the fool represents in embodied form the conscience of Lear. If this be so, one wonders at the fact that Lear's conscience has no effect upon him. When a person acts as if he were unaffected by a conscience we generally say that he has no conscience. Perhaps what is really meant is that the fool represents what would have been Lear's conscience if he had had one. This would, perhaps, explain the fact that he speaks only to Lear and that there is no more of him when Lear has lost his mind.

I think, however, that there may be another explanation of the function of the fool. Recall the tempestuous character of the king. We are always looking for an explosion greater than the one before. Now the fool throughout is saying things that would cause such an outbreak of temper had they been said by any one else in the play. It is only because they originate with the fool that Lear is able to control himself. Yet we are constantly wondering how long the king will be able to exercise this slender self-control which hangs by such a trifling thread. The behavior of the fool, then, seems to me to be intended to produce the effect of lighted matches left carelessly in the neighborhood of gunpowder. It may go off at any moment. If it escapes an accidental ignition this time it may not the next. At any rate there is sure to be an explosion some time. Just when will it come? And what will it bring with it?

The great moment comes on the heath. And after this, there being no further need of the fool, he does not appear again.

12. Perhaps it would not be amiss at the conclusion of this set of questions to say a word or two as to the degree of cruelty displayed in the story. Though I have no sympathy with the suggestion, it has been suggested that the degree of cruelty displayed in *Titus Andronicus* is sufficient to throw doubt upon its Shakespearian origin. If this were true, one might use the same line of argument in regard to *Lear*. The truth, however, is that neither play is so cruel as it seems when read in the closet. I do not mean to say that they are not hard, stern stories, almost too repulsive to read, according to our modern standards. I merely mean that, from the Elizabethan point of view, they were not so revoltingly cruel as they are to us.

That was a cruel age. People went habitually armed. They were used to bloodshed. It was a part of the education of the young women of the family to learn to dress and care for wounds. I imagine that an Elizabethan woman who had never seen a violent death would be as rare as a woman to-day who had never seen a horse mistreated in the streets. Death was the penalty for many petty crimes. People dressed in their best and made a holiday occasion of a public execution. To some people to-day football is a brutal sport, brutal enough by nature to warrant association with bull-fighting. But this is a humorous idea to college students or to players on the team. I mean to imply that we may look upon the brutality of these plays as excessive, while the Elizabethans looked upon it as normal. Football is a good hard game for men, it is not tiddlety-winks. So the Elizabethans would look upon *Lear* and *Titus* as hard, stern stories, but not to be judged adversely because either of them had gone too far.

And there is another point to be borne in mind. How was this brutality enacted on the stage? Consult your own feelings for a moment. Suppose you read in the paper that A plunged a knife into B's heart. Are your feelings the same as they would be if you had stood at A's elbow at the moment? One might faint at the latter situation, but hardly over the newspaper account.

Now what is the situation in the theater? Does not the manner of presentation have something to do with the result, something to do with the effect produced, sufficient to take the edge off the cruelty, so to speak? The cruelest act in *Lear* is the gouging out of Gloucester's eyes. But they are not really gouged out on the stage. He turns his back at the moment, and does not let the audience see his face plainly again till he enters blindfolded. It is a hard act, to be sure, and meant to be so taken. But the effect on the stage is nothing to the real deed. And if an effort were made to suddenly apply an artificial mask, or something that would show the vacant bloody sockets in their repulsiveness the device would be considered clap-trap and inartistic. Everything diminishes in effect upon the stage. Therefore, in order to make something on the stage seem cruel, it must be designed as very cruel.

Take the instance in *Titus* where the arms of Lavinia are cut off. This horrible mutilation of her body is not real. Lavinia wore his arms throughout the play. How was it staged? I do not know. But I can guess several ways. The boy who acted the part may have kept his arms behind him. Not being seen, they were imagined gone. I think it more likely that he wore gloves. There is some reason to believe that there was a conventional color that in those days stood for invisibility. Doubtless Ariel wears a cloak of such material in certain parts of *The Tempest*. So here, Lavinia may have worn gloves to the elbow of this material, and the audience would have assumed that this was a mere device meant to suggest that there was nothing to be seen below the elbow. However it was done, we may be sure that the actual presentation conveyed far less of the repulsive element than we are prone to imagine as accompanying the actual deed.

CHAPTER XIX

MACBETH

I. Introductory

THE state of the original text of *Macbeth* is so chaotic that editors have encountered great difficulties in bringing it to its present state of comparative perfection. There are still inconsistencies and contradictions remaining. This state of affairs should be borne in mind at several points of the play. It is also thought that the play was either written in collaboration, or finished by another hand. (See Introduction, The Tudor Edition.)

II. Notes on the Text

I. i. This scene serves to forecast the weird and serious tone of the drama, and suggests, by coming first, how important a part the witches will play in the development.

This scene, and other similar scenes to follow, were probably acted on a partly darkened stage. How was this managed in the open Elizabethan playhouse? (See chapter on *The Merchant of Venice*.)

I. ii. Many editors believe this scene not written by Shakespeare. The meter is slovenly and the sergeant's speech bombastic and inconsistent. I am inclined to think that Shakespeare worked with a collaborator and that he fashioned in detail only the parts of the two Macbeths. (See below.) Considering the loose Elizabethan practice, however, it is hardly justifiable to assume mere carelessness of style to be a good reason for rejecting a passage as Shakespeare's.

I. ii. 52. Note that subsequently Macbeth must know that Cawdor is not what he calls him in I. iii. 73, " a prosperous gentleman."

I. iii. Return to the darkness of the first scene. Perhaps the curtains are partly drawn during the progress of the scene, lightening it towards the end.

I. iii. 38. " So foul and fair a day." In spite of the different explanations that have been offered concerning this passage, it is altogether of no moment. Macbeth's part was taken by the principal actor of the company. This is his first entrance, a moment always accompanied by some emotion, if not actual applause. Naturally the first few lines spoken during this period are of little importance. If the audience missed them altogether, nothing significant would be lost. The passage needs no special explanation.

Note that only two of the speeches made by the witches are prophetical. Macbeth is already Thane of Glamis.

It is my belief that Macbeth, at the opening of the play, is an honest, high-minded man outwardly, who has as yet entertained no ideas of guilt. Everything in the play, with one possible but not probable exception, bears this conception out. Hence the degree of emphasis laid on the subject.

I. iii. 51. Banquo calls attention to the fact that Macbeth starts. And an innocent Macbeth should start. The thought that he may be king has doubtless been often in his mind, as it has in his wife's, and in the minds of the people throughout Scotland generally. There is a good chance of his becoming king in the natural course of events without the necessity of crime. The crown did not always go in direct succession—for instance, see *Hamlet*. The two possible successors are Malcolm and Macbeth. One is young, inexperienced, and keeping away from the battlefield when he should be making his reputation. Yet he has the direct blood claim. The other, not so near in blood, is older, experienced, and at present appearing as the savior of his country from the double danger of foreign invasion and domestic insurrection. Banquo does not speak as if he believed the possibility of Macbeth's succession as at all untenable. It is hardly possible that Macbeth, even had he been the soul of honor, would have escaped the hope. Now he hears supernatural creatures in whom he believes, declare the future fulfilment of his desires. Of course he starts. And there is no reason to believe it a guilty start.

He is immediately cast into a brown study. He is not planning his crimes. He is merely wondering how it will all come about. He has no doubt of the fact.

I. iii. 73. Macbeth speaks of Cawdor whom he has just overthrown in battle as " a prosperous gentleman." (See note on I. iii.) Macbeth knew better. The messengers knew that he knew better. There is no point in his assertion. It cannot be explained. It is mere contradiction. It may be due to a corruption in the text; or to careless collaboration; or to a change of plan on the part of Shakespeare while working. It is time wasted to puzzle over it.

Note that, throughout, Banquo is not so superstitious as Macbeth. Had Macbeth been less so, he might have escaped his ruin. (See note on V. v. 43.)

I. iii. 104. Ross and Angus have come to give Macbeth an "earnest." This word implies that something much greater is to follow. What does Macbeth think it is? He believes, thanks to the witches, that he will be king. The present king's support in favor of his succession will probably make it possible. Is this the way chance will crown him? Does he not believe that this is what the messengers refer to? Do they think so themselves?

I. iii. 120. That trusted home: means, if you trust too implicitly to what the witches have said you may be led into bringing about by bad means what you now believe will come about naturally. Note, also, that it is Banquo, the most upright man in the play, who first puts the idea of possible wrong-doing in the future into the mind of Macbeth.

I. iii. 127-142. Macbeth believes in the outcome. Yet he is unable to see how it will come about. He knows that witches are considered malignant beings; yet they cannot be bad in the present instance, because what they have foretold has turned out true, in part, at least. (Suggestion in line 134 means temptation.) Yet, on the other hand, they cannot be altogether good, else he would not be so upset by the idea of temptation that Banquo has put into his head. A man already guilty in thought would not be so overcome by the idea of his possible enactment of a crime. The very thought of such a thing (line 139) is repugnant to him in the extreme. He will not even contemplate such a course (line 143). The meaning of the line is: " If chance, that is, fate, will have me king, fate must bring it about, not I. And this may be (line 147), as one can never tell what will happen." And immediately Macbeth has disclaimed any personal responsibility he begins to feel relieved.

I. iv. This is the scene in which Duncan appoints his son Malcolm the Prince of Cumberland. This title implied that he would be the successor to the crown. Let us analyze the situation.

Sufficient attention, it seems to me, has not been given in the modern discussion or staging of this scene. The announcement is a fearful slap in Macbeth's face, whom every one has considered as a possible successor to the crown. Macbeth is coming home in triumph. Why should the *kindly* Duncan select this public moment of all others to dash Macbeth's hopes forever? The action is so unlike the nature of the gentle king that it requires a justification—at least, an explanation. Duncan has met Macbeth with a warm welcome. His mouth has outrun itself in fashioning extravagant expressions of gratitude. The most he can do is too little for Macbeth's deserts. But this is all rhetorical flourish. He does not mean a word of it literally. Macbeth, however, who remembers the witches' prophecies and the " earnest," is now taking all this in a literal sense. Perhaps Banquo and the others share this impression with him. Instead of relegating this to a mere scene in front of a middle drop as is so often done nowadays it should be carefully staged. The eyes of the many persons present turn towards Macbeth as their ears drink in the promises of the king. Gradually positions shift, more people grouping themselves about Macbeth, the successor, than about Malcolm, whose youth and inexpericuce have caused him to be passed over.

This, however, is all due to a mistake. Duncan suddenly realizes what is happening. Lest it be too late to correct it to-morrow he determines to correct it now. The gist of what he says is this: Macbeth is worthy of everything I can do within reason. But do not misunderstand me. I intend my son to succeed me. Therefore I appoint him the Prince of Cumberland.

There is a splendid opportunity for stage effect in this sudden opposite turn of affairs.

I. iv. 48. "That is a step." Macbeth means that it now looks as if the witches' prophecy could not possibly come true. Or else, if it does, it will only come true by his taking some means to overcome this new obstacle. That is what Banquo suggested. Macbeth is afraid even to think of what this implies. This is certainly not the line of thought of a man already hardened to the contemplation of crime.

I. v. Lady Macbeth is reading a letter. Throughout the play we discover that husband and wife are very close together. (Search the play throughout for additional proofs of this assertion.) In the first part of the play he reports everything to her. She knows his character through and through. Her speech, which follows the text of the letter in this scene, is a soliloquy. Hence there is no reason for her not speaking the truth.

She says that Macbeth is too full of the milk of human kindness. Modern readers frequently misunderstand kindness to mean sympathy, or tenderheartedness. In this line the word is used in its old sense of naturalness—as we have it in the Biblical phrase "the kindly fruits of the earth." Human kindness, then, is equivalent to, inherent qualities of human beings. Milk implies soft, or weak, with a touch of disapproval, perhaps not quite so strong as contempt. The sense of the phrase is almost opposite to that implied as a rule when it is quoted in modern speech. The attribute implied is anything but complimentary, even less so on the lips of such a stern woman as Lady Macbeth.

Furthermore, she says positively that, though ambitious, her husband would achieve his desires by holy means. We must at least acknowledge that if Macbeth entertained criminal intents at this time his wife was ignorant of the fact. But she could not possibly be ignorant. And she immediately voices (line 23) the fatal defect of his character—he would profit by the wrong-doing of others. It is upon that that she depends. If he will but put the management of this great business into her hands for her to despatch all will be well. This soliloquy alone is sufficient to outline Macbeth's character at the beginning of the play.

I. v. 63. If Macbeth were already a guilty man at heart his wife would not find it necessary to coax him not to show in his face that such ideas are new to him. She would not find it necessary to impress upon him the fact that his natural behavior was altogether inconsistent with a career of crime. If, perchance, she were misjudging him he would seize this opportunity to make an explanation. He does not, because she is right.

I. v. 72. "We will speak further." Does this

conversation ever take place? On or off the stage? When and where?

I. vi. This is a division scene. During the interval Lady Macbeth has talked with her husband. (See above, line 72.) She has persuaded him, as she thinks, to follow her lead, and to do the deed she has suggested. Doubtless she found the task difficult to accomplish. At the opening of scene vii. Macbeth is still in this mood, but he is at the threshold of reaction, and soon drifts back to a more honorable state of mind.

I. vii. See above. Macbeth for a moment has given up to his worse nature. He soon begins to draw back. At first his objections are due to physical fear of the consequences. Then his thoughts take a higher turn and he objects upon moral grounds. At last he resolves not to do the deed at all.

I. vii. 28. At the entrance of his wife he tells her of his change of mind. This, to her, is the milk of human kindness in his nature asserting itself. She realizes that her task of persuasion is all to be done over again. She begins by irritating him with the charge of cowardice.

I. vii. 48. Lady Macbeth says that he broke the enterprise to her. Evidently he did not. The passage, therefore, is hard to explain.

In the first place, it may be due to a corruption of the text.

Or, she may not be telling the truth, trusting to his excitement to prompt him to overlook the fact, hoping it will lead him to fall in with the notion that he is drawing back from something that he really did propose.

Or, what I believe is more likely, in the off-stage conversation (see I. v. 72) she may have insinuated her ideas to him so skilfully that he did in reality actually phrase them first though she virtually proposed them.

In other words, the passage may or may not be construed in accordance with the view here set down of Macbeth's character. If the latter interpretation is assumed we should remember that this single couplet is opposed to many and frequent indications of the contrary. This fact robs it of its value.

One reason why I am so insistent on this view of Macbeth's character is that it rounds out the picture of his personality so much better than any other conception, and is better dramatic construction. There are evidences that Shakespeare has worked out the character of Macbeth carefully, both before and after the play begins. Later in the play Macbeth says there was a time when his senses would have cooled to hear a night-shriek. I think that Shakespeare conceived Macbeth as one of those persons who have a great repugnance to physical suffering. He had, at first, for instance, to steel himself against the horrible sights of a battlefield. But the training of war had gradually made him callous to bloodshed. He had undergone the change that so many sensitive surgeons have gone through.

Later in life he goes through the same process in regard to moral wrong. The whole of the change is included in the present play. It takes up the history at the very beginning of the change, not after it has already progressed to a considerable degree, and carries him on relentlessly to the end.

At the end of this scene Macbeth is once more persuaded to carry out his wife's plans.

A preliminary word as to the character of Lady Macbeth: Remember that in Elizabethan times her part was taken by a boy. Not until the time of Mrs. Siddons was her part looked upon as the principal part of the play. We should not lose sight of the fact that she is to be dominated by her husband so far as the stage presentation goes. Her character is simple, and not beyond the immature acting of a boy.

At first she is painted as a stern, ambitious woman, and one who is capable of shrewd character analysis. She is absolutely unscrupulous, and willing to do anything to urge her husband to a great crime. She is also tactful, and able to see quickly the possibilities of a new situation. On the other hand, she is not a monster. She has tender feelings regarding her child. She is affected by the similarity of the king to her father. She is as ambitious for her husband as for herself. Yet she is not able to continue under the strain indefinitely. (See II. iii. 131, the discussion as to whether Lady Macbeth faints or not.) And she ends with utter collapse in the sleep-walking scene. This shows that, though she can commit a crime, she cannot do so without compunction, as her more callous husband learns to do before the end of the play.

Search for passages throughout the play illustrative of the above characteristics.

II. ii. 1. What is the antecedent of "that"? Is it drink? or merely the situation? That which has demanded that the grooms be drugged has demanded that I be bold?

This scene involves the time of the murder. II. iii.

59, etc., implies that there was a terrible storm at the time. Yet Lady Macbeth could hear the owls and the crickets, sounds not usually very prominent in a storm. In fact, a stage storm at this point ruins the effect and was not intended. Furthermore, violent noise here ruins the effect of the subsequent knocking on the gate. (See De Quincey's essay on this subject.)

Yet the contradiction implied by II. iii. 58, etc., is not a blemish, or something to be condoned. It is an intentional stage device. During this scene the audience gets all the advantageous effect of weird, uncanny silence and soft sounds. These are interrupted with tremendous effect by the knocking on the gate which brings the audience back to the every-day life they have left shortly before. Later, when reference is made to a terrible storm, Shakespeare was merely making use of the contemporary belief that a storm accompanied a great crime. The greater the storm the greater the crime, and *vice versa*.

II. ii. 53. "Give me the daggers." This should not be uttered too dramatically. All is hushed and quiet. If Lady Macbeth were to assume a bombastic air of superiority over her husband she would ruin the effect, as most actresses I have seen do. Yet the task must be done, and by her. She should act as if she sympathized with her husband, yet is able to do, though reluctantly, that which he has not been quite equal to.

II. ii. 56. It is often suggested that Lady Macbeth's pun on guilt and gild implies a grotesque touch of humor. Any one who is familiar with Elizabethan conditions would be inclined to deny the above assertion.   In fact, the Elizabethan attitude towards puns was altogether different from ours.

In our day and generation we either laugh at or with a punster.   The possibility of a laugh is assumed. Three hundred years ago the laugh was accidental.

The vocabulary was rapidly increasing.   A good punster needed a full command of the vocabulary, and a ready memory that could instantly recall all the words of similar sound, though of different meaning.   The ability to do so excited admiration rather than mirth.   The Elizabethan attitude towards a punster was like our attitude towards a sleight-of-hand juggler.   A funny piece of jugglery makes us laugh, but one that is not funny arouses our admiration for the skill displayed and the juggler's control over his muscles.

Hardly any one would discover a touch of humor in the repeated puns uttered by the dying Gaunt in *Richard the Second.*   The dexterity displayed by them merely suggests that, though dying, the great statesman is still in full possession of all his senses. Else he would not be able to pun.   So here.   Lady Macbeth is sufficiently cool and self-controlled to pun. There is no question of humor.

Why is the knocking on the gate of the castle introduced?

Compare its effect following a violent stage storm with its effect under the conditions of the setting suggested above.

Note how many details of this scene are recalled in the sleep-walking scene.

II. iii.   The porter's speeches were comic to the

Elizabethans. People of that day demanded a certain mingling of the comic element with the most tragic themes. This was commoner in the days of the Miracle Plays; almost intolerable to-day. It was more frequent in the plays of other Elizabethan dramatists than in the plays of Shakespeare.

II. iii. 24. Enter Macduff. In the structure of this play Macduff is the opposite of Macbeth. He is the second main character, for the structure is like that of *Othello* and *Hamlet*. Yet, in the development of the play, the character and the function of Macduff are so slighted that one may easily miss the significance of his part. It is not possible to account for this neglect. Perhaps it is due to the corrupt condition of the text; perhaps to the mediocre work of a collaborator; perhaps to the fact that the play was either not quite finished, or finished hurriedly without actually being completed.

II. iii. 69. Imagine the strain on the Macbeths while they are waiting the discovery of the murder, and its effect, especially upon Lady Macbeth.

II. iii. 131. Does Lady Macbeth faint or pretend to faint?

It has been urged that Lady Macbeth pretends to faint because she can in this way distract attention from her husband. Heretofore her presence has been the only sufficient control over him. To say the least, it would be unwise of her to withdraw this control when at the most it would only serve as a momentary distraction.

It has been suggested that Lady Macbeth pretends to faint in order to convince others of her horror of the murder. This is slightly more plausible than the above. Still, she must face the risk of leaving her husband unassisted.

There is, however, a still more plausible explanation. Macbeth's murder of the grooms, which was not in the original plan, was a blunder from all points of view. Lady Macbeth realizes this fact and is horror-stricken. But all her wits are about her. Macbeth's extemporaneous attempt to justify himself (line 114, etc.) is a stroke of genius on his part. It is very convincing and genuine. Lady Macbeth immediately realizes that he has at last found himself able to rise fully to the occasion. The milk of human kindness, which she formerly deplored, is overcome forever. He can now take care of himself. He no longer needs her assistance. A great wave of relief sweeps over her. It is the last straw. Her endurance snaps. And she really faints.

Note that the sons of the king, immediately recognizing foul play, resolve to fly. There is no indication that they at once suspected Macbeth more than another, or others. And Malcolm appeared almost as a coward at the opening of the play.

II. iv. Enter an old man. In the Elizabethan plays such a nameless character usually indicates public opinion. The "old man" here implies that suspicion has begun to get abroad in general, rather than harboring in one particular person's breast.

Macduff suggests that the sons of the king have done this deed, suspicion resting upon them because they have fled. *If he is telling the truth* it is not much to the credit of his common sense. They would not have planned a murder that would have required them to fly the moment it was successfully accomplished, thus compelling them to give up all the advantages to be derived from it. Besides, Malcolm has nothing to gain from such a crime. He has already been appointed Prince of Cumberland. *But Macduff is probably not telling the truth.* His actions subsequently show that he really suspected Macbeth. It is just possible, however, that he did not acquire this suspicion till after the murder of Banquo.

III. i. By this time Banquo has begun to see through Macbeth. It is time for him to act in order to guard against this new danger.

III. i. 10. Stage direction. In the meantime the coronation has taken place off-stage.

III. i. 15-42. Note the phrases: Ride you this afternoon? Is't far you ride? Goes Fleance with you? These are so buried in the conversation that Banquo has no idea why they are asked. Why are they asked?

III. i. 48, etc. Would Macbeth make such unfavorable comparisons between himself and Banquo?

The Elizabethan soliloquy serves a double purpose: 1. It gave the inmost thoughts of the person speaking. 2. It served as a direct means of communication between the author of the play and the audience. As an illustration of the former read *Macbeth*, I. v. 16, etc. As an illustration of the latter, read *Henry the Fourth*, Part I, I. ii. 218, etc. This is not in keeping with the character of Prince Hal. It is Shakespeare's apologetic message to the audience that he is not permanently trifling with the character of the great king, Henry the Fifth.

III. ii. In the last scene we learned that, now that he is king, Macbeth's troubles are really just beginning. In the present scene we learn that his wife, in spite of her former confidence, is in the same condition.

The question arises as to why Macbeth, who was formerly so in harmony with his wife, did not take her into his confidence regarding the murder of Banquo.

1. In the beginning, she wished to rouse him to the point of taking the initiative. If she could do this her work was done.

2. Macbeth has so far progressed in crime by now that it is getting easier to him, and he is willing to take the initiative himself. He desires his wife's good opinion and thinks that this independent course will please her. It is not a sign that he has lost confidence in her.

III. iii. There has been much discussion regarding the identity of the third murderer. Such discussion is time wasted. There is no indication in the play as to who he is. To assume that he is Macbeth is to make of the latter a man of poor judgment and clumsy behavior. The supposition is also contradictory to his behavior in the banquet scene. Show how this is.

III. iv. The Banquet Scene. It is well to draw a stage plan showing how the persons should be placed.

Should the ghost of Banquo actually enter, or not? It has been staged both ways.

III. iv. 46. How can Macbeth say that the table is full without recognizing the ghost?

Note how alert Lady Macbeth is to divert attention from her husband. Part of her lines are to her husband as asides. When she speaks of the air-drawn dagger she evidently does not see anything in Banquo's chair. But she knows from the direction of her husband's eyes that whatever he sees is there.

The moment the ghost disappears Macbeth grows more calm, but he goes to pieces again the moment it reappears.

III. iv. 119. Notice that Lady Macbeth dismisses the guests in a hurry. Why does she do it at just this moment?

She dismisses them at a moment when her husband was really in a little better control over himself than shortly before. It is hardly, then, because he is going to pieces that she does it.

At this point I think she sees the ghost; and it is because she fears she will go to pieces herself that she sends the guests away.

1. This is quite in accordance with the contemporary belief in ghost-lore.

2. It constitutes an intermediate step in her own nervous and mental breakdown.

3. When the room is empty she would have questioned her husband as to what he saw, if she did not already know.

4. Similarly Macbeth would have told her what he has seen if he did not know that she had herself seen the ghost and understood.

5. This supposition gives the actress a much better opportunity to display her powers than if she is supposed not to see the ghost.

6. Lady Macbeth probably thinks now that the others will see it, too.

III. iv. 142. Lady Macbeth seems to have lost

interest in her husband's plans. She sees that the game is up. This apathy is the beginning of the decline that ends in the sleep-walking scene.

III. v. Note the additional witch, and the change in meter. Perhaps the later witch scenes are interpolated, or written over later by another hand than Shakespeare's.

III. iv. Somewhere about here is the location of the technical turning-point. It is not possible to defend one exact moment rather than another. Note how little has been made of Macduff up to this point, and how poorly his character has been carried out in the remainder of the play. Compare with *Othello*, a model of perfection of this kind of construction, where the two opposing figures are Iago and Othello.

IV. i. Note the ambiguous characteristics of the second set of prophecies as compared with the literal directness of the first set.

IV. i. 111. "A show of eight kings." These are the Scottish Stuarts, the last of which was on the throne of England at the time Macbeth was written. Those seen in the glass merely indicate the hope, on the part of Shakespeare, that there would be many more. This sort of anachronism was not objectionable to the Elizabethans. There is another example of it in the play. The scene describing the touching for the king's evil refers to the revival of an obsolete custom in the reign of King James.

IV. ii. The character of Macduff is very poorly drawn. Examine his knowledge of the dangerous state of Scotland, which he shows he is familiar with in a later scene where he discusses the subject with Malcolm. Under such circumstances he would not have left his wife and children unprotected. And his wife, though she calls him such, did not believe him a coward. Nor was he.

Before we condemn Shakespeare for the cruelty of a scene like this we should bear in mind the temper of the time. Both sports and laws were cruel to such an extent that a mutilation or a killing offended the audience no more than a hard beating would offend to-day. (See the subject discussed in the chapter on *King Lear*.)

IV. iii. This poorly written scene is sometimes said not to be by Shakespeare's hand. It may not be. There is no positive way of telling. It is well to note, however, that it is written as if it belonged to a much longer play than the present play. It may be from another play, from another and more lengthy draft, or it may be poor writing on the part of Shakespeare, or of a collaborator. Note also that the character-drawing of Macduff and Malcolm is poorly done.

IV. iii. 76. Malcolm's lies are preposterous, and Macduff is a fool to believe them. How do they serve as a test of Macduff's honesty?

V. i. Why is the sleep-walking scene considered so great?

The value of this scene is not in its words. Rather in the way the scattered exclamations of Lady Macbeth manage to review the whole play for us in a moment. Note how each detail touches some important point, some great moment of the play. In other words, this scene is a digest of *Macbeth*, and the greatness of the scene is but a reflection of the greatness of the play as a whole.

From here to the end of the play we have merely

the dramatization of the remainder of the narrative, the result of which had been already guessed by the audience.

There is, however, one point of unusual interest (see V. v. 43), "to doubt the equivocation of the fiend." This phrase means, "to suspect the double-dealing of the witches."

The audience was already familiar with the historical story of Macbeth, and was, therefore, familiar with the double meaning of the prophecies long before the truth was discovered by Macbeth. The audience would be on the watch for his behavior when he made the discovery. All along Macbeth has proceeded on the assumption that the witches were altogether right. Now he realizes that they were not; that it was his own failure to understand them as well as Banquo would have understood them which has driven him to his present state of ruin. This is the real nemesis that comes to him in the play. He has been deluded and fooled to his destruction. In comparison to his mental anguish at this moment his death is a welcome relief.

III. THE CHARACTER OF MACDUFF

Macduff should be a character that vies with Macbeth in importance, but he is not. Go through the whole play noting: 1. How little is told of Macduff. 2. What is actually told of Macduff. 3. The characteristics of Macduff to be inferred from his actions, and from what others say of him. 4. Is the picture of him consistent? 5. Is the picture of him complete?

IV. Was there a Collaborator?

It is not safe to conclude that because we find evidence of careless work in the play it is therefore not wholly by Shakespeare. He was often careless. On the other hand, it is a notable fact that parts of this play show the greatest evidence of care and skill.

The play seems to drop in interest in the middle, both in artistic and dramatic quality. Most of the praiseworthy points are to be found in the first half; most of the blamable details are to be found in the second half. Most of the blamable details of the first half have to do with those scenes in which the Macbeths do not figure. Most of the praiseworthy parts of the second half have to do with those scenes in which the Macbeths do figure.

Is it not, then, a fair inference that Shakespeare himself worked out the characters of Macbeth and of Lady Macbeth, and that a collaborator worked out the Macduffs. This theory implies that the two principal parts of the play were composed by different hands.

(See the chapter on dramatic structure in explanation of the suggestion that Macduff should be of equal importance with Macbeth. The structure of this play is of the type to which is referred *Othello* and *Hamlet*.)

CHAPTER XX

THE TEMPEST

I. INTRODUCTION

SIR G. SOMERS was wrecked on the shores of the Bermudas in 1609. In 1610 three accounts were published of this shipwreck. These were probably before Shakespeare, yet fresh in the popular mind, when he wrote *The Tempest*. A careful consideration of them, together with the external evidence, suggests some time early in 1611 as the date of the appearance of this play.

Several contemporary writings, and the history of Italy, suggest innumerable details of the play. There is, however, no single original to which the author is indebted for the major portion of the drama.

The duration of the action is a few hours following the shipwreck.

The play was first published in the Folio.

Some critics see in *The Tempest* an element of autobiography. Prospero is Shakespeare. His ending his work of necromancy symbolizes Shakespeare's retirement from the stage, and the theatrical world in general. It is, however, not necessary to believe this fact, hard in any case to prove, in order to appreciate the play.

The play has appeared in the Variorum Edition and

has also appeared in the Dowden Edition. The latter gives a full account of the wreck of Somers and the published descriptions.

II. Notes on the Text

In the *Century Magazine* for December, 1911, there appeared an article by the eminent scholar and student of Elizabethan conditions, Mr. Corbin, dealing with the Elizabethan setting of *The Tempest*. There will be found a very suggestive illustration of the stage setting for the first scene. I have followed some of the suggestions of this article elsewhere in the present volume; others therein mentioned were, however, conclusions arrived at independently.

I. i. The scene is of the nature of a little preliminary pageant. It is referred to in the next scene but is hardly sufficient to get the story fairly started. The real story of the play deals with the love affair of Ferdinand and Miranda.

I. ii. With the details of Mr. Corbin's article fresh in mind, let us imagine this scene acted with the fallen chains and other paraphernalia of scene i. still upon the stage. Instead of being a detriment this will help to link the scene to the first one and thus bring out the continuity of the story even before the relation is made clear by the words of Prospero.

This scene starts the principal thread of the story, that of Ferdinand and Miranda; and gives to the audience the necessary introductory matter. Note how much introduction there is and how long drawn out.

I. ii. 15. Note how quickly and how emphatically

we are told that the storm of scene i. is a mere sham. There is no real danger, and the tone of all is mere playfulness.

I. ii. 37. Though Miranda has never heard the story of her life Prospero tells it here in detail in reality for the information of the audience. This, the story of Ariel, and that of Sycorax and Caliban, constitute the introductory material. Query: Is there too much of it? Could it be shortened to advantage? Could the material be differently distributed? Would anything be gained by getting the entrance of Ferdinand and Miranda earlier in the play?

I. ii. 57. It was Shakespeare's custom not to fool the audience. He is here engaged in informing fully as to what has happened. Contrast in this respect the practice of Ben Jonson. See, for a good example of the opposite, *The Silent Woman.*

I. ii. Let the student recall some of the earlier plays of Shakespeare. In them we often encounter long speeches which are monotonous to read and still more monotonous to hear upon the stage. Here we find a much more skilful method of procedure. The long account of Prospero is broken up by the occasioual remarks and questions of Miranda, for the purpose of interrupting the montony of what would otherwise be a long address from her father.

I. ii. 189. We have already been told in so many words that the subject-matter of this play is all trivial, it is a mere comedy from the beginning, altogether light-hearted. The reference to Prospero's power over the storm, to his magic mantle, and now the appearance of Ariel tell us once for all that this is a fairy-story. And it should thus be taken by the reader, or by the audience. There is nothing serious about it. Some critics, however, see in it: 1. Shakespeare's farewell. 2. A psychological study of a woman raised absolutely alone. 3. Merely a delightful tale. If one delights in either the first or the second interpretation he must, perforce, be grateful to the author. But, for my part, I owe a sufficient debt to Shakespeare not to increase it by such an additional burden.

I. ii. 195. Ariel describes his behavior at the time of the event related in scene i. There was, however, probably no attempt to stage these antics of the spirit. Though Ariel says he caused amazement, there is no reference to him or his eccentricities in scene i.

I. ii. 244. Ariel is universally good-natured and obedient with a willing heart throughout. This momentary "moodiness" is introduced merely to give Prospero a chance to tell the elfin's story for the benefit of the audience.

I. ii. 374. The entrance of Ferdinand marks the real beginning of the story, or, at least, the main thread of it.

II. i. The first 180 lines of this scene are mere by-play. There is more of this sort of writing than usual in one of Shakespeare's plays—that is, text that fails to advance the plot or to delineate crucial points of character.

II. i. 215. What becomes of this conspiracy?

II. ii., III. ii. Caliban, Trinculo, and Stephano form the low comedy element of the play. What becomes of this conspiracy? In fact, should one raise this question seriously at all? Or should one accept their antics as a mere comic parody of the other more serious conspiracy, and expect nothing of it? Does, and if so, why should, Prospero take more pains— perhaps I should say, more space—to nullify their efforts than the efforts of the other conspirators?

III. ii. 136. Here and for some time Ariel has been invisible. How would this fact be suggested on the Elizabethan stage? In some scenes in the plays a person is visible to the audience, yet supposed to be invisible to those on the stage. He has no difficulty in carrying his part. The illusion of the situation is produced by the behavior of the others. Again, the invisible person is not on the stage at all, yet the audience is able easily to infer his presence. There is reason to believe that on the Elizabethan stage a conventional color to a garment represented invisibility. Thus, in *Titus Andronicus* there is a point where Lavinia enters after her arms have been cut off at the elbows. When I have an opportunity to add an account of this play to the present volume I shall try to show that the play does not deserve its usual treatment at the hands of critics regarding its un-Shakespearian element of cruelty. Lavinia at the entrance alluded to above probably wears gloves of this conventional color, thus rendering her hands in the imagination invisible, that is, cut off. Here Ariel is probably garbed in a cloak of the same color. He is undoubtedly present and visible to the audience, for it is the appearance of the spirit that gives point to the allusion to the picture of Nobody. Yet Trinculo, who makes the remark, probably does not see Ariel.

IV. i. 139. Prospero drops the mask and takes up the matter of the more trivial conspiracy with extreme suddenness. (See the former note on Caliban's conspiracy. Is Prospero justified in being so greatly moved on the present occasion?)

III. ANALYSIS OF THE PLOT

I. i. Alonso and his companions are wrecked in an enchanted storm off Prospero's island. There are no forecasting allusions to subsequent portions of the play, and no names are mentioned.

I. ii. This scene opens by showing that Prospero raised the storm that figures in scene i.; and Prospero tells Miranda that no real harm was done by the storm. Thus both scenes are linked together, and we catch both the playful and the magical elements.

Prospero outlines to Miranda their early history; and the same is done in connection with Ariel; and the same with Caliban.

Then enters Ferdinand, with whom Miranda immediately falls in love. As this could easily have been prevented by her magical father, we are left to suppose that it is really the result of his machinations. Here is where the main story in reality begins. Prospero assumes a harshness towards Ferdinand which he does not feel.

Note that though some of the other characters have appeared in scene i., they are not really introduced till II. i. This is unusual.

II. i. The principal survivors enter and talk about the shipwreck, and are finally put to sleep by Ariel. Sebastian and Antonio plan the murder of Alonso, but are prevented by his sudden awakening by Ariel.

II. ii. Caliban meets Stephano and Trinculo. They form a sort of confederacy.

III. i. Ferdinand and Miranda disclose their love for each other.

III. ii. Caliban and his fellows hatch out the comic conspiracy against Prospero.

III. iii. The banquet which mysteriously vanishes. Ariel appears in the form of a harpy. Prospero upbraids Alonso and the rest for their treatment of him.

IV. i. Prospero approves the love of Ferdinand and Miranda. Then follows the mask, which is entirely an undramatic digression introduced for the mere purpose of spectacular entertainment. This is suddenly dropped at its end, after which Caliban and his fellows are chased off the stage by hounds.

V. i. Prospero reveals himself to the others. All are happily reconciled. Caliban and his fellow-conspirators are let off with a merciful neglect.

This complicated plot may be resolved into the following threads:

1. Prospero's banishment, which is eventually the means of bringing all the characters of the play happily together at the end.

2. Alonso's wreck, which brings him into contact with Prospero.

3. The love of Ferdinand and Miranda. This is the main thread of the story.

4. The plot against Alonso by his equals, suddenly dropped, however, without being brought to a conclusion.

5. The comedy-element plot against Prospero by Caliban, etc., which is a parody of thread number 4.

6. A mask in celebration of the love of Ferdinand and Miranda, really a part of thread number 3.

The plot may be graphically represented, as in the

following diagram. The figures in the top line refer to the thread numbers mentioned above. The numerals in the left column denote act and scene. The dots represent the appearance of the particular part of the story.

	1	2	3	4	5
I. i.		•			
I. ii.	•		•		
II. i.		•		•	
II. ii.					•
III. i.			•		
III. ii.					•
III. iii.		•			
IV. i.			•		•
V. i.	•	•	•		•

Note further. The story begins with 2, which forms a sort of framework. The second scene brings in 1, which consists mainly of preliminary material necessary to the understanding of what follows.

3 is the main story. It is simply told. There is no opposition or complication save Prospero's momentary harshness to Ferdinand. Relatively it oc-

cupies less space than is usual with the principal thread.

4 looks for a while as if it were intended to exemplify nemesis on Alonso. But it comes to naught and is left unfinished. What frustrating there is is due to Prospero, who is heaping coals of fire.

In the last scene all threads are brought together except 4, which, however, is alluded to as immaterial: 1. Prospero's banishment is over. 2. Alonso recovers his ship. 3. Ferdinand and Miranda are happily married. 5. Caliban and his fellows are reproved but not punished.

IV. THE CHARACTER OF PROSPERO

Many a man has whiled away an evening in a country store by telling a good yarn. His purpose is to pass the time and to please his audience. Perhaps the same man on another occasion attempts to correct the follies of his child by relating in familiar guise the story of the Prodigal Son. To infer from the latter situation that the former is impossible, that the elder never speaks without intending some dark and hidden significance to his words, is to imply, to say the least, an extraordinary lack of human quality.

There seems to be a tendency on the part of some persons who have written about the subject-matter of Shakespeare's plays to deny to the author this human quality, to deny the possibility of his writing as so many have written, merely for the purpose of passing the time with a delightful narrative. There is a great idea of moral consequence dominating *Hamlet*. I can find nothing but a pleasing tale in *A Mid-*

summer Night's Dream.   Nor does the mere fact that
The Tempest is probably the last of Shakespeare's
plays convince me that it contains an abridged ency-
clopedia of all the author's knowledge of all things.
It may be, as a recent critic thinks, that Caliban is
a remarkable embodiment of the supernatural, the
social order of the day, and Elizabethan politics.   I
say, it may be true, but it is not clear.   To me it is
a monster such as Othello speaks of, such as Shakespeare read about in the numberless travel narratives
of the day.

The Tempest, I take it, is one of the pleasantest
stories ever written for the stage.   There is a kindly
geniality about it, the loveliness of serene maturity.
And if there be an underlying moral lesson, is it
more than that one does well to forget an injury, to
turn away wrath with a soft answer? to disarm an
enemy by turning to him the unstricken cheek?   This,
at least, is the example of the play, and it is acted
out most significantly in the character of Prospero.

He is a man of high social rank, a lover of books,
and so well trained and educated that he can teach
his daughter Miranda all that she needs to know.
With it all he has acquired the art of magic, through
the possession of which he works a bad beginning into
a good end.

Though he has been badly treated, there is no
malice in his nature.   He is quick to affirm that no
harm will come of the shipwreck.   He has his old
enemies in his power.   His first thought, however, is
not to punish them, or revenge himself, but to reform
them, and to bring good results out of the chance
meeting.

It is easy to comprehend why the common people of Naples loved him. He is kindly and genial to all. Careful of details for others' good, his main interest is in the welfare of his child. When Ariel exasperates him he is, for a moment, petulant, but it is only a momentary rebuke that follows. Ariel is soon pleased again and ardent to do his master's bidding. Prospero never fails to praise a well-done task. Even his relations to Caliban, harsh as his words sometimes are, are illustrative of his forgiving nature and his forbearance. And when he treats Ferdinand harshly for the sake of future benefit he does it with a naïve clumsiness, as if the rôle were unfamiliar.

Most notable among Prospero's characteristics is his treatment of his enemies. He has been harshly treated himself, but there is no lingering desire for revenge in his composition. When his enemies come unbidden to his door his one impulse is to make them friends. He entertains no ill feeling against Ferdinand. He keeps a supernatural watch which frustrates the attack upon Alonso, which is so like the earlier conspiracy against himself, and which Alonso so justly merits. He does not scruple to expose the conspirators' wickedness, but he does so gently, and magnanimously refuses to reveal the plot of the traitors now that it has come to naught and their hearts have changed.

Prospero is throughout the great, genial, lovable, and loving man, who works miracles by the power of his gentle personality.

V. The Elizabethan Staging

The play requires in reality but two sets. One is used in the first scene, and not used again. The other is used throughout the rest of the play.

1. The shipwreck would probably be set as suggested by Mr. Corbin. (See *Century Magazine*, December, 1911.)

2. The other set is arranged so that it can be used in two ways. The outer stage is bare. Properties are introduced on the middle stage to suggest out-of-doors on the island. These are probably brought in while the traverse is drawn during the first 185 lines of II. i. The inner stage is concealed by a drop helping the illusion of " out of doors." Behind this Prospero's cell is set up on the inner stage. Raising and lowering this drop accommodates all the succeeding scenes.

INDEX

Act division, 71
Acting, 106
Actor, Shakespeare as, 5
Actors, companies of, 4, 25; customs of, 29; of women's parts, 179; boy, 179
Acts, music between, 34
Admiral's Men, 4
Admission to theaters, 29
Alleyn, 4
Anachronisms, 226, 242
Antic disposition passage, 222
Audience, 30; seating, 31; on the stage, 40; character of, 42

Balcony scene of *Romeo and Juliet*, 158
Bale's *King Johan*, 87
Bankside, 26
Battle scenes, 107, 108, 149
Bear Garden, the, 28
Beginning and end of a play, 66
Bible as known to Shakespeare, 2
Blackfriars, the, 29
Blank verse, 56, 156
Bolingbroke, character of, 130
Boy actors, 179
Brutus, structural relation to *Julius Cæsar*, 191
Buckingham, character of, 108
Bugle call at the beginning of a play, 33

Burbage, James, builder of The Theater, 26

Cæsar, Julius, notes on the text, 190; structural relation of Brutus in, 191
Catastrophe, the, 68, 70
Character drawing, Shakespeare's method of, 177
Character study, 108
Children in Shakespeare's plays, 104
Chorus, 143, 144
Chronicle play. *See* History plays.
Cloths, painted, 33
Comedy, structure of, 180; mixed with tragedy, 219
Companies of players, 4, 5; of actors, 25
Construction of *Romeo and Juliet*, 114
Contradictions, apparent, 274
Costume, stage, 36, 193
Cruelty of the time, 262, 282
Cumberland passage, Prince of, 268
Curtain, The, 27
Curtain, traverse, 33

Darkening the stage, 47, 188, 245, 264
Declamations, 108, 143, 144, 158, 175
Derby's actors, 4
Devil lore, 220

297

|

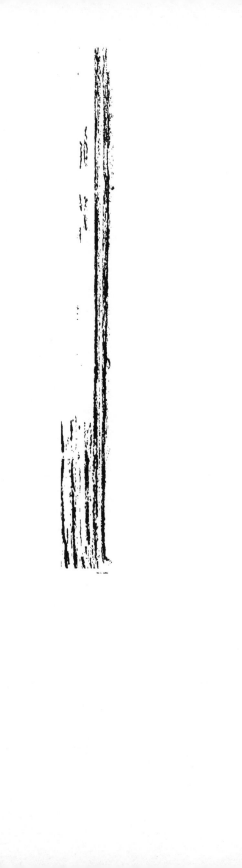

FELIX E. SCHELLING'S ENGLISH LITERATURE DURING THE LIFETIME OF SHAKESPEARE

8vo. $2.50 net; by mail, $2.70.

"A philosophy of literature. . . . Suggestive, interesting, learned. . . . A most illuminating chapter on Shakespeare's contemporary dramatists. . . . Well thought out and inspiring. . . . He has shown the great Elizabethan dramatist's real literary character by pointing out the stock of which his genius was the supreme efflorescence."—*Literary Digest*.

H. T. STEPHENSON'S THE ELIZABETHAN PEOPLE

With 70 illustrations. $2.00 net; by mail, $2.16.

A vivid account by an authority of such matters as "Country Life and Character"; "Amusements in General"; "Celebration of the Calendar"; "The Love of Spectacles"; "Popular Superstitions"; "Birth, Baptism, Marriage, Death"; "Domestic Life."

"Gives us a human insight into the character and daily life of Shakespeare's audience. The account is well ordered and thorough. The style is easy and entertaining."—*The Bookman*.

H. T. STEPHENSON'S SHAKESPEARE'S LONDON

With 42 illustrations. $2.00 net; by mail, $2.15.

A vivid portrayal and scholarly study, largely from contemporaneous sources, of the topography, customs, and picturesque side of Elizabethan life. The illustrations are mostly from old prints.

"It is something more than a mere topographical survey; the daily life of the people is described as vividly as their streets, their houses, and the mere external aspects of their week to week existence. . . . Brings each scene directly before the eye of the reader."—*Boston Transcript*.

STOPFORD A. BROOKE'S ON TEN PLAYS OF SHAKE-SPEARE

8vo. $2.25 net; by mail, $2.38.

Midsummer Night's Dream, Winter's Tale, Merchant of Venice, As You Like It, Richard II., Richard III., Macbeth, Tempest, Romeo and Juliet, Coriolanus not so much analyzed as "appreciated" in a thoroughly sympathetic spirit and genial style.

"A more delightful volume of criticism it would be hard to find."—*Boston Transcript*.

TEN BRINK'S FIVE LECTURES ON SHAKESPEARE

The Poet and the Man; The Chronology of Shakespeare's Works; Shakespeare as Dramatist, as Comic Poet, as Tragic Writer.—Translated by JULIA FRANKLIN. $1.25.

"No single volume on the great dramatist is, in our judgment, superior in value to this modest but extremely able work."—*Outlook*.

HENRY HOLT AND COMPANY

34 WEST 33D STREET   NEW YORK

ARCHIBALD HENDERSON'S THE CHANGING DRAMA

Its Contributions and Tendencies. By the Author of "George Bernard Shaw: His Life and Works," "European Dramatists," etc. 12mo. $1.50 net.

The pioneer book in English in its field. While a number of good books, taking up important dramatists and discussing them one after another, are available, this is probably the first that describes the significant changes and movements in the drama of the last half century, illustrating them by the work of leading dramatists and by apt citations of and quotations from their plays. The author, publicist as well as dramatic critic, aims to show the expression of the larger realities of contemporary life in the drama, the widening of social influence of the stage, the new technic, form, and content of the play, the substitution of the theme for the hero, the conflict of wills for that of arms, etc. In short, to give a brief but authoritative general survey with a more detailed appraisal of some of the chief creative contributions.

The chapter headings indicate the content and scope of the work: Drama in the New Age; The New Criticism and New Ethics; Science and the New Drama; The New Forms—Realism and the Pulpit Stage; The New Forms—Naturalism and the Free Theatre; The Battle with Illusions; The Ancient Bondage and the New Freedom; The New Technic; The Play and the Reader; The New Content; The Newer Tendencies.

The author, though an American, has also studied the drama in the theatres of Great Britain and the Continent, and has before this demonstrated that he is a dramatic scholar and a keen, clear-eyed, entertaining critic. His articles have appeared in *La Société Nouvelle, Mercure de France, Deutsche Revue, Illustreret Tidende, Finsk Tidskrift, T. P.'s Magazine,* etc., etc.

Maurice Maeterlinck said of his "Interpreters of Life" (now incorporated in his "European Dramatists"): "You have written one of the most sagacious, most acute, and most penetrating essays in the whole modern literary movement."

"It is a really great work," said Professor William Lyon Phelps of "George Bernard Shaw: His Life and Works."

Of his "European Dramatists," *The Dial* said: "The criticisms of their work are keen and lucid, and have the advantage of coming from one who has studied the plays exhaustively."

HENRY HOLT AND COMPANY

PUBLISHERS   vii'14   NEW YORK

HALE'S DRAMATISTS OF TO-DAY

ROSTAND, HAUPTMANN, SUDERMANN,
PINERO, SHAW, PHILLIPS, MAETERLINCK

By PROF. EDWARD EVERETT HALE, JR., of Union College.
With gilt top, $1.50 net; by mail, $1.60.

Since this work first appeared in 1905, Maeterlinck's SISTER
BEATRICE, THE BLUE BIRD and MARY MAGDALENE, Rostand's
CHANTECLER and Pinero's MID-CHANNEL and THE THUNDER-
BOLT—among the notable plays by some of Dr. Hale's dramatists—have been acted here. Discussions of them are added
to this new edition, as are considerations of Bernard Shaw's
and Stephen Phillips' latest plays. The author's papers on
Hauptmann and Sudermann, with slight additions, with his
"Note on Standards of Criticism," "Our Idea of Tragedy,"
and an appendix of all the plays of each author, with dates of
their first performance or publication, complete the volume.

Bookman: "He writes in a pleasant, free-and-easy way. . . . He
accepts things chiefly at their face value, but he describes them so ac-
curately and agreeably that he recalls vividly to mind the plays we
have seen and the pleasure we have found in them."

New York Evening Post: "It is not often nowadays that a theatrical
book can be met with so free from gush and mere eulogy, or so weighted
by common sense . . . an excellent chronological appendix and full
index . . . uncommonly useful for reference."

Dial: "Noteworthy example of literary criticism in one of the most
interesting of literary fields. . . . Provides a varied menu of the
most interesting character. . . . Prof. Hale establishes confidential
relations with the reader from the start. . . . Very definite opinions,
clearly reasoned and amply fortified by example. . . . Well worth
reading a second time."

New York Tribune: "Both instructive and entertaining."

Brooklyn Eagle: "A dramatic critic who is not just 'busting' himself with Titanic intellectualities, but who is a readable dramatic critic.
. . . Mr. Hale is a modest and sensible, as well as an acute and sound
critic. . . . Most people will be surprised and delighted with Mr.
Hale's simplicity, perspicuity and ingenuousness."

The Theatre: "A pleasing lightness of touch. . . . Very readable book."

HENRY HOLT AND COMPANY

PUBLISHERS   **NEW YORK**

Lightning Source UK Ltd.
Milton Keynes UK
UKHW020741060119
335045UK00011B/957/P

9 781330 232194